Dear Pastor

Thank You Dr. Ben
for the material from
Dr. Piper (page 40) also
J page 265!

— Dan

Dear Pastor

Only You Can Rescue America

Jay Menefee

The hope of the world is the local church Teaching and living the Truths of Jesus Christ as found in God's Word, The BIBLE.

DUNHAM
books

Dear Pastor
© 2014 DearPastor.Net

For information on licensing or special sales, please email Dunham Books at info@dunhamgroupinc.com.

Unless otherwise cited, all Scriptural references are from the New American Standard Bible. The writing in the Appendices has not been edited from the original; thus, many words in the Old English are frequently spelled differently than American English.

Trade Paperback ISBN: 978-0-9837456-7-9
Ebook ISBN: 978-0-9851359-0-4

Library of Congress Control Number: 2015931331

Printed in the United States of America

This book is dedicated to my dear friend
"Bun" Blossom and the trustees
of Crossroads Foundation.

Table of Contents

PREFACE

Pastor, I am not coming to you in this little book as some "great expert" to share with you out of my vast intellect. Quite the contrary! I believe the Lord has blest me with just the right amount of simple-minded ignorance to be able to see His straightforward instructions and commandments on how we should live together and govern ourselves. In other words: How exactly do we "Love our neighbors as ourselves?" I believe God used Balaam's donkey to provide His message to Balaam. I believe God is using me to bring this message to you. I do ask that as you approach this book, you would pray to God to relieve you of any preconceived notions, prejudgement, and other distractions you may harbor.

With that disclaimer…

If you are a believing pastor… who takes God at His word when He tells us: "All Scripture is inspired by God and profitable for teaching, for reproof, for correction, for training in righteousness; that the man of God may be adequate, equipped for every good work…" (2 Timothy 3:16-17), then this book is for you.

This little book is written to you because I am convinced that it is your leadership and only your leadership that can rescue our nation! I think this falls under your commission from God to equip the saints for service and good works, as discussed in Dear Pastor Letter Twenty-Two (22), "The Mission of the Church." We must look to you to teach us what God's Word means when He commands us to "love our neighbor as ourselves." In fact, Dear

Pastor, Letter Sixteen (16) explains precisely why I think you have this responsibility.

The scripture from Judges that you used recently in your sermon pretty well sums up where we are now: "And all that generation also were gathered to their fathers; and there arose another generation after them who did not know the LORD, nor yet the work which He had done for Israel. Then the sons of Israel did evil in the sight of the LORD..." (Judges 2:10-11).

Almost everyone I talk to believes that our country has been drifting, at an ever increasing pace, into a godless morass that, in many respects, is exactly opposite what God requires of us in His Word. Take a moment to look up Hosea 4:6: "My people are destroyed for lack of knowledge..." Please take that passage before the Lord and ask Him if it applies to the church of today. It should be very discomforting, but...

What is so surprising is that, historically, this phenomenon is a very recent thing! You would never have been able to convince my grandfather, just a couple of generations back that this country could have even gotten close to where we are today! We, as a nation, are quickly marching towards judgment! This little book explores how and why that happened. And, from God's Word, it explores how we could rescue the nation from His judgment.

What is so exciting, Pastor, is that God's Word tells us, as a nation, how to return to godliness and prosperity. It is not that we wrongly interpreted His Word... We simply chose one day to begin to overlook those particular scriptures! Working together, we can rescue our nation. This little book, using God's Word, points the way. Pastor, it can be done! Why would we not do this?

I have heard some say: "It is just too late...We are so ungodly we cannot go back!" Determined to do what I could to change our direction, back in 1980 some friends and I started an organization called Ohio Roundtable. Our efforts were joined to those of the Christian Coalition, the Moral Majority, and many others to educate Americans about the changes needed to alter our direction.

I was so excited...Ronald Regan was elected president and many conservatives sent to Congress. Many pastors appointed church members to organize voter registration, voter guides were distributed, many churches organized "candidate nights" and "get out the vote" drives were held in quite a few as well. A few churches even started having Bible studies on "governance." Wow! It was working. Pastors were getting involved...It could actually be turned around!

Over the next two to three years federal spending was cut significantly, many federal regulations were curtailed, and many programs were relegated back to the states. I was filled with hope, thinking we had begun to turn the corner to rescue our country!

I soon began to see that support for this reformation, even though it was a mile wide, turned out to be less than an inch deep! Unaware what God's Word had to say about this, most pastors assumed they had won the day, lost interest, and turned their attention to other areas! Secular liberals then began to regain their positions of influence and reverse the progress of reducing the federal government. Soon we were multiplying federal agencies and federal budgets with a vengeance. Although there remains a modicum of support for conservative, Biblical ideas, the process of secularizing the country, centralizing power, suffering sluggish financial growth, and increasing indebtedness continues today at an even greater speed.

The most important thing I learned over that period is that until you, Pastor, understand what God's Word has to say about living together and governing ourselves and take leadership in this area…support will remain shallow and ineffective! And our country will continue, as Judge Robert Bork put it, "slouching towards Gomorrah."

The second most important thing I learned is that it is not too late! With your leadership and teaching, Pastor, this is by no means a lost cause. It was easy to see that when pastors led in teaching us how to "love our neighbor as ourselves" the nation could be turned to godliness. And that is not only encouraging…It is downright exciting!

Finally, Pastor, how do you think we are doing today with God's "Great Commission" to make disciples of our nation? Are you happy with our progress? How are American families doing? Is divorce in steep decline? Do you think we are on the verge of another great awakening?

Did you realize that from 1609 all the way through 1900, nearly three hundred years, we evangelized most of our countrymen, including a great many Native Americans and many African-Americans who, incidentally and to our shame, found themselves entrapped in slavery? We also led the world in sending missionaries across the globe. No other nation came close! By the late 1800s regular church attendance was near eighty percent and still growing. Divorce in America was a rare event! Mark A. Noll, in his book *A History of Christianity in the United States and Canada*, called that period in America the "Protestant Century." He quotes Alexis de Tocqueville when, in the early 1800s, he said "…there is no country in the world where the Christian religion retains a greater influence over the souls of men than in America."

This commitment to God's Word, incidentally, had a material effect on our nation as well. Pastor, from 1700 to 1900 our industrial output grew to twice that of Great Britain and over half that of all of Europe! GDP increased by 1,000-fold. God raised us up from a wilderness of axes and log cabins to being the greatest, most powerful nation on the planet! Over the first three hundred years we had no national debt and government was, for the most part, limited to defending the shores and keeping the peace.

Pastor, during the time of my grandfather, *pastors made an abrupt change* and our nation followed them! Just two generations later, church attendance has now shrunk by half to less than forty percent. Europe, of course, being more modern has reduced church attendance to less than four (4) percent! In fact, every year we now have fewer and fewer followers of Christ in America. When my grandfather was a young man in the late 1800s, Bible-believing pastors abruptly abandoned public life and the way they had led the church over the previous three hundred years. They disengaged and, so to speak, "led the church up the mountain" to protect us from worldly contamination to wait for the Lord's return. It was folly. The famous evangelist, Charles Finney, who was part of the "Second Great Awakening," prophetically predicted our situation in 1878 and put his finger precisely on what would cause it. In one of his last sermons he stated:

> If there is a decay of conscience, the pulpit is responsible for it. If the public press lacks moral discernment, the pulpit is responsible for it. If the church is degenerate and worldly, the pulpit is responsible for it. If the world loses its interest in Christianity, the pulpit is responsible for it. If Satan rules in our halls of legislation, the pulpit is responsible for it. If our politics become so corrupt that the very foundations of our government are ready to fall away, the pulpit is responsible for it.

Finney was precisely right; when pastors disengage from teaching us how to Biblically educate our children and justly govern ourselves as God requires, we indeed suffer a "decay of conscience." In fact, we now find ourselves well along in that bleak process.

There is good news, however…We have a choice. Or, more correctly, I should say, you have a choice. You can once again teach and encourage us to obey God's instructions laid out in His Word, as occurred in the first three hundred years of our nation's history and momentarily in 1980. I was part of the 1980 revolution…and can witness to that firsthand…It can be done!

Because of the gift God has given you as a pastor, you and only you are able to do this. You can lead us, once again, into the blessings of Mount Gerizim (Deuteronomy 28:1). Or, you can continue what you have been doing, until Christianity finally dwindles into insignificance and we find ourselves in the curses of Mount Ebal (Deuteronomy 27:4).

∽

If you are a believer but not a pastor… I would caution you not to attempt on your own to lead fellow believers in your church to carry out the suggestions in this book, including Steps One through Four. This can only be successfully initiated and led by your pastor. To attempt this without the pastor's leadership will create contentious factions within the congregation and do more harm than good.

It would certainly be commendable to lobby your pastor to get involved in this effort. You could even gift your pastor with this book and encourage him to read it. You could also tell your pastor that your inspiration is from Luke 18:5: "…because this widow bothers me, I will give her legal protection, lest by continually coming she wear me out." Please be advised; this tactic has limited chance for success.

Probably the more productive thing to do is to quietly find a church that is already engaged in these steps to rescue our nation and energetically join them.

∽

If you are a pastor or believer who does not accept that the Bible is the Word of God and that "…all Scripture is inspired by God and profitable for teaching, for reproof, for correction, for training in righteousness…" (2 Timothy 3:16), you still may want to join this effort. In fact, I would recommend you read and give serious thought to Appendix One…you just might change your mind and conclude that the Bible is far more than a collection of spiritual or religious allegories. No matter what your belief may be, whether Jewish, Libertarian, or simply one who would like to see the country recover some of the unalienable rights we enjoyed in our first three hundred years…You are welcome to join the effort. Doing all we can to regain our God-given freedoms is an exercise we all should engage in.

∽

A word of explanation as to how this book began a couple of years ago: Letter One (1) was written to a real pastor. He was not interested, so I decided to continue to write to a new "imaginary" pastor who, while not entirely convinced, was willing to at least hear me out. It was an amazing journey where one revelation led to another in God's Word and the experiences of my last thirty-five years began to fit into place.

You do not need to read the book "in order," front to back. It is largely a Biblical "how to" book that can be utilized as needed. In fact, probably the most pressing problem we need to address is covered in Section One ("Education") Part I, beginning with Letter Eighteen (18).

Letters One through Seven consist of my exploration of God's Word, attempting to understand what He requires of we who are, His creation, when it comes to living together and governing ourselves.

Letters Eight and Nine examine what nations, if any, governed themselves Biblically and also examine our American Constitution to see if it was Biblically-based. Letters Ten through Fourteen look at our Declaration of Independence to see how Biblically-based it is. And, finally, Letter Fifteen looks to see if there is any evidence of our nation fulfilling these Biblical requirements. Letter Sixteen offers ten conclusions regarding God's instructions and Letter Seventeen examines the responsibilities God requires of Pastors and what responsibilities He requires of believers in general.

Letters Eighteen through Thirty-Eight lay out a plan in four steps that I am convinced will successfully rescue our nation should our Nation's pastoral community choose to lead us through them. Letter Thirty-Nine offers some conclusions.

Only our pastors can do this… No one else can.

∽

Appendix One contains a few of my thoughts on God's Law, both natural and for us, His creatures. God, being a god of reason, and order left none of His creation ungoverned. This appendix contains some interesting thoughts that were passed over lightly or, in some cases, skipped completely in the Letters. Nonetheless, they should strengthen your faith or perhaps even cause you to come to believe the Bible to be God's actual word and not just stories and allegories.

Appendices Two and Three are sermons by Reverend Charles Chauncy, a famous pastor in Boston, and Doctor Joseph Sewall, pastor of Old South Church, also in Boston. Although both were from the mid-eighteenth century, they are presented here because of their timeliness to our current situation.

Both of these sermons are taken from a collection of sermons entitled "Political Sermons of the American Founding Era," Vol. 1 (1730-1788), reprinted by permission from the Liberty Fund. Both volumes are available online at no charge and come highly recommended. Pastor, please read these two volumes to see just what was coming from the American pulpit before the pastors of my grandfather's era disengaged and gave up on the second command of the "Great Commission," "...teaching them all I commanded you..." Truly, our nation is being destroyed for lack of knowledge and you and you alone can rescue us! Pastor, please lead us to repentance and change! Many pastors did this in 1776 and paid for it with their lives. I pray God will give you courage!

LETTER 1

Is God Concerned with America?

Dear Pastor,

I know that this has nothing to do with our personal salvation, but I've been thinking about whether God involves Himself with nations, particularly ours, and I have some questions. Does God still concern himself with nations today the way He seemed to in the Bible? Everyone knows about His judgment on Sodom, and then there was Jonah who went to Nineveh. That city was not Jewish or even close to Israel and yet it says that they repented and prayed to God for forgiveness and He spared them of His judgment. In the New Testament, Jesus also talked about God's judgment on the cities of Bethsaida and Capernaum.

I read in Jeremiah 18:7: "At one moment I might speak concerning a nation or concerning a kingdom to uproot, to pull down, or to destroy it;" in verse 8 that "if that nation against which I have spoken turns from its evil, I will relent concerning the calamity I planned to bring on it;" in verse 9, "Or at another moment I might speak concerning a nation or concerning a kingdom to build up or to plant it;" and in verse 10, "if it does evil in My sight by not obeying My voice, then I will think better of the good with which I had promised to bless it."

I don't think God changed His mind from this prophecy since the Bible also says: "For I am the LORD, I do not change" (Malachi 3:6). And "…the Father of lights, with whom there is no variation or shadow of turning" (James 1:17). Aren't there other places in God's word where it says…God doesn't change?

One question, Pastor, is how do you think we, as a nation, are doing in God's sight? I am not even sure if I know what criteria God uses to evaluate a nation. In Nineveh's case, they certainly didn't become Jewish or start to practice any ceremonial law to gain God's favor. It just says: "They turned from their evil way and God relented." What is it that a nation does that God considers evil and what does He consider good?

I see in Ezekiel 16:49-50 that "Look, this was the iniquity of your sister Sodom: She and her daughter had pride, fullness of food, and abundance of idleness; neither did she strengthen the hand of the poor and needy. And they were haughty and committed abomination before Me; therefore I took them away as I saw fit."

Although some of this description sounds uncomfortably familiar, I don't think we are there yet. Do you? But, do you think we might be practicing "brinkmanship" with the Lord to not pay attention to this until we get to the limit of God's grace with us? It seems to me that we, as a nation, might be heading the wrong way. Do we know what God requires of us, as a nation? Shouldn't we actually be trying to do what we can to please God, as a nation, since we have been so wonderfully blessed? Shouldn't we at least know?

It would be sad if Hosea's prophesy applied to us: "My people are destroyed for lack of knowledge. Because you have rejected knowledge, I also will reject you from being priest for Me; Because you have forgotten the law of your God, I also will forget your children" (Hosea 4:6).

Since we are a self-governed, democratic republic, we would surely have no one to blame but ourselves if we don't get this right! I sincerely would like to know what you think God would like to see us do as a nation, Pastor. If you don't help us understand God's word on this, who will?

Sincerely yours,

LETTER

Has God Said How We Should Live Together?

Dear Pastor,

I have been thinking about my letter to you and it occurred to me that I was off a little. My initial thoughts make it sound like God is some kind of stern umpire just waiting for us to cross the lines He has drawn before He punishes us. That does not fit the picture God portrays of Himself in His word. There He is a loving and long-suffering god, slow to anger and quick to forgive!

It dawned on me that the nature God gave us, as humans, determines the requirements, rules, laws, etc. for our wellbeing. I think God then surely gave us these in His word so that we would know how to please Him and live together in peace and prosperity.

In his book, *Legal Foundations: The Framework of Law*, Gerald R. Thompson of Lonang Institute put it this way: "When God created the heavens and the earth, He imposed order (law) upon the entire earth (universe) and [all of] its inhabitants. Not one area of life or aspect of creation [chemical, physical, or biological] was left ungoverned."

Pastor, I just don't think a loving God would have placed us on this planet without instructions for how to live together. Do you? Surely He would not expect us to come up with them on our own. On every occasion in history in which man invented his own rules, the results were always disastrous!

The question I have, then, is what are these rules? Can we find them in God's word?

My first guess would be the laws, principles, requirements, etc. that Moses codified in Exodus through Deuteronomy and summarized by God Himself as the Ten Commandments. Clearly, some of those are ceremonial in setting the Jewish people apart as "chosen," plus those that deal with the priesthood and temple worship. I do realize, Pastor, that it is these latter laws that point forward to our Lord Jesus Christ who fulfilled them as He provided our personal salvation. I think most could sort out, though, which laws are ceremonial and which are not.

One problem with assuming these are God's requirements for humans, of course, is that Moses lived at least a couple of thousand years after creation. People had been living together with success, more or less, for a long time before Moses. Were these laws known and did they apply to people before Moses codified them into Scripture? I'm talking about the non-ceremonial laws governing how we should live together.

Pastor, don't you think this is something we should know? Would you help me sort this out?

Yours in Christ,

LETTER 3

Didn't God Have the Same Rules Before Israel as After Israel?

Dear Pastor,

In my second letter to you, I ask if the Mosaic Law was known or applied before Moses lived. Pastor, I reread Genesis to see if I could find any mention of it. Wow, the substance of the Ten Commandments is referred to all the way through the book and they are applied to Egyptians, Canaanites, and Sodomites as well as to Adam, Noah, Abraham, and all those people. Canaanites and Egyptians were even quoting God's requirements to Abraham about right and wrong! Of course, in Jonah, well after Moses, they are also apparently applied to the Assyrians. Here is what I read in Genesis:

In Genesis 2:3 God says that He blessed the seventh day and made it holy, which is the fourth commandment.

In Genesis 4:9 Cain told God he didn't know where his brother Abel was, which is bearing false witness, the ninth commandment, and of course, when he murdered Abel he was violating the sixth commandment: "do not commit murder." Cain clearly knew both were wrong.

In Genesis 9:24, when Noah woke up from his sleep he was dismayed that his son, Ham, had violated him, which is against the fifth commandment: to honor your father and mother.

Then, in Genesis 12:17 it says that God plagued Pharaoh and his house because he took Sarai, Abraham's wife, which, of course, involves commandment seven, "thou shall not commit adultery." Here it is Pharaoh who reprimands Abraham!

Also, in Genesis 14:11 it says that they (the kings of the north) took all the goods of Sodom…and went their way, which violates the eighth commandment: "Thou shall not steal." There is no question in the account that this was wrong.

In Genesis 20:9 Abraham again provides a "false witness" by telling the Canaanite king, Abimelech, that Sarai (now being called Sarah) was only his sister and God then punished the king because he believed Abraham and took her for a wife (Thou shall not commit adultery). It was Abimelech, however, who had to call out Abraham on this. Poor Abimelech (or, more likely, his son) even had the same sham pulled on him later (in Genesis 26:7-11) by Abraham's son Isaac.

Regarding the tenth commandment, "thou shall not covet," I found in Genesis 27:19 Jacob swindling Esau's blessing by fooling his father and in Genesis 29:25 Laban, the Chaldean, swindling Jacob by giving him Leah when he had promised Rachel. In Genesis 31:19 Rachel then violates the eighth commandment by stealing Laban's idols, something she clearly knew was wrong because she hid them when Laban showed up to look for them.

Even the marriage laws as part of the seventh commandment are noted in Genesis 34 where Shechem, who had raped Jacob's daughter, offered to provide the Mosaic dowry required in Deuteronomy 22:28, and Judah admitted in Genesis 38:26 that Tamar, his daughter-in-law, was more righteous than he because he did not give her to his youngest son. This refers to the "duty of the husband's brother" of Mosaic Law in Deuteronomy 24:5.

The first and second commandment of having no other gods before Me, and not having any idols, are found in Genesis 35:2 wherein Jacob tells those with him to put away the foreign gods (idols) they were possessing and purify themselves (to God).

Finally, Pastor, just to confirm that these instances of God's Commandments weren't some cultural norms that existed at the time, I read in Genesis 26, verses 2 and 5: *"Then the LORD appeared to him (Isaac) and said: … 'because Abraham obeyed My voice and kept My charge, My commandments, My statutes, and My laws…'"*

Pastor, don't you think that these commandments, statutes, laws and charge are almost certainly the non-ceremonial laws that Moses codified in Exodus through Deuteronomy? I believe this occurred over 400 years before Moses was even born.

This is amazing! "Abraham obeyed My voice and kept My charge, My commandments, My statutes, and My laws…"

The only conclusion is that these commandments and laws were written and understood by most of the then-civilized world 400 years before Moses and probably all the way back to Adam!

Pastor, it sure seems like God's rules for establishing a just society were pretty much the same before the nation of Israel as they were after. You also get the idea that they applied to pretty much everyone, whether Egyptian, Chaldean, Jewish, or Canaanite. It does seem reasonable, that God's rules for establishing a just society would apply to everyone and be the same for all time. Don't you think they apply to America today? If they do, don't you think we should be doing something? I don't think any of us know what these laws are and how to apply them. Pastor, don't you think we should? I believe we really need help here, Pastor, don't you?

Yours in Him,

LETTER

What Did Jesus Say About Rules for Living Together?

Dear Pastor,

In talking with someone a while ago about the laws in the Old Testament, he said "Look, we are no longer under the law; we are now under grace. And besides, those laws only worked for Israel because they were a theocracy; they would not work in a democracy." Wow, where do you begin to answer that?

Well, first I pointed out that, thankfully, we are not a democracy, but a democratic republic and that limits what we can do, constitutionally, no matter what the majority wants. Secondly, I pointed out what I wrote to you in my third letter. Namely, that those laws for Israel (the non-ceremonial laws) were clearly applied to everyone in the book of Genesis for thousands of years before the nation, Israel, even existed. Further, they were applied to Nineveh, the capital of Assyria, through Jonah after Israel. And Nineveh was nowhere near Israel; it was certainly not Jewish and it clearly was not a theocracy!

After saying that, I realize that it is not exactly correct. As I thought about it, Pastor, isn't the whole earth a theocracy? I mean, we certainly believe that our Lord Jesus created us. And we certainly believe Jesus when He says: "...All authority has been given to Me in heaven and on earth" (Matthew 28:18). In other words...He is king and ruler of us all. Pastor, doesn't that constitute a "theocracy?" In Luke 17:20-21: "He answered them and said, 'The kingdom of God is not coming with signs to be observed; nor will they say, 'Look, here it is!' or, 'There it is!' For behold, the kingdom of God is in your midst."

Anyway, to say "we are under grace and not the law so we can dismiss the law" sort of misses the point. It confuses our "salvation" with our "governance." We all know that when we believe in the Lord Jesus Christ we are forgiven our lawlessness and given eternal life. However, even as forgiven Christians, we need rules to live peaceably with one another. Besides, that misses what we have seen so far, that God's laws seem to be for all people for all time!

Pastor, I thought I would see what the Lord Jesus, Himself, had to say about this. First, in my reading, I found that over the years there have been a lot of scholars who have opined about it. These people, while clearly educated and bright, all seem to have their own "axe to grind" and, as a result, they all came to completely different conclusions. They may have been incorrect conclusions, but they were never in doubt! You can just about pick any position you wish to take and find a big-name scholar to justify whatever it is.

As a result, I really think it would be best to take the Berean approach of Acts 17:11: "...examining the Scriptures daily (themselves), to see whether these things were so."

Also, Pastor, I don't think we even need the help of any "theologians" here for a number of reasons. First, I have heard you say many times, "the main things are the plain things and the plain things are the main things!" We are not looking for some fine point, small nuance, or obscure meanings; we are looking for the main, plain things.

We also should keep in mind that God's Word is not that complicated. Martin Luther put it this way: "I have often said that whoever would study Holy Scripture should be sure to see to it that he stays with the simple words as long as he can and by no means departs from them unless an article of faith compels him to understand them differently. For of this we must be certain no simpler speech has been heard on earth than what God has spoken."

I also like the way the not-very-religious Mark Twain put it: "It's not the hard to understand things in the Bible that bother me. It is those things that are easy to understand."

Anyway, I looked at what the Lord said in the Gospels. Jesus, in Matthew 5:17-19, said: "...Do not think that I came to destroy the Law or the Prophets. I did not come to destroy but to fulfill. For assuredly, I say to you, till heaven and earth pass away, one jot or one tittle will by no means pass from the law till all is fulfilled. Whoever therefore breaks one of the least of these commandments, and teaches men so, shall be called least in the kingdom of heaven; but whoever does and teaches them, he shall be called great in the kingdom of heaven." Wow, Pastor, do you think we could be called "great" if we have some Sunday-school classes on God's Laws?

In John 14:15 Jesus, giving final instructions to his disciples, said: "If you love Me, keep My commandments."

Jesus identifies these commandments in Matthew 19:18 when the rich young ruler asks: "Which ones?" Jesus said, "'You shall not murder,' 'You shall not commit adultery,' 'You shall not steal,' 'You shall not bear false witness,' 'Honor your father and your mother,' and, 'You shall love your neighbor as yourself.'"

He then included the first four commandments by telling the young man to sell all he had and follow Him...that is, to put God first in his life. Pastor, I believe these are the same Ten Commandments that are listed in Exodus.

Pastor, I even find that Jesus several times quoted Old Testament Law to criticize those of His day. For instance, in Matthew 23:23 Jesus says: "Woe to you, scribes and Pharisees, hypocrites! For you tithe mint and dill and cumin, and have neglected the weightier provisions of the law: justice and mercy and faithfulness; but these are the things you should have done without neglecting the others." And again in Luke 11:42 Jesus says: "But woe to you Pharisees! For you pay tithe of mint and rue and every kind of garden herb, and yet disregard justice and the love of God; but these are the things you should have done without neglecting the others." Isn't Jesus saying here, that they were right to obey God's command in Deuteronomy 14:22 ("You shall surely tithe all the produce from what you sow, which comes out of the field every year.") but were making a mockery of justice, mercy, faithfulness and all of the more important commands God has given us? I read in Matthew 15:3-8:

> And He answered and said to them, "And why do you yourselves transgress the commandment of God for the sake of your tradition? For God said, 'Honor your father and mother,' and, 'He who speaks evil of father or mother, let him be put to death.' But you say, 'Whoever shall say to his father or mother, "Anything of mine you might have been helped by has been given to God," he is not to honor his father or his mother.' And thus you invalidated the word of God for

the sake of your tradition. You hypocrites, rightly did Isaiah prophesy of you, saying, "'This people honors me with their lips, but their heart is far away from Me.'"

Pastor, isn't Jesus criticizing them for using some man-made rules to avoid God's command to "Honor your father and mother?" I was surprised to realize that Jesus—twice in the Gospels—quoted Old Testament Law to His disciples to give credence to what He was saying. This was in Matthew 10:10 wherein He says: "...or a bag for your journey, or even two tunics, or sandals, or a staff; for the worker is worthy of his support." Again, in Luke 10:7 wherein Jesus says: "... And stay in that house, eating and drinking what they give you; for the laborer is worthy of his wages..." In both of these instances, Jesus is quoting the Old Testament case law in Deuteronomy 25:4, which says, "You shall not muzzle the ox while he is threshing." We know that these both are correct interpretations of the Deuteronomy law because Paul, in 1 Corinthians 9:9-11, not only quotes the same law but also gives the interpretation: "...For it is written in the Law of Moses, 'You shall not muzzle the ox while he is threshing.' God is not concerned about oxen, is He? Or is He speaking altogether for our sake? Yes, for our sake it was written, because the plowman ought to plow in hope, and the thresher to thresh in hope of sharing the crops. If we sowed spiritual things in you, is it too much if we should reap material things from you?"

Now I am aware of the passage in John 15:10 in which Jesus says: "If you keep My commandments, you will abide in My love, just as I have kept My Father's commandments and abide in His love." I understand that some of those big-name scholars have tried to say that "See, Jesus' commandments are different from God the Father's, so now we can disregard the Old Testament commands!" Pastor, do you really believe that the laws and statutes that God applied to everyone, including Canaanites, Chaldeans, Egyptians, Jews, and Greeks from creation down to Jesus' time suddenly were changed? That sure does not sound plausible to me. I think I should probably study what the apostles had to say to the new believers in the rest of the New Testament.

What is your opinion, Pastor, about all these things Jesus said about God's Law?

Yours in Him,

LETTER 5

What Did the Apostles Say about Living Together?

Dear Pastor,

Well, I spent some time looking at the rest of the New Testament to see what the apostles and disciples had to say about God's laws and statutes for living together. I was surprised to see how much was there.

When I read their comments, I did have to put myself in their context. I doubt that any of them could even imagine living in a self-governing nation whose original laws were actually based on Biblical law! Most of them lived and wrote during the rule of the Roman Republic. As I understand, Roman law, during the time of the Republic, was more or less just but by no means Biblical. In fact, parts were pretty brutal. For instance, a father held his wife and children as chattel property and could dispose of them at his pleasure. I once saw a copy of a papyri found in Egypt that was a letter from a Roman soldier to his wife back in Italy. It said that if the baby she was expecting was a boy, she should take care of it, but if it was a girl she should "expose" it. (Expose meant to discard the baby in an open field.) Also, while Roman government left a little room for independently settling disputes there could have been no thought whatsoever of establishing an independent state! Finally, the New Testament writers expected the Lord's return was eminent and had no idea that many empires would rise and fall and 2,000 years later we still wait expectantly.

That being said, here is what I found. Paul reiterates the Ten Commandments for those living in Rome: "…You shall not commit adultery," "You shall not murder," "You shall not steal," "You shall not bear false witness," "You shall not covet," and if there is any other commandment, are all summed up in this saying, namely, "You shall love your neighbor as yourself" (Romans 13:9).

Of course, we know that these commandments are just the summary statements for different categories of God's rules. We can see that when Paul quotes Deuteronomy 25:4 to make the point that being a minister should be considered a full-time job worthy of pay. Paul says: "For it is written in the Law of Moses, 'You shall not muzzle an ox while it treads out the grain'" (1 Corinthians 9:9), falling under the categorical law "thou shall not steal." Paul would certainly not be quoting Mosaic Law if it had been preempted by some other set of rules.

Pastor, I believe a passage in 1 Corinthians 6 is really instructive on this subject, wherein Paul writes:

> (1) Does any one of you, when he has a case against his neighbor, dare to go to law before the unrighteous, and not before the saints? (2) Or do you not know that the saints will judge the world? And if the world is judged by you, are you not competent to constitute the smallest law courts? (3) Do you not know that we shall judge angels? How much more, matters of this life? (4) If then you have law courts dealing with matters of this life, do you appoint them as judges who are of no account in the church? (5) I say this to your shame. Is it so, that there is not among you one wise man who will be able to decide between his brethren, (6) but brother goes to law with brother, and that before unbelievers? (7) Actually, then, it is already a defeat for you, that you have lawsuits with one another. Why not rather be wronged? Why not rather be defrauded? (8) On the contrary, you yourselves wrong and defraud, and that your brethren.

My first observation is…here are believing Christians under the tutelage of Paul, himself, taking each other to court! So much for the idea that if we were just all Christians we would not need God's Law to settle disputes between us.

Secondly, from verse five, it seems that ignorance of God's law has been a perennial problem in the church: (5) "…to your shame. Is it so, that there is not among you one wise man who will be able to decide between his brethren."

Thirdly, Pastor, do you know anyone in our church who knows enough about God's Law to sit in judgment between angels!? I don't think we are even ready to deal with the here and now!

Fourthly, I think there is no doubt here that we have the clear responsibility to study God's law and be able to properly apply it to ourselves.

Pastor, I will admit that in my reading on being "under the law" in the New Testament, I did find some statements that at first seemed really troubling. Particularly in Galatians 3:1-2: "You foolish Galatians, who has bewitched you, before whose eyes Jesus Christ was publicly portrayed as crucified? This is the only thing I want to find out from you: did you receive the Spirit by the *works of the Law, or by hearing with faith*?" (emphasis added). This seems to be the "proof text" for all those who say we are now under "grace" and not "under the law." But, after some thought, I realized why Paul was saying this so strongly. I believe all these kinds of statements in the New Testament were directed at the so called "Judaizers," who were still holding on to the ceremonial law such as circumcision, kosher laws, etc. as requirements for following Christ. After all, Temple worship was still going strong through most of the writing of the New Testament, and had been for nearly a thousand and five hundred years before that. In fact, in the first ten or twelve years of the early church there was not a single record I could find of one uncircumcised Gentile in the church, which had, by that time, grown to be many thousands of Jews.

In fact, some twenty-eight years after the church was established at Pentecost, Paul made his last visit to Jerusalem. He reported there to the Apostles what God was doing among the Gentiles through his ministry. The Apostles rejoiced but cautioned Paul: "You see, brother, how many thousands there are among the Jews of those who have believed, and they are all zealous for the Law; and they have been told about you, that you are teaching all the Jews who are among the Gentiles to forsake Moses, telling them not to circumcise their children nor to walk according to the customs" (Act 21:20-21). So as to not "rock the boat" they even talked Paul into making a "ceremonial vow" to appease the Jerusalem Jewish believers.

Twenty-eight years into the history of the church and they are still arguing about whether it was necessary to follow the ceremonial law to be a follower of Christ!

Pastor, to put this in perspective, think about what would happen today if two guys called Peter and Paul showed up and proclaimed they had a new revelation from the Lord! According to this new revelation, baptism and the Lord's Supper are to be done away with because it was pure legalism! They could prove it because the Lord, Himself, told the thief on the cross that he would be with Him in Glory that very day and the thief certainly didn't get baptized or observe the Lord's Supper. Also in Ephesians 2:8-9 it clearly states that we are "saved by faith," not the legal proceedings of baptism and the supper thing. Now think about what would happen if more and more people began signing on to this "new revelation." I know this is preposterous, but what kind of conflict in churches do you think that would produce? Don't you think it might be something just short of World War Three? Pastor, thinking about it that way, it is amazing that there is actually so little written about no longer being under the ceremonial law. In fact, Pastor, I would urge you to go back and re-read Galatians with this in mind.

After Galatians 3:1 quoted above, Paul only talks about being enslaved or under "the law" four more times. In 4:9, he is speaking of ceremonial "months and seasons" connected to Temple worship and the remaining three references of 5:1, 5:11, and 6:12 are all about no longer requiring believers to be circumcised. I don't think it even occurred to him that his readers might think he was referring to not being under God's rules for living together in Galatians or any other epistle he wrote.

Paul puts this idea to rest with what he says in Corinthians: Circumcision is nothing, and uncircumcision is nothing, but *what matters is* the keeping of the commandments of God (1 Corinthians 7:19).

Pastor, I think we have been seriously misled with this idea of no longer needing God's commandments because we are "no longer under the law." What do you think?

Yours in Him,

P.S. You know, Pastor, to bring the question down to earth a bit more, can't you just see the new Christian in traffic court. The judge asks, "Are you guilty or not guilty?" The new Christian says, "Judge, I am not guilty. See here in Galatians 3:1 it says that I am 'not under the law;' that means I am not guilty!" I am sure that the Judge would say something like, "That will be $50 and you can pay at the window on your way out...next case." Pastor, I think you will have to admit, we are always under someone's law. And in this country it is up to us whether it is God's Law or someone else's law!

LETTER

Would Behavior Change If Everybody Were Christian?

Dear Pastor,

Along the line of saying "we are under grace and not the law" I was thinking more about my friend saying "If we just get everybody saved we would be okay." I think that comes from the Christian mantra of "Jesus changes lives" or "Jesus gives us the power to obey." Even though we all go around saying that, and this is going to sound like heresy, but Pastor, I don't think it's true. At least it isn't true the way we think it is.

Yes, of course, there is a wonderful change when we surrender our lives to Jesus. We experience an amazing spiritual birth, become a new creature, and have all of our sins forgiven, just to name a few of the blessings that come with salvation. I know, firsthand, what a wonderful change that is. However, I don't think Jesus includes in that process zapping us into suddenly being wonderfully holy and Christ-like people. The Lord Jesus provides forgiveness and restoration *but he doesn't deliver us from our human nature.*

Pastor, I believe God's word teaches us that our behavior is determined both before and after our commitment to the Lord by these three things acting on the free will God gives all of us:

- The extent or absence of Biblical training and discipline.
- The cultural or social acceptance of what is right or wrong.
- The restraints of doing wrong provided by Biblical civil and criminal law.

Here is why I came to these conclusions. First, God's word frequently talks about both His discipline for us and our own self-discipline. In Hebrews 12:5-11, Paul explains in detail how God disciplines us. In verses 9 and 10 he says: "Furthermore, we had earthly fathers to discipline us, and we respected them; shall we not much rather be subject to the Father of spirits, and live? For they disciplined us for a short time as seemed best to them, but He disciplines us for our good, that we may share His holiness." Now discipline here is not punishment and it is certainly not some instant change but a long and continuing process of training. In his book, *The Power of Family Unity*, author Rashid Rashad explains:

> To discipline means to instruct a person to follow a particular code of conduct or order. In the field of child development, discipline refers to methods of modeling character and of teaching self-control and acceptable behavior: for example, teaching a child to wash her/his hands before meals. Here, washing hands before meals is a particular pattern of behavior, and the child is being disciplined to adopt that pattern.

Pastor, I spent some time in the U.S. Navy and we were disciplined from the day I went in till I was honorably discharged. We were repeatedly trained to respond this way or that or trained to do a task or operate some piece of equipment with equal precision whether in a laboratory or surrounded by blinding, choking smoke and ear-splitting noise! I can assure you, Pastor, that did not happen overnight…It took a lot of time and repeated effort. Maybe an even better example is learning to fly an airplane using instruments. When you are flying in cloud cover, unable to see the horizon, the only way to know the orientation of the plane is an instrument on the dash. It takes an amazing amount of discipline and nearly two hundred hours of training to fly using the little instrument. What the instrument tells you is completely opposite from what your senses are telling you. In fact many pilots who are not trained to fly with instruments lose control when they try to fly into clouds and invariably crash. They feel no danger only to find too late they were actually in a spin.

Watchman Nee uses the Scripture "The sun rose upon him as he passed over Penuel, and he limped upon his thigh" (Genesis 32:31) in his August 7th devotion to make this observation:

> Here at Penuel, met face to face by God, Jacob received the new name of Israel. Yet the narrative continues to call him

Jacob! There is a reason in this. The truth is, of course, that nobody can completely change in one night...For Jacob, Penuel was not the touch of perfection; it was the beginning only of a new and transforming experience of God.

Pastor, while our forgiveness occurs in an instant of God's grace, BECOMING a Christian is a lifelong process! As the T-shirt says... "Forgive the mess; I'm still under construction!"

Now, besides taking a long time, what exactly is the discipline or training that God's word encourages us to embrace and not resist? It says in Deuteronomy 6:6-7: "And these words (God's commandments), which I am commanding you today, shall be on your heart; and you shall teach them diligently to your sons and shall talk of them when you sit in your house and when you walk by the way and when you lie down and when you rise up." Again in Psalm 119:8-10 it says: "I shall keep Thy statutes; ...How can a young man keep his way pure? By keeping *it* according to Thy word... Do not let me wander from Thy commandments." Even the Lord Jesus, Himself, says in Matthew 5:19 "Whoever then annuls one of the least of these commandments, and so teaches others, shall be called least in the kingdom of heaven; but whoever keeps and teaches them, he shall be called great in the kingdom of heaven."

We can, of course, resist proper discipline in our lives. But, Pastor, I think, first and foremost Christ-like behavior must come from a long period of embracing the study and discipline of God's precepts, principals, statutes, and laws. In fact, an inner-city pastor once told me, "If you want a Christ-like young man, you need to start the program about six months before his mother is born!"

Secondly, while some will want to discount the cultural or social environment as a factor, I just need to ask you, Pastor, how many times do you encounter the statement "What could I have done... Everyone else was doing it!" In my first biology class, the Professor walked into the room and said: "Now, the first superstition we need to lay to rest is that man came from a naked Hebrew stirring a clay pot in the desert!" "You need to decide now...Do you want to be an objective scientist or a religious fanatic?" This can have an effect on young minds. In fact, the most telling study along these lines was a doctoral thesis done at Southern Theological Seminary in Louisville Kentucky in the late seventies or early eighties. The seminary had, incidentally, become very liberal in its teaching at that time. One of the Th.D. candidates constructed and normalized a survey of orthodoxy. It asked such questions as "Was Jesus born of a virgin?" and "Was Jesus actually raised from the dead?" He administered the survey to Southern Baptist ministers who had no formal training had no formal seminary training, those who had received their Master of Divinity at Southern, and those who graduated from Southern with a Doctor of Divinity. He found that the most orthodox ministers were those with no formal seminary training and the least orthodox were those who had the most formal seminary training. That thesis, incidentally, started a revolt in the Southern Baptist Convention that virtually changed the entire hierarchy. Pastor, we can be influenced by that to which we expose ourselves.

Finally, our behavior is clearly modified by the laws and statutes we live under. At the extreme, if you research what produces criminal behavior, you will find experts who attribute it to everything from genetics to poverty and even the shape of the skull...It was called "phrenology." James Q. Wilson, one of the most noted scholars in this area, concluded that man is a rational being and will refrain from a crime when the cost is certain and significantly greater than the reward obtained from the crime. I suspect he didn't, but he could have concluded this from reading Deuteronomy 13:11, 17:13, 19:20, and 21:21. Verse 20 of Chapter 19, for instance, says: "And the rest will hear (of this penalty) and be afraid, and will never again do such an evil thing among you."

As I mentioned in my last letter, the sadist experiment we have just made that proves this beyond any doubt is our marriage laws. When our nation's marriage laws were fairly near Biblical marriage law, the divorce rate was less than five or ten percent. Now that we gave this process over to those who discount Biblical teaching we, including Christians, suffer a divorce rate of fifty percent and more. I don't know what we were thinking; do you?

Finally, Pastor, I will admit that religious commitment or fervor can be a factor in our behavior, but I am convinced that it can fade just as quickly. I am convinced that it is the things laid out above that is really the determinate factors. What do you think? Am I off-base here?

Yours in Christ,

LETTER

The "Great Commission" Says Nations, Not People Why?

Dear Pastor,

In looking at some of the church's study material, I saw that the "Biblical Purpose" of the church was pretty much wrapped up in the "Great Commission" given in Matthew 28:19-20:

> Go therefore and make disciples of all the nations, baptizing them in the name of the Father and the Son and the Holy Spirit, teaching them to observe all that I commanded you; and lo, I am with you always, even to the end of the age.

Mark 16:15 and Luke 24:45-49 are also listed, describing this command in slightly different words.

Before I go further, Pastor, you know that I believe without doubt that our "salvation" is strictly personal. I also know that there is no such thing, in any form, that can be even thought of as "collective salvation." That is not where I am going. That said, here are two things I noticed about these scriptures.

The first is: Why did the Lord use the word "nations" instead of "people" when He tells us to make them disciples?

The second is: What did the Lord mean when He said to teach these "nations" to "observe" all My commandments?

Pastor, I began to think the Lord's instructions here go considerably beyond just preaching personal salvation, telling them to live holy lives and showing them how to pass the "Gospel" on to others! *I think He is commissioning us to teach nations His commandments and then*

do everything we possibly can to see they do His commandments! I think
the Lord intended just what I have been saying in my previous letters.
Here is what I did to look at these important scriptures.

Admittedly, with only three semesters of Greek, I know just
enough to be dangerous. With that disclaimer, I went to my Greek
New Testament and found that the word "nations" used here is the
Greek word εθνη (eth'nay). This Greek word is used 52 times in the
New Testament and about 336 times in the Septuagint (the Greek
translation of the Old Testament done about a century before Christ
was born.) The first instance occurs in Genesis 10:32 wherein it says
that out of the sons of Noah came all the nations (εθνη) of the world.
In fact, it was at this time in world history that God first created
nations by creating a different language for each tribal group, which
He then called nations at Babel. Throughout the scriptures it always
refers to a group or groups of people that are in some way identifiable
as a unit...typically through a common language. All through the
Old Testament (and every time the Old Testament is quoted in the
New Testament) it is used to refer to "Gentile" nations or people. In
the 22 other times εθνη is used in the New Testament it is referring
to "nations" in general. This is especially true in the many times it
is used in the book of Revelation. Pastor, it is never used to mean
"people" in general!

Interestingly, I just ran across a more complete study of this very
thing by Reverend John Piper, pastor of Bethlehem Baptist Church
in Minneapolis, Minnesota. He wrote a paper entitled "Discipling
All the Peoples" published in a book called *Perspectives* (Chapter 17,
pp. 113-117). His conclusion is that Matthew 28 is not saying "all
individuals," but rather the focus of the command is the discipling of
all the "people groups" of the world.

At this point, I wondered if perhaps this was the only Greek word
available to express "all people." When I went back to check on this,
I found that there was a perfectly good noun to express "people" in
the Greek word ψυχη (sue' kee). In fact, it specifically includes in its
definition the concept of a person as being both spiritual and physical
rather than just another creature. While it has a plural form, it can be
paired with the pronoun πασα (pas' sa), meaning "all" or "every," to
make it even more inclusive. There are several other Greek word forms
and combinations that could have been used had the Lord wanted to
say "every person" or just "all people in general." By the way, Pastor, I
didn't stop here, I looked up all these Greek words in the 10-volume

dictionary of the New Testament, known as "Kittel." Each one of these words has about 8-10 pages of discussion of how they were used and defined in Greek literature, the Greek Old and New Testaments, and other contemporary Greek writers. It confirmed what I said above: when the Lord said "nations" he meant NATIONS!

Pastor, if God uses the term "nations" in His instructions to the church, I clearly think we should go back to God's Word and take a closer look at that term.

In the Septuagint (Greek translation of the Old Testament), God told Abraham three times that through his seed all the nations (ἔθνη) of the world would be blest. He told him a fourth time, but used the term "families of the world" or "clans." I know that this "seed" of Abraham surely refers to Jesus, our Savior, as explained in Galatians 3:16. So, no doubt, part of this "blessing" is our personal salvation through Christ Jesus. But does that mean that a nation with a large population of believers is a "blest" nation? Pastor, it surely includes more than this. If this was all there was to it, then you would have to say that Haiti, Nigeria, or Bolivia were as "blest" as America because all have about the same percentage of believers. And, you would have to say that the inner-city ghetto (where there are a very high percentage of believers) was more "blest" than our affluent suburbs where the percentage is lower. That is clearly ridiculous!

Pastor, don't you believe this blessing of a nation has to include one where God's justice prevails and the freedoms he has given us are enjoyed? That is surely missing in the ghettos and the nations mentioned above and as a result it would be silly to call them blest.

Incidentally, we have no need to speculate about what a blest nation is or is not…The Lord has given us that definition in Deuteronomy 28:1: "Now it shall be, if you will diligently obey the Lord your God, being careful to do all His commandments which I command you today, the Lord your God will set you high above all the nations of the earth." (As an aside, Pastor, "above all the nations of the earth" is where we find ourselves today, but don't hold your breath. If we don't do something pretty quickly we won't be here much longer!) It goes on to say: "And all these blessings shall come upon you and overtake you, if you will obey the Lord your God." Pastor, it goes on for 14 verses describing the blessings of obedience and you really should re-read it. It will blow you away.

There is yet another reason, I believe, the Lord uses the word "nations" instead of everyone or all mankind or the like, and that is the "disobedience" God really, really dislikes is *violence, defrauding the innocent and injustice within a nation.* By that I mean where murder and violence goes unpunished and where through fraud and injustice the widow, the orphan, the helpless or disabled and such are treated unjustly. Ezekiel 16:49 says: "Behold, this was the guilt of your sister Sodom: she and her daughters had arrogance, abundant food, and careless ease, but she did not help the poor and needy." And in Isaiah 10 it says: "Woe to those who enact evil statutes, And to those who constantly record unjust decisions, So as to deprive the needy of *justice*, and rob the poor of My people of their rights, in order that widows may be their spoil, and that they may plunder the orphans." Even Jesus, as I mentioned in an earlier letter, said:

> But you say, "Whoever shall say to his father or mother, 'Anything of mine you might have been helped by has been given to God,' he is not to honor his father or his mother." And thus you invalidated the word of God for the sake of your tradition. You hypocrites, rightly did Isaiah prophesy of you, saying, "This people honors Me with their lips, But their heart is far away from Me..." (Mat 15:7-8 NAS).

Micah 6:8 says: "...what does the Lord require of you but to do *justly*, to love mercy, and to walk humbly with your God?" (emphasis added).

Pastor, a single believer cannot "do justly;" in fact, not even a church can "do justly." A single believer cannot try and enforce penalties against violence, theft, or fraud; in fact neither can a church. It takes a government (nation) to practice justice or injustice, try criminals and execute murderers.

And, Pastor, a lot of God's rules for living together that involve fraud, theft, violence, and murder that clearly can only be enforced or not enforced by a nation.

So, since individuals and churches cannot practice "injustice" or "record unjust decisions," it begins to make sense that the Lord would tell us to "...make disciples of all *nations*" and "teach them" His commandments. As the Bible commentator Matthew Henry, writing in 1721, says about this passage, "...bring the nations to be His subjects; setting up a school, bring the nations to be His scholars..."

Pastor, if you look closely at Jesus' second command in this passage, it goes even further. He does NOT say to "teach" the nations His commandments...He says to "teach them to *observe*" His commandments!

Observe can mean to "see" or "understand" as in: "I *see and understand* the speed limit sign says 30 miles per hour." Or it can mean: "Sir, you did not *observe* the speed limit…Here is your citation for driving 45 miles per hour!"

Jesus, in this command, uses the Greek word τηρειν (ter · ein'), the infinitive present active of τηρεώ (ter · eh · oh). It basically means to guard, keep, preserve, do, or obey. In fact the Revised Standard Version and the New International Version of the Bible both more correctly translate the word as "obey!"

In the Old Testament, the Lord, through Moses, says: "You shall therefore obey the LORD your God, and do His commandments…" (Deuteronomy 27:10). The word "do" is the Hebrew word "asah" which, in the Septuagint, was translated into the Greek word τηρεώ…the same word that Jesus uses in His command above.

Pastor, doesn't it seem to you that Jesus is telling us that we have a responsibility beyond teaching the nations His commandments? Are we not also to call them to task when they do not do them?

Clearly, God created nations to govern societies. And it appears to me that we may be "selectively" obeying God's commission to the church. Pastor, haven't we turned our backs on this second part.

Pastor, I think this "silence" may be the very reason that our nation is in cultural decline. What do you think?

Yours in Him,

P.S. Just for the record, I discovered something very interesting. I discovered that after the Lord creates the "new Jerusalem," does away with death and dying, and when there will be no more wars…that is in the "new heavens and the new earth"… there are still going to be "nations!" Just go back and read Micah 4:2-4 and Revelations 21:23-27 and 22:1-2.

Also interesting is that in my Bible, the New American Standard Version, the words "sin" or "sins" appears 623 times and, of course, that is no surprise. But what is surprising is that the words "nation" or "nations" appears even more times…at 644! I believe we are missing something if we think that God is not interested in nations.

LETER

Are There Any Governments Modeled After the Bible in History?

Dear Pastor,

I have tried to see which nations, if any, modeled their government after what the Bible teaches and how they fared. What I did is, of course, very precursory and certainly not scholarly, but even at this level I discovered some very interesting things.

Now I know that God's word does not specify exactly what form of government is correct in terms of whether we should have a parliament and prime minister or congress and president or something else. But it is certainly not without advice on the subject. In 1 Samuel 8:9, God tells Samuel: "…you shall solemnly warn them and tell them of the procedure of the king who will reign over them." In the following verses He then tells them, in no uncertain words, that if they allow a king to govern them, a good king will multiply wealth to himself and a bad king will turn them into peasants! The Bible also seems to make it clear that you cannot have someone who is a ruler or king and also a priest. Jesus, alone, can be both priest and king! The Bible is also really clear as to how to appoint judges and just how they should judge. It also rules out the so-called socialist forms of government. It is probably not true, but I have heard that Karl Marx said that the only thing that stood between him and his socialist economic ideas was the "eighth commandment." (Thou shall not steal.) Our founding fathers in America were convinced, as am I, that God, in His word, gives us the rights of "life," "liberty," and "the pursuit of happiness (or property)." In fact, I believe a case can be made that the Bible considerably limits the role of government in our lives. Finally, there is the whole body of laws, statutes, etc. in the Old Testament on tort law, criminal law, etc. I think the important thing here is that anyone with a reasonable mind can look at some government and say: "yes, that seems to agree with God's word," or "no, that doesn't," at least on the main things.

Looking at Bible history, Moses set all these ideas before Israel and prophesied that if they would do them, they would be blest out of site. They had a pretty good start under Joshua, but as a kind of federation of twelve tribes they could never quite keep it together. (As an aside, Pastor, the similar "Articles of Confederation" we started out with in this country never worked either!) Plus they started adopting poor ideas from the very local population they were supposed to displace. It was not until David that they started to get it together and then under his son Solomon they momentarily flourished. Solomon, as kings always do, bled a lot of wealth off to himself and then fell in to disrepute with his foreign wives. His son was a total loss, and Israel never really got it back together enough to make a difference after that. It is true, over the years, that they had some revivals, but those were never complete changes and they came and went depending on which king was in power at the time. Push comes to shove; Pastor, except for Solomon's early years, Israel simply never became the nation that God offered to make them!

History offers some kingdoms and empires that are portrayed to be pretty big deals, such as Alexander the Great and the Greek empire, the Pharaohs and their Egyptian kingdom and then dwarfing these was the great Roman Empire. None of these nations came close in nature to anything Biblical, and to put them in perspective, you could have fit the entire Roman Empire, including the Mediterranean Sea, into one side of Canada, just to our north!

As a comparison, the British Empire, at its peak, had control over one fourth of the planet's land mass and one fourth of the earth's population. France, Spain, and the Netherlands developed empires but they were much shorter-lived and far less extensive. However, the whole idea of an empire of colonies does not strike me as fitting very well with the Biblical teaching of governance and, in practice, it was clearly not very stable.

While Britain, as a nation, dates back to Roman times, it did not really flourish until the early 1600s. It would seem to correspond to two changes. First, thanks to Wycliffe's translation of the Bible into common English in the late 1300s followed by Martin Luther's reformation in the 1400s more and more people in England had firsthand access to the Bible and its teaching. Secondly, at about this same time the power of the monarch was being eroded and was all but extinguished by the Whig revolution of 1688-89. In the early 1700s, Sir William Blackstone was commissioned to codify English common law. He did so, and it is available today in his four-volume work, *Commentaries on the Laws of England*.

Blackstone, in his Prologue, divided law into two categories. The first he called "the law of nature" and described these laws as given at creation and "dictated by God Himself." He states that while we can use our "reason" to discover these laws, we are limited. As Blackstone describes it: "…If our reason were always, as in our first ancestor before his transgression, clear and perfect, unruffled by passions, unclouded by prejudice…we would need no other guide but this." "But every man now finds the contrary in his own experience: that his reason is corrupt, and his understanding full of ignorance and error."

Thus, Blackstone points out that God in his providence "…has been pleased, at sundry times and in diverse manners, to discover and enforce its laws by an immediate and direct revelation." "The doctrines thus delivered we call the revealed or divine law, and they are to be found only in the Holy Scriptures."

Blackstone concludes "Upon these two foundations, the law of nature and the law of revelation, depend all human laws; that is to say, no human laws should be suffered to contradict these."

As stated in the introduction of these volumes: "Sir William Blackstone's Commentaries on the *Laws of England* (1765-69) is the most important legal treatise ever written in the English language. It was the dominant law book in England and America in the century after its publication and played a unique role in the development of the fledgling American legal system."

The conclusion here, Pastor, is that Britian came somewhat close to Biblical law over this period, from 1300 to 1700, and gained influence over about a quarter of the planet. They had an enormous handicap, however, of nearly nine centuries of baggage that kept dragging them off in other directions until the "Enlightenment" finally got them largely distracted.

Pastor, this makes me think we should see just how we, as America, got started and whether we have any claim to being close to the Biblical model.

Yours in Christ,

LETER

Was American Government Modeled After the Bible?

Dear Pastor,

As I mentioned in my last letter, I have now looked at whether we in America have any claim on trying to model our government after Biblical teaching. What I found was amazing to me!

First, America was, in 1600, a completely blank slate. The country was a wilderness with no settled cities, towns, or organized government. Unlike many other countries in the world, the original settlers in this country had no existing traditions, laws, government, or culture to compete with. They were free to start from scratch in establishing American culture and government.

Secondly, most of these settlers were strongly religious and coming to America for refuge. The first paragraph of a document from the Library of Congress says it best (http://www.loc.gov/exhibits/religion/rel01.html):

> Many of the British North American colonies that eventually formed the United States of America were settled in the seventeenth century by men and women, who, in the face of European persecution, refused to compromise passionately held religious convictions and fled Europe. The New England colonies, New Jersey, Pennsylvania, and Maryland were conceived and established "as plantations of religion." Some settlers who arrived in these areas came for secular motives--"to catch fish" as one New Englander put it—but the

great majority left Europe to worship God in the way they believed to be correct. They enthusiastically supported the efforts of their leaders to create "a city on a hill" or a "holy experiment," whose success would prove that God's plan for his churches could be successfully realized in the American wilderness. Even colonies like Virginia, which were planned as commercial ventures, were led by entrepreneurs who considered themselves "militant Protestants" and who worked diligently to promote the prosperity of the church.

Their intent to establish Biblical government in America is shown in a 1630 address given to the Massachusetts Bay colonists by Governor John Winthrop on or just before passage to America (http://religiousfreedom.lib.virginia.edu/sacred/charity.html):

> ...And to shut this discourse with that exhortation of Moses, that faithful servant of the Lord, in his last farewell to Israel, Deut. 30. "Beloved, there is now set before us life and death, good and evil," in that we are commanded this day to love the Lord our God, and to love one another, to walk in his ways and *to keep his Commandments and his ordinance and his laws,* and the articles of our Covenant with Him, that we may live and be multiplied, and that the Lord our God may bless us in the land whither we go to possess it.... *(emphasis added)*

He warned, in this same sermon, that: "The eyes of all people are upon us, so that if we deal falsely with our God in this work we have undertaken, and so cause us to withdraw His present help from us, we shall be made a story and a byword through the world."

Pastor, one of the most quoted sermons during the American revolutionary times was by Samuel Sherwood, a *Connecticut pastor. His text was Revelations 12: 14-17. He uses this text to propose that God actually destined the American colonies to save the church, as the woman of the text was given wings to fly into the wilderness and escape the serpent. It is really a moving sermon, Pastor. Please go to the reference here and read it yourself. The title of Mr. Sherwood's sermon is "The Church's Flight Into The Wilderness: An Address On The Times."* You can also find it in Volume One of the two-volume work, *Political Sermons of the American Founding Era,* which includes a Foreword by Mr. Ellis Sandoz. This is available through Liberty Fund, Inc. at http://oll.libertyfund.org/?option=com_staticxt&staticfile=show. php%3Ftitle=816&chapter=69264&layout=html&Itemid=27.

What really clinches the argument of whether American government is modeled after Biblical teaching can be found in the proceedings of the Constitutional Convention, which finally established how America would be governed. What I am referring to, Pastor, is a speech given by Benjamin Franklin. (This speech was found, a considerable time later, as an insert in James Madison's diary in Franklin's own handwriting!) (http://www.wallbuilders. com/LIBissuesArticles.asp?id=98) He begins by saying:

> Mr. President,
> The small progress we have made after 4 or five weeks close attendance & continual reasonings with each other, our different sentiments on almost every question, several of the last producing as many noes and ays, is methinks a melancholy proof of the imperfection of the Human Understanding. We indeed seem to feel our own want of political wisdom, some we have been running about in search of it. We have gone back to ancient history for models of Government, and examined the different forms of those Republics which having been formed with the seeds of their own dissolution now no longer exist. And we have viewed Modern States all round Europe, but find none of their Constitutions suitable to our circumstances.

As I said before, Pastor, they are starting from a blank slate! They have looked at every form of government, past and present and rejected them all. Franklin goes on to say:

> ...how has it happened, Sir, that we have not hitherto once thought of humbly applying to the Father of lights to illuminate our understandings? In the beginning of the Contest with G. Britain, when we were sensible of danger we had daily prayer in this room for the divine protection. Our prayers, Sir, were heard, and they were graciously answered. All of us who were engaged in the struggle must have observed frequent instances of a Superintending providence in our favor. To that kind providence we owe this happy opportunity of consulting in peace on the means of establishing our future national felicity. And have we now forgotten that powerful friend? I have lived, Sir, a long time, and the longer I live, the more convincing proofs I see of this truth- that God governs in the affairs of men. And if a sparrow cannot fall to the

ground without his notice, is it probable that an empire can rise without his aid? We have been assured, Sir, in the sacred writings, that "except the Lord build the House they labour in vain that build it." I firmly believe this; and I also believe that without his concurring aid we shall succeed in this political building no better than the Builders of Babel...

They then adjourned for three days of prayer, asking God to provide the framework for the new nation. Pastor, our God is faithful and just and I know that if we humbly ask His guidance, He is certain to give it! Thus, within the limits of human frailty, I believe that God indeed provided them the framework for which they asked. In fact, Pastor, in light of this, I would venture to say that our Constitution was God-given! Wouldn't you?

They were here, only concerned with how the states would be represented, limiting the powers of the federal government, etc. The laws of the land were already well established by the writings of Sir William Blackstone. In fact, one of the Congressional attendees actually studied under Blackstone himself in Great Britain. As pointed out in my last letter, Blackstone's conclusion was: "Upon these two foundations, the law of nature and the law of revelation, depend all human laws; that is to say, no human laws should be suffered to contradict these." To put it another way, any law that differs from the laws, statutes, and commandments of the Bible are not legitimate laws and should not be tolerated!

Pastor, is it as clear to you as it is to me that for the first time since Israel was given the promised land, men sat down and, from scratch, tried their best to form a government and establish laws as laid out in God's word and as they felt directed by the Lord, Himself?

Pastor, I apologize for the length of this letter...It is way too long. However, I hope you are as excited as I am about this research. I think I should also check the Declaration of Independence since this was the original rationale for separating ourselves from Great Britain and forming a separate nation.

Yours in Christ,

LETTER

Is the Declaration of Independence Biblical?
Part I: The Right to Life

Dear Pastor,

In my last letter I asked if American government was based on Biblical Law. It occurred to me that I had better check the Declaration of Independence to see if it was based on secular reasoning or Biblical Law. I was astounded! The first sentence of the document includes these words:

> "...to assume among the powers of the earth, the separate and equal station to which the Laws of Nature and of Nature's God entitle them..."

Pastor, as you remember from previous letters the "Laws of Nature and of Nature's God" was explained by Sir William Blackstone, the British legal scholar of that era, as simply the contemporary way to say "Biblical Law." Pastor, do you think our children are being taught that our nation's founding fathers appealed to Biblical Law as the philosophical basis and rationale for declaring independence from Britain? I don't think so! The very next paragraph of this document says:

> We hold these truths to be self-evident, that all men are created equal, that they are endowed by their Creator with certain unalienable Rights; that among these are Life, Liberty and the pursuit of Happiness...

Pastor, most of us are so familiar with this statement I think we might have failed to really reflect on what these men are saying. *They are declaring here that this new independent government they intend to establish is going to be based on rights given us by God, Himself,* and I can assure you, Pastor, when they used the term "Creator" here, they are referring to God, Himself.

Now, the question is...

Does God's Law really give us the unalienable rights of life, liberty, and the pursuit of happiness (better known as property rights)? Is this Biblical? Is this really in God's Word?

Pastor, let's take these "rights" one at a time and see if they really are in God's Word.

We should probably start with the right to *life*.

Pastor, I presume you would look at this first regarding our right to life after birth. I think I would start with Genesis 1:27: "And God created man in His own image, in the image of God He created him; male and female He created them." Because we are created in the image of God, He gives us in His Law: "You shall not murder" (Exodus 20:13). And "...do not kill the innocent and righteous" (Exodus 23:7). Now I know that God's Word does allow for exceptions in the taking of human life involving self-defense, certain capital offenses and during a justifiable war, but we could consider these at another time.

You and I would both agree, however, that abortion is certainly not one of these exceptions! Pastor, I know that you agree with me on this but because some think the Bible might equivocate on this issue I thought I should share what I found. Dr. R. Rushdoony in his book *The Institutes of Biblical Law*, puts it this way: "Abortion, the destruction of the human embryo or fetus, has long been regarded by Biblical standards as murder. The grounds for this judgment are the sixth commandment, and Exodus 21:22-25." He first cites Cassuto's "explanatory rendering" of this latter passage:

> When men strive together and they hurt unintentionally a woman with child, and her children come forth but no mischief happens—that is, the woman and the children do not die—the one who hurt her shall surely be punished by a fine. But if any mischief happens, that is, if the woman dies or the children die, then you shall give life for life. (From *Commentary on the Book of Exodus* by Umberto Cassuto; Jerusalem: Magnes Press. The Hebrew University, 1967.)

He then cites the Old Testament commentary of Keil and Delitzsch, The Pentateuch, II (134f):

If men strove and thrust against a woman with child, who had come near or between them for the purpose of making peace, so that her children come out (come into the world), and no injury was done either to the woman or the child that was born, a pecuniary compensation was to be paid, such as the husband of the woman laid upon him, and he was to give it... by (by an appeal to) arbitrators. A fine is imposed, because even if no injury had been done to the woman and the fruit of her womb, such a blow might have endangered life...The plural...is employed for the purpose of speaking indefinitely, because there might possibly be more than one child in the womb. "But if injuries occur (to the mother or the child) thou shall give soul for soul, eye for eye, wound for wound": thus perfect retribution was to be made.

Finally, Dr. Rushdoony makes these comments:

The importance of Exodus 21:22-25 becomes all the more clear as we realize that this is case law, i.e., that it sets forth by a minimal case certain larger implications. Let us examine some of the implications of this passage: First, very obviously, the text cites, not a case of deliberate abortion, but a case of accidental abortion. If the penalty for even an accidental case is so severe, it is obvious that a deliberately induced abortion is very strongly forbidden. It is not necessary to ban deliberate abortion, since it is already eliminated by this law. Second the penalty for even an accidental abortion is death. If a man who, in the course of a fight, unintentionally bumps a pregnant woman and causes her to abort, must suffer the death penalty, how much more so any person who intentionally induces an abortion? Third, even if no injury results to either the mother or the fetus, the man in the case is liable to a fine and, in fact, must be fined. Clearly, the law strongly protects the pregnant woman and her fetus so that every pregnant mother has a strong hedge of law around her.

The understanding that God considers abortion to be murder has been consistent from the first century as noted in the Didache—a catechism for children and new believers from around 70 AD—which states "... thou shalt not murder a child by abortion nor kill that which is begotten." This belief is also echoed by Josephus, the first century Jewish historian, in his *Against Apion* wherein he says: "The law, moreover, enjoins us to bring up all our offspring and forbids women to cause abortion of what is begotten, or to kill it afterward…"(2:202). For a modern discussion of what the Bible has to say, here are references from Protestant, Catholic, and Orthodox Jewish teachers:

- Biblical Basis for a Pro-life Position: (Protestant)
  http://www.godandscience.org/doctrine/prolife.html
- Bible's Teaching Against Abortion: (Catholic)
  http://www.priestsforlife.org/brochures/thebible.html
- Judaism and Abortion: (Orthodox Jewish)
  http://www.angelfire.com/mo/baha/judaism.html

Now, if we believe the Bible is the inspired word of God, there does not appear to be any question that God does grant us a right to life from conception to natural death. Pastor, it seems that when our nation's founders claimed that God, in His law, gave us the "unalienable right to life" they were exactly right. Pastor, in the some 400 years of this country's history, it is only in the past 30 or so that we have abandoned this unalienable right in our laws. Don't you think we should go back to honoring that right?

The unsettling thing here, Pastor, is that I don't think that our congregation knows this or has given it much thought. If they knew that the first assumption in forming our government was that God has given us the right to life and that God's word considers abortion to be murder and a clear violation of that right to life, I don't think we would be where we are as a nation.

To bring this down to a personal level, Pastor, there is a little girl who lives only a mile or two from us. In about twenty years she is going to get pregnant. If we go right on doing what we are doing now, she will have her baby aborted. What will we say, Pastor, to that baby when we get to Glory…Why we did not take the trouble to save his life? What will we say to our Lord?

Did you know that if we—along with other Bible believing folks—simply went to the trouble to make sure everyone in our congregation was registered to vote, and then voted for the presidential and senatorial candidates who pledged to support the right to life, and we did that for the next five election cycles (about 20 years), abortion would no longer be legal in our country? Just a few weeks of work over the next twenty years and we could easily save that baby's life! Pastor, this letter is way too long, but later I will show you how unquestionable this fact is. In fact our elections are so close that even if half of Bible- believing folks did this, it would still happen. Don't you think our congregation should be aware of this?

Pastor, do you think we should have some sermons on Matthew 18:14… "Thus it is not the will of your Father who is in Heaven that one of these little ones perishes?"

Yours in Him,

LETTER 11

Is the Declaration of Independence Biblical?
Part II: The Right to Liberty – Religious Liberty

Dear Pastor,

In my last letter, we found that the "unalienable right to life" mentioned in the Declaration of Independence was clearly included in God's Word and His Law. So now I thought we should look at our "unalienable right to liberty" in the Declaration of Independence. The "unalienable right to liberty" is so broad I also thought we should break it into "religious liberty" and "civil liberty."

Let's start with religious liberty since that is surely in contention these days. Pastor, I am referring to the Federal mandate that requires religious schools, hospitals, charities, etc. to provide abortions or abortifacients to their employees through their health insurance plans. Since Judeo-Christian law and teaching clearly forbids that, they are being required to act against their beliefs and thus have had their religious liberty abrogated. Pastor, should that be allowed? Should we do something?

This seems to raise the question: What are legitimate religious liberties and how are they determined? Do we simply vote and if the majority of us think it is okay, it then becomes okay?

For example, what if some families who traced their roots back to the Mayan culture of Central America migrated to this country, and they decided that their corn crop would be much better if they sacrificed a young girl to their god? Should they be allowed that religious liberty? What if everyone voted and the majority decided that it would be okay as long it was one of their young girls and not one of ours? Should that be allowed? Or if the Middle-Eastern family in our country decided to kill their daughter because she left her faith to marry a Christian boy...Would that be okay? You know, Pastor, that is accepted as all right in more than one country...even today!

Obviously, when the fifty-six signers of the Declaration of Independence read that document those thoughts never entered their minds. As we saw in my last letter, I am sure they limited this liberty as that which was endowed by our Creator...God Himself. In fact, just to see what they were thinking at that time, I looked up "religious liberty" in Noah Webster's *American Dictionary of the English Language*, published in 1828. He defines "religious liberty" as:

> Religious liberty is the free right of adopting and enjoying opinions on religious subjects, and of worshiping the Supreme Being according the dictates of conscience, without external control.

Pastor, there was no argument, at that time, about who the Supreme Being was! It was unanimously understood that it was the Creator, the God of the Bible.

So then, Pastor, what does God's Word say about religious liberty? Is religious liberty allowed in God's Law? As I began to look into this, I realized that, yes, of course, He gives us this liberty.

Beginning with Adam, whom God gave the *liberty* to believe Satan and disobey God's command all the way through to the Israelites, whom Joshua told to "*Choose* you this day, whom you will serve" God has extended us the liberty to choose to believe Him or reject Him! In the New Testament as well, John tells us:

> He who believes in Him is not judged; he who does not (choose to believe) believe has been judged already, because he has not believed in the name of the only begotten Son of God (John 3:18).

Two very important things come to mind here. First is the obvious that we can only *love* God when we are given the choice to reject Him. In other words, you cannot be *loved* by an automaton. Such a thing would not have the independence to choose anything for which it had not been programmed. Love is, by definition, volitional! So God does give us the "religious liberty" to love and obey or reject and disregard.

Secondly, we are strictly forbidden to even make religious judgments about someone. The Bible makes this clear:

> For who among men knows the thoughts of a man except the spirit of the man, which is in him...? (1 Corinthians 2:11)

God, in fact, reserves all such judgment to Himself. He, of course, does judge and condemns those who choose to reject Him. But, because of our inability, He warns us *not to make such judgments.*

> But the Lord said to Samuel, "Do not look at his appearance or at the height of his stature, because I have rejected him; for God sees not as man sees, for man looks at the outward appearance, but the LORD looks at the heart" (1 Samuel 16:7).

And, through Jeremiah God tells us:

> "I, the LORD, search the heart, I test the mind, Even to give to each man according to his ways, According to the results of his deeds" (Jeremiah 17:10).

Pastor, I don't think we are aware of this, but the Bible actually even commands us to be hospitable to foreigners! We are told:

> "When a stranger resides with you in your land, you shall not do him wrong. The stranger who resides with you shall be to you as the native among you, and you shall love him as yourself; for you were aliens in the land of Egypt: I am the LORD your God" (Leviticus 19:33-34).

Jesus, Himself, said

> "For I was hungry, and you gave Me something to eat; I was thirsty, and you gave Me drink; I was a stranger (a foreigner), and you invited Me in..." (Matthew 25:35)

So does God, in His Law, allow these "strangers" to carry out any "religious" practice they think is required by their faith? Should we allow people to kill their children or cut off the thief's hand or what ever else their religion requires?

Emphatically not!

While the Bible gives everyone the liberty to believe and worship as they will, it *does not* allow them to have their own *law.* Repeatedly, God's Word tells us:

- "The *same law* shall apply to the native as to the stranger who sojourns among you" (Exodus 12:48-49).

- "There is to be ONE LAW and one ordinance for you and for the alien who sojourns with you" (Numbers 15:16).

- "You shall have *one law* for him who does anything unintentionally, for him who is native among the sons of Israel and for the alien who sojourns among them" (Numbers 15:29).

Pastor, it sure seems clear to me that God does, in fact, give us religious liberty, and in fact, commands us to extend that liberty to everyone else. At least, to the extent that any particular religious acts do not conflict with God's Law.

So, the Declaration of Independence, when it said that our new government was going to be based on the "unalienable right to (religious) Liberty," was certainly within the teaching of the Bible!

Sadly, Pastor, we have been losing those liberties of late. For example, do you feel the liberty to speak out about a person doing right or wrong when that person is a politician? Pastor, it seems to me that God has even given us a command to do this very thing.

> When I say to the wicked, "You shall surely die"; and you do not warn him or speak out to warn the wicked from his wicked way that he may live, that wicked man shall die in his iniquity, but his blood I will require at your hand (Ezekiel 3:18).

I think that most pastors these days feel "gagged" by the fear of losing their non-taxable status and am afraid of saying or doing anything in this area. *Pastor, that is a loss of religious liberty that is not only wrong; it is against Biblical teaching.*

Would you believe that in our 400-year history, we just lost this particular liberty in my lifetime! Senator Lyndon B. Johnson, in 1954 added an amendment to another bill that prohibited 501(c)3 organizations from being involved in a political campaign. Progressive liberal "rulers" really do not like criticism, especially about what they might be doing right or wrong. There is also no doubt that they will continue to chip away in this area until all of the Judeo-Christian voices are completely silenced.

Pastor, I firmly believe that we need to do something about this. Please go to the website below to see how the American Catholic Bishops are planning to fight our loss of religious liberty: http://www.usccb.org/issues-and-action/religious-liberty/our-first-most-cherished-liberty.cfm.

Pastor, we still have just enough liberty in this area left to us that if we act soon we can begin to reverse this and regain those liberties. *And we can regain them* if we roll up our sleeves and go to work.

However, if we fail to act and just keep on doing what we have been, we may well become so isolated that change will be beyond our grasp!

Because of my thirty-some years of experience leading tax-exempt 501(c)3 organizations…even through a couple of IRS audits, I can tell you how we can go about this safely. In some of my later letters entitled "God's Word and governing ourselves" I will explain how this can be done.

Pastor, right now though, we need to explain to our congregation how we are losing our religious liberty. I sure hope you feel as strongly as I do about our liberties.

Yours in Christ,

LETTER

Is the Declaration of Independence Biblical?
Part III: The Right to Liberty – Civil Liberty

Dear Pastor,

In the last letter, I think we showed that our *religious liberties*, as part of the "unalienable right to liberty," mentioned in the Declaration of Independence, was clearly given to us in God's Word. In this letter I thought we could consider whether *civil liberties* are also given to us by the Bible. By civil liberties, I mean the unrestrained freedom to contract with one another through employment, buying and selling, leasing, manufacturing, etc.

Pastor, to prove a negative—e.g. "the Bible does not restrict commerce…"—is very difficult. However, you can come pretty close because the Bible is, in fact, so brief when it speaks to this subject.

Orthodox Jewish teaching commonly recognizes 613 Commandments in the Bible (specifically the first five books or the Torah). These were organized by subject and cataloged by the 12th-century rabbi Maimonides. Of these, over 450 relate to Temple worship and kosher laws. In fact, of the remaining 150 or so, I could only find 53 that related even slightly to commerce. Of these, *none restrict one from doing something, so long as it does not damage life or property*. When it comes to commerce, Pastor, the Bible is more libertarian than Libertarians! So that you can see this for yourself, I will include the web site that lists these commandments as a P.S.

Three things I have discovered, Pastor, in considering these laws: First, we need to be careful because with some of God's Laws we are not authorized to make judgments or exact sentences. In these cases, it is God who makes the judgment and punishes the violator. God's laws require us to make provision for the poor to provide for themselves from our production or produce—"Now, when you reap the harvest of your land, you shall not reap to the very corners of your field, neither shall you gather the gleanings of your harvest" (Leviticus 19:9). Even though this is a clear commandment, nowhere in Scripture is there instruction requiring us to penalize those who disobey. That is not to say that there is no punishment for neglecting the poor, just that the punishment will come from God, Himself, not us. The point here, is that there are many of God's laws where government is NOT authorized to legislate, regulate, license, or in any other way restrict activity or punish some violation.

Pastor, I believe *we should be as careful about what the Bible does NOT say as we are about what the Bible does say*!

The second thing I have discovered is that Biblical Law is "case law." For example, the Apostle Paul cites the law: "You shall not muzzle the ox while he is threshing" (Deuteronomy 25:4). He does this to make the point that a minister is worthy to be paid for his work. Paul goes on to explain: "...God is not concerned about oxen, is He? Or is He speaking altogether for our sake? Yes, for our sake it was written, because the plowman ought to plow in hope, and the thresher to thresh in hope of sharing the crops" (1 Corinthians 9:9-10). In other words, the Bible gives us example cases from which we are to deduct how to handle all other similar situations. For example, the Bible says: "And if a man opens a pit, or digs a pit and does not cover it over, and an ox or a donkey falls into it, the owner of the pit shall make restitution; he shall give money to its owner, and the dead *animal* shall become his" (Exodus 21:33-34). This law, number 456 in Maimonides' list, provides a "case" in which a hazard, the pit, created by a person has caused damage, loss of the animal, and dictates that the proper restitution is a fine equivalent to replace the loss...no more...no less. From this we can know, Biblically, how to settle the case of when I invite my neighbor over for coffee and he runs over the rake I left in the driveway, the hazard, and destroys two tires...the damage caused by the hazard. My responsibility in this case is to give him the money to replace the tires...no more...no less. I cannot tell him he should have seen the rake and avoided it and he cannot tell me that I should buy him better quality tires because I created such a hazard.

I guess we could define "Case Law" as this: God gives us a basic, simple situation where something went wrong...the Case, and then tells us that His Law...the Law, requires this particular *payment* or *action* to make restitution. That is, to make the situation "right." We are then to use that *case* as an example to properly deduce restitution in future cases. Thus, by using "case law," Biblical Law becomes timeless. That is, it is good for all time.

Pastor, case law precludes "regulatory law." When it comes to commerce, case law allows us to do anything we wish and then gives us cases to determine the proper restitution when life or property is damaged by our actions. Regulatory law, on the other hand, limits what we can do at every turn. It dictates that we must do something only a certain way. It tries to keep bad things from happening by eliminating all possibilities of failure. Regulatory law, basically, tries to eliminate all risks.

The problem, however, is that regulatory law grows like a cancer! Every day thousands of regulators sit around thinking of new things that can go wrong and then coming up with new regulations, licenses, fees, permits, and the like to prevent the wrong. This then quickly grows into a mountainous labyrinth of laws and regulations that completely smother out commerce. That is where we are today!

Which brings me to the third thing I have learned, Pastor: The Bible actually forbids us to do this. It says: "Whatever I command you, you shall be careful to do; you shall not add to nor take away from it" (Deuteronomy 12:32). Maimonides lists this commandment as number 580 and 581. (There is a slight difference between chapter and verse numbers between Jewish texts and Christian texts.)

- 580: Not to add to the Torah commandments or their oral explanations (Deut. 13:1)

- 581: Not to diminish from the Torah any commandments, in whole or in part (Deut. 13:1)

Pastor, it sure is clear to me that when it comes to the "unalienable right to liberty in commerce," God has given us *complete* liberty. In fact, He commands us to avoid losing that liberty by adding to His laws.

My conclusion here is that the Bible gives us total freedom to engage in commerce in any way we wish. It then gives us about 50 examples (case laws) of how to make restitution when something goes wrong. Then God commands us to keep it just that simple! In fact, if we don't we are disobeying God.

Pastor, do you think we have allowed ourselves to be dragged into disobedience by progressive liberals who believe they can create a utopia if they can just pass enough regulations? Do you think we have squandered our God given freedom here?

Yours in Christ,

P.S. Here is the website listing the 613 commandments listed by Rabbi Maimonides: http://www.aish.com/print/?contentID=48945081&section=/h/sh/se

LETTER 13

Is the Declaration of Independence Biblical?
Part IV: The Right to Liberty

Dear Pastor,

Well, we have been looking at the Declaration of Independence and asking if, when it says we have God given rights to life, liberty and property, are those Biblical? We found that God's Law clearly protects our right to life from conception to natural death. We also found that within the constraints of Biblical Law, God gives us religious liberty to worship whatever or whomever we like. There are, of course, consequences when we choose not to obey and worship God, but He reserves judgment and punishment here to Himself. Finally, He, most emphatically, gives us the civil liberty to freely do business and contract with one another in any way we choose.

There is, however, one area of God's Laws wherein we have completely turned the idea of liberty upside down...That is the area of what we might call personal liberty as it relates to the family. Here, we have quietly turned our backs and allowed liberties to be taken where God gives us absolutely NONE.

Pastor, as I think about God's creation, it seems clear that He created us "social" beings. That is to say, we always tend to come together to form communities. Nowhere is there evidence that we were meant to be lone creatures roaming around without relationships. God also created, within our nature, an amazingly strong sexual drive that we might procreate and maintain our species. I know that these observations are self-evident and beyond disagreement, but I point them out to say that in the society He created us to live within, He created the "family" as the basic building block. In fact, the very first thing God did after He created human beings was to create and define the family. "For this cause a man shall leave his father and his mother, and shall cleave to his wife; and they shall become one flesh" (Gen 2:24).

Now I know there is no place in God's Word where it is specifically stated that the family is the basic building block of society. However, it is an unavoidable conclusion that this is true when we examine what His Word has to say about the family and the laws He gave us to govern families within society. The laws God gave us to protect the family are possibly among the strictest and they also carry the most severe of penalties. Almost all of the laws prohibiting adultery, incest, and sexual perversion are capital offenses and God's Word holds us accountable to enforce them. Divorce is also very restricted.

Pastor, it seems to be a reasonable conclusion that if we fail to enforce these laws God has given us, then the family will slowly disintegrate and society will begin to unravel.

Today, between 30 to 60 percent of our children are born out of wedlock and about half of the weddings you perform will wind up experiencing adultery and divorce. There is also, of course, the growing number of those engaging in homosexuality or other sexual perversions. In fact, Pastor, we send our children to schools that teach them that this kind of behavior is perfectly normal and acceptable!

Pastor, do you think this qualifies as a "disintegration of the family?"

It seems such a sad experiment we have engaged in, failing to enforce God's Laws in order to see if they are really necessary! Clearly, they are.

You are probably aware, Pastor, that historically, this is a fairly recent turn of events. For the first 300 years of our country's existence, God's Laws were largely enforced. It is only since about 1900 that we began to abandon them. As a result of their enforcement, in 1800 the divorce rate was somewhere less than five percent. Sexual perversions were considered so abhorrent that Sir William Blackstone, in his *Commentaries on the Laws of England* would not name them and instead listed them as "crimes against nature committed with either man or beast." He states "This, the voice of nature and of reason, and the express law of God, determine (the penalty) to be capital." The penalty in 1769 was hanging! I haven't studied the history here but I suspect there was very little sexual perversion...at least not in public.

The point I am trying to make, Pastor, is that so-called liberties in this area are certainly not unalienable rights given by God and they were never even imagined by the writers of the Declaration of Independence!

Our failure here, in abandoning God's Laws, has been slowly growing over the last three or four generations. I would guess that it would take us close to that amount of time to regain that obedience even if we started today and tried our best.

Pastor, don't you think we should at least repent here? Shouldn't we at least give this serious thought as to how we might return to God's Word? What are your thoughts?

Yours in Christ,

LETTER 14

Is the Declaration of Independence Biblical?
Part V: The Right to the "Pursuit of Happiness"

Dear Pastor,

To complete my examination of the basis of our American government given in the Declaration of Independence, I looked at the unalienable right of "the pursuit of happiness." Now, that certainly does not mean, as we might interpret in today's terms, that we have some right to go around trying to feel "happy." First and foremost, it was understood in that era to be the "right to property." We can see this in a document crafted by many of these same people just two years earlier. The very first resolution listed by the American Continental Congress in a document they sent to England in 1774 stated:

> Resolved, N.C.D. 1. That they are entitled to life, liberty and property: and they have never ceded to any foreign power whatever, a right to dispose of either without their consent. (The Declaration and Resolves of the First Continental Congress, October 14, 1774)

Some have speculated that the writers of the Declaration of Independence intended to extend this right to "property" beyond just "real" property by stating it more broadly as the "pursuit of happiness." In other words, we are to have the right to safely hold not just our "things" but also the "intangibles" such as "reputation," "acquired privileges from contracts", etc.

Pastor, of all the unalienable rights, this may be the easiest to find in God's Word. We both would probably start with the commandment in Exodus 20:15 "You shall not steal" and repeated by the Lord Jesus in Matthew 19:18 "You shall not steal." Or when God commands: "You shall not oppress your neighbor, nor rob him"(Lev 19:13).

We would then broaden the idea with the commandment: "You shall not covet your neighbor's house; you shall not covet your neighbor's wife or his male servant or his female servant or his ox or his donkey or anything that belongs to your neighbor" (Exodus 20:17). That is to say, you must not desire to the point of taking anything that belongs to your neighbor through trickery or deceit. In other words, to swindle is to covet!

As an aside, Pastor, in our day and time we have some pretty tricky ways to covetously swindle our neighbor. For example, some farmers may complain to the state or federal government that they are being harmed by foreign competitors selling more cheaply. To remedy this, they convince the government to use the taxes they collect to guarantee them a "fair" price for their crops. This results in the government taking money from others to give to the farmers. That is clearly covetously swindling from your neighbor. Just because they are getting a third party, the government in this case, to take the money does not make it any less against God's Law. As I began to think about this, I realized that at this point in time just about everybody and their brother has discovered they are a victim of something or other and are now getting some kind of good or privilege from the government at the expense of their neighbors.

Pastor, this is another problem I think we should repent of and begin to make changes.

Incidentally, God extends our responsibility in this area even more when He commands:

> When a person sins and acts unfaithfully against the LORD, and deceives his companion in regard to a deposit or a security entrusted to him, or through robbery, or if he has extorted from his companion, or has found what was lost and lied about it and sworn falsely, so that he sins in regard to any one of the things a man may do; then it shall be, when he sins and becomes guilty, that he shall restore what he took by robbery, or what he got by extortion, or the deposit which was entrusted to him, or the lost thing which he found, or anything about which he swore falsely; he shall make restitution for it in full, and add to it one-fifth more. He shall give it to the one to whom it belongs (Lev 6:2-5).

Note here that the fine of 20 percent does not go to the government! It goes to the victim from whom it was taken!

God finally gives us the ultimate responsibility in this area when He commands "… but you shall love your neighbor as yourself; I am the LORD" (Lev 19:18). Paul repeats this command in Romans 13:9-10 saying "You shall love your neighbor as yourself. Love does no wrong to a neighbor…"

Pastor, I'm sure you would agree now that when our Declaration of Independence claims we have the unalienable right to "pursue happiness," it is certainly confirmed as being Biblical! In fact, as we see above, it is Biblical and then some!

In the last few letters, we looked at whether the basis of American government as laid out in the Declaration of Independence was Biblical. Before that we looked at whether our Constitution was based on Biblical principals and precepts. As we saw, within the limitations of human frailty and within the limitations of mitigating circumstances, it was absolutely uncanny how close they came.

Pastor, there is one last thing I would like to look at. That is to see if there is any evidence that would indicate whether American government was Biblical.

Yours in Christ,

LETTER

Is There Evidence That American Governance Was Biblical?

Dear Pastor,

In one of my earlier letters, I quoted Deuteronomy 28:1 wherein Moses is giving instructions to the Israelites. He tells them that if they will obey all of the commandments, etc. he has just laid out for them that God would bless them in many incredible ways.

I think, Pastor, before we try to apply that scripture to America we need to see first if it is limited only to the nation of Israel and secondly did America fulfill the requirements. Pastor, I am sure I remember you preaching on Galatians 3:29: "And if you belong to Christ, then you are Abraham's offspring, heirs according to promise." And also Galatians 4:28 "...And you brethren, like Isaac, are children of promise." Now, if it is true that even we, as God's adopted children can claim His promises, I see no reason why then this promise would not apply to us as Americans or any other nation that fulfills His requirements. Finally, did early America fulfill the requirements of the promise? Well, clearly, they did not have everything right. Plantation-type slavery is certainly un-Biblical and if you look close at Blackstone's writings you can find things, here and there, that aren't quite Biblical. However, it is uncanny how close they came. And under any circumstances, it is clear that they were consciously trying their best. What was the result? Pastor, I looked carefully at that reference and here is what I see.

First it says in Deuteronomy 28:1 (b) "...the LORD your God will set you high above all the nations of the earth." A Wikipedia reference chart of Gross Domestic Product says it all:

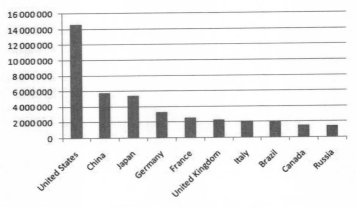

2011 Gross Domestic Product

http://en.wikipedia.org/wiki/List_of_countries_by_GDP_(nominal)

Pastor, we have actually been slipping in the past decade or so, but if this is not "*high above*" all nations tell me what is!

In verse 5 it says: "Blessed *shall be* your basket and your kneading bowl." Pastor, we have always been an exporter of food and never in our history of four hundred years has any American ever died of famine. In fact, if I understand correctly, the biggest food problem today in the lower socioeconomic levels is OBESITY!

In verse 7 it says: "The LORD will cause your enemies who rise up against you to be defeated before you; they shall come out against you one way and shall flee before you seven ways." Now, admittedly once or twice we have chosen to give up a fight and come back home, but since colonists first landed in the 1600s we have never once lost a war! Today, we are the most militarily powerful nation on the planet and no nation would dare attack us.

In verse 12 it says: "The LORD will open for you His good storehouse, the heavens, to give rain to your land in its season and to bless all the work of your hand; and you shall lend to many nations, but you shall not borrow." Pastor, we have recently been seriously slipping here but until that we indeed were always lenders and never borrowers among the nations. And, for that matter, world commerce even today is denominated by the American dollar!

Pastor, surely this is as clear to you as it is to me, America started out doing its very best to govern themselves according to God's instructions and guidance and to live according to God's laws. As you can see God, in His faithfulness, has in turn blest us out of all understanding! In fact, Pastor, until I began laying this out in my letter I had never fully realized just what all God had done for us and how richly He has actually blest us! Pastor, it is way, way, way beyond anything we deserve. I don't think you could find a better "Thanksgiving day" sermon if you tried.

Pastor, I believe there are two really important things to consider here. In the mid to late 1800s Christians completely abandoned the helm of state to the liberal progressives and only concerned themselves with witnessing and personal holiness. Our "ship of state" is a very large one and our founders, with God's help, designed it so that "change" would be slow and hard to effect. However, the progressives, who believe they have better ideas than those in God's word, have been both patient and enthusiastic in their efforts to bring about change. And our country, I think you would agree, is now drifting away from God's laws. Pastor, I believe we are now far enough along on that road that we are really testing the Lord's patience and long suffering. What do you think?

The second is when I hear Bill O'Reilly on Fox News and others talk about "American exceptionalism," and how we are a "noble" nation. Yes, there is an element of truth in that we, as a nation, are concerned for those at home and around the world that have suffered from disasters and we try our best to take care of those who are needy or hungry. It is also true that, as a nation, when we have conquered other nations who attack us we immediately set about helping them to rebuild and then set them free. But, Pastor, I believe the danger here is for us to think ourselves somehow better than others. You know we could start to think that we got all this wealth and power that we enjoy simply because we are smarter, stronger and more talented than the rest of the world! Really!???

Pastor, as you know, this is one of the first warnings Moses gives to God's people before they went in to possess the land. Deuteronomy 8:12-14 says "...lest, when you have eaten and are satisfied, and have built good houses and lived in them, and when your herds and your flocks multiply, and your silver and gold multiply, and all that you have multiplies, then your heart becomes proud, and you forget the LORD your God." And again in verse 17 we read: "Otherwise, you may say in your heart, 'My power and the strength of my hand made me this wealth.'"

I believe we may be on borrowed time here. Pastor, please call us, as God's people, to repent and ask His forgiveness. Call us to once again learn His principles, precepts, statutes, laws, and commandments. Please call us to begin, once again, to live by them and once again seek to convince our fellow countrymen of the blessings that this will bring for us, our nation, and our children after us. Pastor, I think that it is going to depend on you. God has made us, by nature, to follow the shepherds He places over us. If they lead us in His ways, we will continue to prosper peacefully, but if they lead us astray we will eventually incur His displeasure. Am I going too far here? What do you think, Pastor?

Yours in Christ,

LETTER

Ten Conclusions about the Ten Commandments

Dear Pastor,

We have now looked at a lot of specific ideas about whether God gave us instructions for how to live together and govern ourselves… in fact, whether He even cares about such things. What we have done, in effect, is to look at a lot of different trees in the forest and considered their individual characteristics. Now I think it would be profitable to, in a sense, lift ourselves up as high as we can and try to look at the WHOLE FOREST! After all, God invites us to "Come now, and let us reason together …" (Isaiah 1:18). Pastor, I hope you will find this not only reasonable but also Biblical.

Here are the "ten conclusions" I have come to about God's "Ten Commandments."

1. **God created man and placed him on the earth.**

   "In the beginning God created the heavens and the earth" (Genesis 1:1). "And God created man in His own image, in the image of God He created him; male and female He created them" (Genesis 1:27).

2. **God created all men with an intrinsic nature (human nature).**
   Having a free will

   "…but from the tree of the knowledge of good and evil you shall not eat, for in the day that you eat from it you

81

shall surely die" (Genesis 2:17). "...choose for yourselves today whom you will serve" (Joshua 24:15).

Drive to Procreate

"For this cause a man shall leave his father and his mother, and shall cleave to his wife; and they shall become one flesh." (Genesis 2:24) "My beloved is mine, and I am his..." (Song of Solomon 2:16) "Now when evening came David arose from his bed and walked around on the roof of the king's house, and from the roof he saw a woman bathing; and the woman was very beautiful in appearance. So David sent and inquired about the woman. And one said, 'Is this not Bathsheba, the daughter of Eliam, the wife of Uriah the Hittite?' And David sent messengers and took her..." (2 Samuel 11:2-4)

Social by Nature

"From that land he went forth into Assyria, and built Nineveh and Rehoboth-Ir and Calah, and Resen between Nineveh and Calah; that is the great city" (Genesis 10:11-12).

3. **Man, by his choice, became fallen and prone to sin (a sinner by nature).**

   "Your first forefather sinned," (Isaiah 43:27) "...for we have sinned against the LORD our God, we and our fathers, since our youth even to this day. And we have not obeyed the voice of the LORD our God" (Jeremiah 3:25). "...for all have sinned and fall short of the glory of God," (Romans 3:23) "...If we say that we have no sin, we are deceiving ourselves, and the truth is not in us" (1 John 1:8). "...For the good that I wish, I do not do; but I practice the very evil that I do not wish. But if I am doing the very thing I do not wish, I am no longer the one doing it, but sin which dwells in me" (Romans 7:19-20).

4. **Thus, men have these two needs...Rescue from their sinful nature and Instructions on how to live together and govern themselves. God is a loving god and would not leave men without these directions.**

   "Know therefore that the LORD your God, He is God,

the faithful God, who keeps His covenant and His loving kindness to a thousandth generation..." (Deuteronomy 7:9) "And his banner over me is love" (Song of Solomon l 2:4). "He does not retain His anger forever; Because He delights in unchanging love" (Micah 7:18).

5. **First, God has given men instructions on deliverance from their sinfulness.**

"And there is salvation in no one else; for there is no other name under heaven that has been given among men, by which we must be saved" (Acts 4:12). "Believe in the Lord Jesus, and you shall be saved..." (Act 16:31) "Now faith is the assurance of things hoped for, the conviction of things not seen. For by it the men of old gained approval" (Hebrews 11:1-2). "For what does the Scripture say? Abraham believed God, and it was accounted to him for righteousness" (Romans 4:3).

6. **Deliverance from sin does not deliver us from our human nature, thus: God has given men all the instructions (in His Word) necessary to best order and govern human society. These instructions are unchanging; they are for all people, all places and for all times. His instructions provide the maximum liberty and the minimum of restraint. These instructions, designed by God and given in His Word, provide for the restraint of violence, the righting of injustices, and the preservation of the family and provide for those unable to provide for themselves.**

"...Abraham obeyed Me and kept My charge, My commandments, My statutes and My laws" (Genesis 26:5). "Or what great nation is there that has statutes and judgments as righteous as this whole law which I am setting before you today?" (Deuteronomy 4:8) "Those who love Thy law have great peace, And nothing causes them to stumble" (Psalm 119:165). "If you love Me, you will keep My commandments" (John 14:15). "Here is the perseverance of the saints who keep the commandments of God and their faith in Jesus" (Revelation 14:12). "Circumcision is nothing, and uncircumcision is nothing, but what matters is the keeping of the commandments of God" (1 Corinthians 7:19).

7. **God chooses and calls certain men (priests, apostles, prophets, rabbis, pastors, shepherds, etc.) and gives them the responsibility to teach and call on men to follow His instructions. As part of our human nature God created in us a propensity to follow these leaders. Even to the point of "drinking Kool-Aid!"**

"And the LORD commanded me at that time to teach you statutes and judgments, that you might perform them in the land where you are going over to possess it" (Deuteronomy 4:14). "…do according to all that the Levitical priests shall teach you;" (Deuteronomy 24:8) "Now it shall come about when he sits on the throne of his kingdom, he shall write for himself a copy of this law on a scroll in the presence of the Levitical priests" (Deuteronomy 17:18). "But we (The Apostles) will devote ourselves to prayer, and to the ministry of the word" (Acts 6:4).

8. **When these leaders energetically and effectively carry out these responsibilities, men will be reconciled to God and follow God's instructions. God then promises to bless such a nation so it will experience a free, peaceful, and prosperous existence.**

Now it shall be, if you will diligently obey the LORD your God, being careful to do all His commandments which I command you today, the LORD your God will set you high above all the nations of the earth. And all these blessings shall come upon you and overtake you, if you will obey the LORD your God. Blessed shall you be in the city, and blessed shall you be in the country. Blessed shall be the offspring of your body and the produce of your ground and the offspring of your beasts, the increase of your herd and the young of your flock. Blessed shall be your basket and your kneading bowl. Blessed shall you be when you come in, and blessed shall you be when you go out. The LORD will cause your enemies who rise up against you to be defeated before you; they shall come out against you one way and shall flee before you seven ways. The LORD will command the blessing upon you in your barns and in all that you put your hand to, and He will bless you in the land which the LORD your God gives you (Deuteronomy 28:1-8).

"At one moment I might speak concerning a nation or concerning a kingdom to uproot, to pull down, or to destroy it; if that nation against which I have spoken turns from its evil, I will relent concerning the calamity I planned to bring on it. Or at another moment I might speak concerning a nation or concerning a kingdom to build up or to plant it; if it does evil in My sight by not obeying My voice, then I will think better of the good with which I had promised to bless it" (Jeremiah 18:7-10). "When God saw their (Nineveh's) deeds, that they turned from their wicked way, then God relented concerning the calamity which He had declared He would bring upon them. And He did not do it" (Jonah 3:10).

9. **However, when these leaders abrogate these responsibilities and refuse to teach God's instructions on how to govern society, that nation will decline. The family will break down, violence will increase, injustice will prevail, and the needy will be ill cared for. That nation will eventually come under God's judgment.**

"My people are destroyed for lack of knowledge. Because you have rejected knowledge, I also will reject you from being My priest. Since you have forgotten the law of your God, I also will forget your children" (Hosea 4:6).

"...Or at another moment I might speak concerning a nation or concerning a kingdom to build up or to plant it; if it does evil in My sight by not obeying My voice, then I will think better of the good with which I had promised to bless it" (Jeremiah 18:9-10).

"When I say to the wicked, 'You shall surely die'; and you do not warn him or speak out to warn the wicked from his wicked way that he may live, that wicked man shall die in his iniquity, but his blood I will require at your hand" (Ezekiel 3:18).

10. **In light of this, our Lord's parting statement when he ascended, called the "Great Commission," contains two commandments and a promise. The first**

commandment is to preach the good news of salvation and baptize those who respond, thus meeting their need for reconciliation. The second is to "teach the *NATIONS* to *OBEY* His commandments," meeting the need of knowing how to live together and govern ourselves. He then promises He will be with us to the end of the age. We must understand that no amount of preaching the "good news" in response to the first command will make up for neglecting the second command to teach the nations to obey God's instructions on how to live together. God forbid that we should continue trying to "selectively" obey His Great Commission.

"Go therefore and make disciples of all the nations, baptizing them in the name of the Father and the Son and the Holy Spirit, teaching them to observe all that I commanded you; and lo, I am with you always, even to the end of the age" (Mat 28:19-20).

What do you think, Pastor? Would you agree that this pretty much sums up what we have discussed so far?

Yours in Christ,

LETTER 17

Is the Church Responsible for Our Situation?

Let us pray God would put a Jonah in every pulpit!
(In fact, take a break and read Appendix Three.)

Dear Pastor,

Thinking about my last letter, I realized how important it is for people to be able to correctly determine the difference between "good" and "evil," "right" and "wrong," etc. In fact, won't that pretty much determine their behavior? Should people look to the church for what is "bad" or what is "good?" Isn't this a subject God is interested in? I'm sure you know that it is.

If we look to God's Word for understanding, we first encounter the subject in Genesis 3:6, when Eve is tested by Satan. Previously God had spoken to Adam, saying:

> And the LORD God commanded the man, saying, "From any tree of the garden you may eat freely; but from the tree of the knowledge of good and evil you shall not eat, for in the day that you eat from it you shall surely die" (Genesis 2:16-17).

From Adam and Eve's perspective, however:

> When the woman saw that the tree was good for food, and that it was a delight to the eyes, and that the tree was desirable to make one wise, she took from its fruit and ate… (Gen 3:6)

So man, using clear logic and all of his senses determined that it was "good," not "evil." How could God have forbidden such a delight? Rabbi Hirsh commented on this scripture by saying:

> Man has to find out what is good and what is bad for him. For that purpose the tree stood for him in all its glory, appealing to all his senses, his whole personal nature must say to him "this is good," and God's word had forbidden the eating of it as "bad." That was to be to him the model, the pattern and the rule for all good and bad for mankind... (Hirsch, Samson Raphael, *The Pentateuch*, Irish University Press, Shannon Ireland, 1963, p73, Vol. 1)

Isn't this what God's Word is saying to us in Proverbs? "There is a way *which seems* right to a man, but its end is the way of death" (Proverbs 14:12), or "Trust in the LORD with all your heart, and do not lean on your own understanding" (Proverbs 3:5).

Biblically, then, it appears that we should carefully study God's word first to learn what he has revealed to us as "evil" and be sure not to practice that and what is "good" that we might seek after that. And also to make sure we vigorously teach these principles, precepts, and commandments to our children. That is exactly what our pastors required of us for the first three hundred years of our country's existence.

In fact, pastors did this so well, the French historian, Alexix de Tocqueville observed in about 1830:

> ...there is no country in the world where the Christian religion retains greater influence over the souls of men than in America. (Knoll, Mark A., *A History of Christianity in the United States and Canada*, Wm. B. Erdmans Publishing Co., 1992, p.163.)

Virtually every American had a strong Biblical conscience, having been taught to read out of the *New England Primer*. American school textbooks quoted Scripture, catechisms, and Christian hymns, and they imparted a sound biblical worldview.

America led the world in missions. Regular church attendance was near eighty percent and growing. Divorce was rare and single-parent homes were only created by the death of a spouse.

Over these three hundred years, God also raised our country from a raw wilderness to the richest, most powerful country in the world! We were exceedingly blest!

When my grandfather was a child, in the later part of the nineteenth century, the "Enlightenment" began to blossom in America. It became very difficult for pastors to defend God's Word as being authoritative when it came to what was "evil" and what was "good." Secular scientists explained to us that since we evolved from lower forms of life, good and evil were completely relative… and furthermore they could prove it! Actually scholars told us that the Bible was just an outdated collection of allegories. As Friedrich Nietzsche (1844-1900) put it: "God is dead. God remains dead. And we have killed him." (*The Gay Science*, Section 125)

Pastors, who had faithfully guarded God's Word for the previous three hundred years, were up against the wall! How could they argue against "scientific proofs?"

Someone then came up with a new theology…God deals with man differently over different periods of time! And we are in the "last times!" God's return is imminent and we must turn our complete attention to the "spiritual" task of getting the Gospel to everyone as quickly as possible. What God had to say in the Old Testament was for the people of those times. Arguing over "good" and "evil" is as much a waste of time as discussing how many angels can fit on the head of a pin! It is in fact a "secular" distraction from the Gospel! Pastors had long since led us to relinquish children's education in our nation over to the "public schools." They had been doing a fair job of teaching a Biblical world view up to that time.

At first, there was not much change, except as this idea (theology) caught on; there was an initial flurry of "prophecy conferences." That was then followed by a number of books such as *The Late Great Planet Earth* by Hal Lindsey. He proclaimed Christ's return was to occur in about 1984. The *Left Behind* series of books and movies describing the imminent "rapture" convinced many the "end" might be tomorrow. All of this expectancy, coupled with the conscience of most Americans that had been developed over the previous three hundred years, kept evangelistic "conversions" moving right along.

Many American pastors felt pleased by this change of affairs…They no longer had to defend God's Word against secular "naysayers," and souls were still being saved! They could now concentrate on "spiritual" things and leave all that other stuff for someone else to take care of. Just "love the Lord your God with all your heart, all your mind and all your soul"…We will then baptize you in the name of the Father, the Son and the Holy Spirit and celebrate the "Great Commission!"

There was an inherent problem with this... It is only half of the Great Commission! In Matthew 28:19-20 it says to "...teach the nations to observe all I have commanded you!" We may have made some converts to Christianity but we have completely failed to teach them to "love their neighbor as themselves!" We turned that over to secular humanists—or "progressives," as they now call themselves. And they gladly began to secularize our nation's children!

Russian Communism, which eliminated private property and promised jobs for all, fell after about seventy years when they began to exhaust the nation's physical assets. In much the same way, our American way of life, built on Biblical teaching, is beginning to fall because of our neglect in teaching each generation the love of God and all He has commanded! With each generation we drift further and further from knowing, Biblically, the difference between good and evil! We are losing a Biblical worldview. And we are losing a Biblical conscience.

We are becoming a nation that "knows not God and what he has done for our country." For nearly three generations we have been secularizing our consciences. We are very close, as a nation, to not knowing Biblically what is "evil" from what is "good." Young people are opting for cohabitation instead of marriage and the fastest-growing institution is "single-parent families." This and many other trends show we are near losing the asset of our consciences!

If a person's conscience has decayed into secular beliefs...he will not be open to evangelism! He will believe he has no need of Christ's offer of salvation!

Charles Finney, the great evangelist, and President of Oberlin College, saw this coming as early as 1873. He prophetically stated in the last paragraph of a sermon titled "The Decay of Conscience":

> If there is a decay of conscience, the pulpit is responsible for it. If the public press lacks moral discernment, the pulpit is responsible for it. If the church is degenerate and worldly, the pulpit is responsible for it. If the world loses its interest in Christianity, the pulpit is responsible for it. If Satan rules in our halls of legislation, the pulpit is responsible for it. If our politics become so corrupt that the very foundations of our government are ready to fall away, the pulpit is responsible for it. *(http://www.gospeltruth. net/1868_75Independent/731204_conscience.htm)*

God's Word puts it far more forcefully and far more personally!

> My people are destroyed for lack of knowledge. Because you have rejected knowledge, I also will reject you from being My priest. Since you have forgotten the law of your God, I also will forget your children (Hosea 4:6).

We are also warned:

> Woe to those who call evil good, and good evil; Who substitute darkness for light and light for darkness; Who substitute bitter for sweet, and sweet for bitter! Woe to those who are wise in their own eyes, And clever in their own sight! ... Therefore, as a tongue of fire consumes stubble, And dry grass collapses into the flame, So their root will become like rot and their blossom blow away as dust; For they have rejected the law of the LORD of hosts, And despised the word of the Holy One of Israel. On this account the anger of the LORD has burned against His people, And He has stretched out His hand against them and struck them down... (Isaiah 5:20-22, 24-25)

In 2011, Dr. Erwin W. Lutzer, pastor of Moody Bible Church, was quoted in a newsletter as saying that we have already crossed that line and lost any chance for restoration. *I do not believe that! Pastor, we can still restore our nation if we start right now! God spared Nineveh, and if we "cry out to God and change our ways," He will surely spare us! As a matter of fact, He has promised us exactly that:*

> (If)...My people who are called by My name humble themselves and pray, and seek My face and turn from their wicked ways, then I will hear from heaven, will forgive their sin, and will heal their land (2 Chronicles 7:14).

Pastor, even though many have been praying for America for more than thirty years...we have yet to *turn from our wicked ways!* We continue doing the same things!

Pastor, please lead us not only to repent but also to change our ways. Teach us, from God's Word, good from evil. Teach us how we should then live. Lead us to teach our nation's children...to observe all that Jesus has commanded us. It is God's commission to the church. It is clearly the church's responsibility. Pastor, don't you believe God will hold us accountable? You and you alone can rescue our nation.

Yours in Christ,

P.S. How you prepare us for these changes is, of course, up to you. A series of sermons along the line of my own journey expressed in this series of letters I have been sharing with you might be useful. A DVD-based study available from Focus on the Family called "The Truth Project" would be great for Sunday School or even Sunday-night services. It is available at "thetruthproject.org." A DVD called "The Role of Pastors & Christians in Civil Government," by David Barton (wallbuilders.com) would also be excellent for Sunday School. Dr. George Grant has some excellent books for this process. I would also recommend a book I am presently reading called *Church & State Being Salt and Light in the Public Square*, by David L. Shelley, PhD. If you are worried about the IRS, skip over to Letter 35, "Appoint for Yourselves Judges and Officers," to see exactly what the IRS has said. Go to Alliance Defending Freedom (http://www. alliancedefendingfreedom.org) for additional information on this subject. See: http://www.speakupmovement.org/church/LearnMore/ details/4702 for how to preach a political sermon!

LETTER

STEP ONE: Education
Part I: The First Step

Dear Pastor,

Hopefully, you agree that God has given us instructions for how to live together and govern ourselves and He expects us to obey. But what exactly is the present road forward to repentance and restoration for our nation? Practically, where do we start? First, I think we need to see where we are and how we got here. In your message some time ago, you quoted a passage from Judges:

> ...and there arose another generation after them who did not know the Lord, They turned aside quickly from the way in which their fathers had walked in obeying the commandments of the Lord; they did not do as their fathers (Judges 2:10, 17).

"...another generation after them who did not know the Lord...They (who) turned aside quickly...from obeying the commandments of the Lord," is clearly where we are today, as a nation. How did we get to this point?

Pastor, when my grandfather, Robert Menefee, was a young man in the late 1800's, Bible-believing Christians did a strange thing. They actually began to let liberal progressives educate our nation's children!

Education was held to be one of the most important tasks by the colonists. So much so, that the first institutions established in the new country were Bible colleges that eventually turned into universities. From the early 1600s through the early 1800s, children were educated in a variety of ways, from homeschooling to community schools and private academies. In almost every case, however, they first learned to read with the *New England Primer*, a thoroughly Biblically-centered textbook.

Did you know, Pastor, from 1690, when it was first published, until the late 1800s the *New England Primer* was the second bestselling book (behind the Bible) in the nation? It was the book from which nearly every American child was taught to read. They learned their ABC's by reciting: A—In Adam's Fall, we sinned all. B—Heaven to find, the Bible mind. C—Christ crucified for sinners died....

All the way through the alphabet.

Among other things, it contained the Lord's Prayer, the Apostles' Creed, the Westminster Shorter Catechism, the Puritan Catechism by John Cotton, Children's Hymns by Isaac Watts and countless Bible verses.

The second bestselling textbooks in America were *McGuffey's Readers*. As noted by an article in Wikipedia (http://en.wikipedia. org/wiki/McGuffey_Readers):

> McGuffey is remembered as a conservative theological teacher. He interpreted the goals of public schooling in terms of moral and spiritual education, and attempted to give schools a curriculum that would instill Presbyterian Calvinist beliefs and manners in their students. The manufacturer Henry Ford cited *McGuffey's Readers* as one of his most important childhood influences. He was an avid fan of *McGuffey's Readers* first editions, and claimed as an adult to be able to quote from McGuffey's by memory at great length. Ford republished all six Readers from the 1857 edition, and distributed complete sets of them, at his own expense, to schools across the United States.

Pastor, from the first settlers in the early 1600s until about 1875 American children were better schooled in Biblical knowledge than those in our own congregation. These were children of parents not just from Britain but from all over Europe and Scandinavia. There were a variety of denominations. In spite of this variation, for the first two hundred and fifty years, American children learned from the Bible and were taught to live according to Biblical standards.

You might think this hodge-podge of homeschooling, academies, community schools, etc. was not doing a good job. Pastor, the 1820

Connecticut Census showed that less than one in five hundred was found to be illiterate. Early American children were not only good Bible students; they were very educated in other areas as well.

It was around 1820 when this process began to change. Massachusetts was the first to start replacing the variety of schools educating children with compulsory public schools. A Wikipedia article notes:

> In 1820, Boston is the site of the first public U.S. high school. And in 1827, a Massachusetts law makes all grades of public school free to all. Massachusetts innovation continues with the state's first Board of Education formed in 1837, headed by Horace Mann. And in 1851, Massachusetts makes education compulsory.

Compulsory public schools spread rapidly throughout the country. While the local community initially retained control, state influence slowly grew over the years. Today, we find growing control of public education by the *Federal* Department of Education. Practically, local communities now have little to no control over content, textbooks or what is to be taught.

Now, what could be so bad about universal, compulsory public education? Basically it is the same thing that is wrong with centralized government. The strongest and most powerful always take control and almost never for the better.

Secular intellectual progressives who came along in the late 1800s immediately recognized that the public education system was the ideal way to further their ideas. The Wikipedia article cited above on *McGuffey's Readers* encapsulates it perfectly:

> The content of the readers changed drastically between McGuffey's 1836-1837 editions and the 1879 edition. The revised Readers were compiled to meet the needs of national unity and the dream of an American melting pot for the world's oppressed masses. The Calvinist values of salvation, righteousness and piety, so prominent in the early Readers, were excluded from the later versions. The content of the books was secularized and replaced by middle-class civil religion, morality and values.

Resistance to this trend was scattered and ineffectual. Protestant Christians, as I pointed out in my last letter, had largely lost concern for education and public policy. But equally because education had by this time become so centralized that nothing short of a public uproar could have intervened.

With weak to no resistance, secular progressives have now totally secularized public schools. Everything supernatural, such as God and His Word, is completely ruled out. Children are taught that they are pointless accidents of evolution and have no purpose in life other than what they happen to choose. The only absolute is that there is no absolute. Right and wrong are only relative. And through "sensitivity training" they are told sexual perversity is perfectly normal. Because of this philosophy drugs and promiscuity are becoming more and more common. There is no end to the nonsense!

So, now we send about ninety percent of American children to secular humanistic government schools and—to our surprise—more and more "do not know the Lord, (and) they have turned aside from the way in which their fathers had walked."

Pastor, it is nothing short of a miracle that any of our children survive this process and retain their faith. Sadly—as you know—many, many do not. In fact many never even have the opportunity to come to faith in the first place.

So, our great folly is now complete. We first let our educational process be centralized and made compulsory, setting it up for a takeover. Then when secular progressives saw the opportunity and began that takeover, we raised little or no resistance.

Now I know, of course, that no individual or organization was maliciously arranging these events as a planned conspiracy. But, I would not be surprised to find that Satan himself had a substantial part in planning it! Regardless, it is a very sad and debilitating event in our nation's history.

Incidentally, Pastor, I am not blaming all teachers here. I know that many of them try very hard to do a good job, and have the very best intentions. They are totally constrained, however, against teaching a Biblical world view. They cannot call on God or mention His Word. In fact, they are limited in making statements regarding right and wrong. They are also under great pressure to follow the textbooks and guidelines that are imposed upon them. Pastor, I can guarantee you that those textbooks and guidelines were not produced with the intention of instilling faith in God and promoting a Biblical world view.

The fact that a large and growing percentage of students coming out of public schools have no faith in God and lack a Biblical world view is *the first and most serious of the school's failings.*

The second and related failing is almost as serious. A self-governing nation, as we are, depends upon a knowledgeable citizenry that actively participates in the process. Public schools and even many Christian schools have now completely dropped instruction on how our government was designed, established and how it works. There is no instruction that when citizens cease to participate in their governance, they will soon become victims of self-serving charlatans who will take away their freedoms and lure them into envy and dependency.

Pastor, we are producing a growing percentage of citizens who have no feeling of personal responsibility for governing our nation. When they do go to the polls, they simply vote for the "coolest" politician, or the one who promises the most "goodies." If this continues, we are certain to lose the wonderful nation that God has so graciously given us!

You can lead us to change all this, pastor, and it is still not too late to do so. In fact, it is not all that difficult to do.

I am certain, however, if the church simply continues doing what it has been doing, our nation could soon be under God's judgment. If you want to see where we are headed, just look to Europe. While regular church attendance in our country has fallen to below forty percent...In Europe it is now below *four percent.* They have traded away their freedoms for dependency. Pastor, are you as concerned about our children and the fate of our country as I am?

I know we are not there yet. We can still recover, but we need to get started quickly. You probably have some ideas on what to do. I am excited about some of the ideas that I have. In my next letter, I will let you know what I have been thinking.

Take courage, Pastor, this war is a long way from being over. And "We have not yet begun to fight!"

Yours in Christ,

LETTER

STEP ONE: Education
Part II: "Train Up a Child"

Dear Pastor,

Let's be part of the "next great awakening" in our country! Wouldn't it be wonderful to see millions of Americans coming to a Bible-believing faith in God every year? I believe God's Word tells us how to do it and our early history shows it can be done. Of course, we are not going to have any great awakening as long as we keep doing what we have been doing! What we have been doing over the last three generations is causing us to lose ground each year and at an ever-increasing pace.

Pastor, to simply keep doing what we have been doing and expect a different result is, I believe, one of the definitions of insanity! We must make a change.

"Train up a child in the way he should go, even when he is old he will not depart from it" (Proverbs 22:6). Whether this is a "promise" or simply God telling us about one of the human characteristics He gave us…it is for certain a Biblical truth. Pastor, as I tried to show in my last letter, this has to be one of our most serious failings in our recent past!

In this letter I would like first to convince you of this through my own personal experience, then through empirical evidence, and finally through the revelations within God's Word.

I went to school in the 1940s in Oklahoma. To put that in perspective, Oklahoma had been a state for less than 35 years, and my grandmother still had letters addressed to her in Wewoka,

Indian Territory, USA. Any notions of secular humanism were still a generation or more in the future, at least in Oklahoma. When I was in school, we still knew that God created us, that we had a divine purpose and there was no doubt in anyone's mind about what was absolutely right and absolutely wrong.

Now there were some weaknesses and failings creeping in at that time but even with this imperfect environment, Pastor, it would have been nearly impossible to not be a believer. In fact everyone I knew was a believer of one denomination or another. From my personal experience I can assure you that if you "Train up a child in the way he should go, even when he is old he will not depart from it!"

Secondly, empirical evidence shows when children are "trained up in the way they should go" by sending them to Christian and/or some private schools they still turn out far better than the secular humanist public schools. A 2011 study from Notre Dame University found:

> In the first study of its kind on K-12 Christian education in North America, University of Notre Dame sociologist David Sikkink, in partnership with Cardus—a public policy think tank—found that while Protestant Christian school graduates show *uncommon commitment to their families and churches, donate more money than graduates of other schools, and divorce less,* they also have lower incomes, less education, and are less engaged in politics than their Catholic and non-religious private school peers (emphasis added).
>
> http://al.nd.edu/news/22059-new-research-on-christian-school-graduates-yields-surprising-results/ (Be sure to click on the "Executive Summary" at the bottom of this report.)

First, Pastor, this is a comparison between Protestant Christian schools and Catholic/private schools—not public schools. Nonetheless, the behavioral outcomes noted are impressive. It is even more impressive when you consider that Christian schools have had almost no support from the church community!

Even more impressive, Pastor, are the empirical results from "homeschooling." The Washington Times reports in a recent article on homeschooling: http://www.washingtontimes.com/news/2009/aug/30/home-schooling-outstanding-results-national-tests/

Five areas of academic pursuit were measured. In reading, the average homeschooler scored at the 89th percentile; language, 84th percentile; math, 84th percentile; science, 86th percentile; and social studies, 84th percentile. In the core studies (reading, language and math), the average homeschooler scored at the 88th percentile. The average public school student taking these standardized tests scored at the 50th percentile in each subject area. In a sentence, homeschooling is a recipe for academic success.

The article also points out that there was little variation between where the students came from and who their parents were.

In a research piece from "examiner.com" homeschooled children were also substantially better socialized, self-reliant, and morally grounded.

… a previous article addressed the fact that research shows homeschoolers are more involved in community groups, service activities, and civic engagement than their public school peers. Likewise, a national survey of homeschoolers in Canada by Deani Van Pelt showed that students educated at home are involved in an average of 8 activities outside the home. After graduation, homeschoolers continue this level of involvement: for example, 76% of 18-24 year olds voted in a national or state election in the past 5 years, as compared with 29% of the same age general population, and 14% worked for a political candidate, party, or cause, as compared with 1% of non-homeschoolers. (http://www.examiner.com/article/top-5-reasons-to-homeschool-for-christian-parents-reason-4)

There is simply no doubt, Pastor, that empirical evidence proves that how a child is *trained up* makes all the difference in the world! Here is what God's Word has to say about educating our children:

"Gather the people to Me, and I will let them hear My words, that they may learn to fear Me all the days they live on the earth, and *that* they may teach their children" (Deuteronomy 4:10).

Now this is the commandment, the statutes and the judgments which the LORD your God has commanded *me* to teach you, that you might do *them* in the land where you are going over to possess it, *so that you and your son and your grandson might fear the LORD your God, to keep all His statutes and His commandments, which I command you, all the days of your life, and that your days may be prolonged.* O Israel, you should listen and be careful to do *it*, that it may be well with you and that you may multiply greatly, just as the LORD, the God of your fathers, has promised you, *in* a land flowing with milk and honey.

Hear, O Israel! The LORD is our God, the LORD is one! And you shall love the LORD your God with all your heart and with all your soul and with all your might. *And these words, which I am commanding you today, shall be on your heart; and you shall teach them diligently to your sons and shall talk of them when you sit in your house and when you walk by the way and when you lie down and when you rise up* (Deuteronomy 6:1-7). (*emphasis added*)

Pastor, everyone agrees on the importance of this command, but did you notice that it comes with a schedule? "When you sit in your house and when you walk by the way and when you lie down and when you rise up!"

It is not just Sunday morning—it is every day of the week! As Dr. Michael Milton puts it, "Oh, that some will draw back from the quenching fires of Molock and run with their little ones in their arms to the loving Savior who brings life abundant and life eternal" (Michael Milton, PhD, Silent No More, Tanglewood Publishing, 2013, p. 251).

- "Come, you children, listen to me; I will teach you the fear of the LORD" (Psalm 34:11).

- "And you, fathers, do not provoke your children to wrath, but bring them up in the training and admonition of the Lord" (Ephesians 6:4).

I am sure you know this, but almost everyone who commits their lives to Christ does so in their younger years. Barna Research, the largest religious polling agency in the U.S., found that the overwhelming percentage of those who are saved have experienced salvation before reaching their fourteenth birthday. The current Barna study indicates that nearly half of all Americans who accept Jesus Christ as their savior do so before reaching the age of 13 (43%), and that two out of three born-again Christians (64%) made that commitment to Christ before their

18th birthday. Called the "4-14 window," both the International Bible Society and researchers in the Nazarene denomination find that 83% of those coming to faith in Christ do so during these years. I distinctly recall, growing up in Southern Baptist Churches, that this was common knowledge more than a half century ago.

Pastor, I am sure you also know that virtually every time God's Word speaks of teaching and education it is referring to *children!*

It seems obvious, that God created us so that we are most impressionable and responsive to ideas during these early years. It is the time when our world view is firmly established. It is clearly why God says "train up a child in the way he should go."

Pastor, don't you think Satan is just delighted when we send our nation's children to government schools where every day they are steeped in secular ideas and thinking?

A recent (June 2013) article in the *Wall Street Journal* by Stephen D. Solomon, entitled "God Is Still in the Classroom" commented on the fiftieth anniversary of the Supreme Court case in which school-sponsored Bible-reading and prayer were disallowed in public schools. His concluding comments stated that schools may now "...provide objective teaching about religion and student-initiated prayer without imposing beliefs on schoolchildren." Really! Pastor, "imposing religious beliefs on schoolchildren" is precisely what the Bible requires us to do! What are we thinking?

> "But whoever causes one of these little ones who believe in Me to stumble, it would be better for him if a millstone were hung around his neck, and he were thrown into the sea" (Mark 9:42).

Pastor, looking at this last scripture, I think we *should tremble in fear, seriously repent, and ask* God's forgiveness. When we send innocent little children to be educated in secular humanist schools we are clearly causing them to stumble in the worst way! This should truly frighten us! *It is no wonder that our nation is in decline—and Pastor...it is our fault!*

The one thing that really stands out as I have been going through God's Word looking for His instructions to us regarding education...*God has given this responsibility to the parents and He clearly requires those He has called as shepherds to make sure parents fulfill this responsibility.*

While in the process of writing this letter, I had the privilege of having dinner with Reverend Premjit Kumar of RIMI ministries. RIMI ministries have Bible schools and orphanages in many areas of India and, as you know, Pastor, India has been very resistant to the Gospel. "I asked Reverend Kumar, what percent of the children that enter the orphanages eventually commit their lives to Christ?" Without hesitation, he said "almost everyone!"

Pastor, God has given us this great evangelistic tool. Of every child we start in preschool and "train up in the way they should go" we know from experience as well as God's Word, almost "everyone" will commit their lives to Christ! America's greatest awakening yet stands before us. How could we turn our backs?

Before I share my thoughts on how all this can be accomplished, I would like to take another look at the "Great Commission" to make sure about who is responsible and for what. But because this letter is so long, I think that will be my next letter to you.

Yours in Christ,

LETTER

STEP ONE: Education
Part III: The Church's Responsibility

Dear Pastor,

So that we have absolutely no doubt about the church's responsibility here, we should take a closer look at what we call the "Great Commission." To do this I would like to share a diagram of this scripture done by Doctor Randy A. Leedy, a professor of Greek at Bob Jones University. It is taken from "BibleWorks 9" Bible software.

"Therefore go and make disciples of all nations, baptizing them in the name of the Father and of the Son and of the Holy Spirit, and teaching them to obey everything I have commanded you. And surely I am with you always, to the very end of the age" (Matthew 28:19-20).

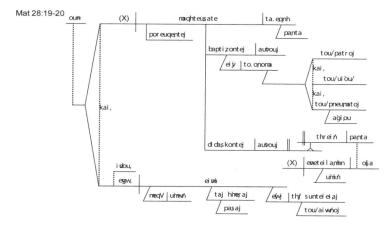

From our high-school sentence diagramming days we see that this is a two-part compound sentence prefaced with ουν (oun—Therefore). The "backbone" is the top line saying μαθητευσατε (matheteusate—Make disciple of) τα εθνη (ta ethna—the nations) with the modifiers of first: πορευθεντεσ (porethentes—Go) and the modifier of παντα (panta—All) referring to nations. So, the back-bone is: "Go…Make disciples of all nations."

This backbone is broken into two clauses. The first starts out βαπτιςοντες (baptisontes—baptizing) and continues with "in the name of the Father, Son and Holy Spirit" as we are all familiar with.

The second clause below that starts out διδασκοντες (didaskontes—Teaching). It continues Teaching αυτους (autous—them) to τηρειν (terein—observe, Obey) all of my ενετειλαμην (eneteilamen—Commandments).

The bottom line in the diagram connected to the top with the word και (kai—and) is the promise that the Lord will be with us in this task until the end of the age.

Thus, this *commission* is a double command and a promise. The double command is to BAPTIZE the nations and to TEACH the nations to obey God's commandments.

Pastor, it is very important to note that both of these verbs, *baptizing* and *teaching,* have as their subject "*all the nations.*" That is to say, we are to baptize all the nations *and* we are to teach all the nations. It does not say to *teach those who have been baptized… it says "teach all the nations.*" Those who have been baptized would, of course, be included but the teaching is not exclusively for them. The grammar simply does not allow that.

This second command could not be put more simply…The church has the responsibility to teach everyone to obey His commandments. It does not depend on some nuance or some particular conjugation of some verb it simply and plainly says: "…teach everyone to obey My commandments." Pastor, this certainly has to be one of the "plain" things…so, as you have said many times before, it must be one of the "main" things He requires of us.

This should not be any surprise since in one of the Lord's very first sermons he proclaimed:

> "Do not think that I came to abolish the Law or the Prophets; I did not come to abolish, but to fulfill. For truly I say to you, until heaven and earth pass away, not the smallest letter or stroke shall pass away from the Law, until all is accomplished" (Mat 5:17-18).

Now, there is no doubt Christ Jesus fulfilled the law…living a sinless life; he became the lamb without blemish to atone for our sins. But, since "heaven and earth" have not passed away, we must still have the non-ceremonial law. Just so there would be no misunderstanding here Jesus went on to say:

> Whoever then annuls one of the least of these commandments, and so teaches others, shall be called least in the kingdom of heaven; but whoever keeps and <u>teaches</u> them, he shall be called great in the kingdom of heaven (Mat 5:19).

Pastor, I think we could sum up these last two letters by saying that Christ's commission was never limited to just preaching the Gospel. The Lord is also commanding the church to be in the teaching business. As the Bible commentator Matthew Henry, writing in 1721, puts it, "…bring the nations to be His subjects; setting up a school, bring the nations to be His scholars…."

Thinking through Christ's commission, these two instructions are very closely related! If someone does not know God's Law how will he understand his need for the Gospel? Paul himself says: "What shall we say then? Is the Law sin? May it never be! On the contrary, I would not have come to know sin except through the Law…." (Rom 7:7)

So, God's commandments show us our need for the Gospel, and… how we should live together and govern ourselves. Paul confirms that when he says: "Circumcision is nothing, and uncircumcision is nothing, but what matters is the keeping of the commandments of God" (1 Corinthians 7:19).

The Lord himself admonishes us: "If you love Me, you will keep My commandments" (John 14:15).

Finally, Pastor, I had someone share with me that we really did not have to worry too much about teaching God's Law because it was written in our hearts. He quoted the Scripture below.

> For when Gentiles who do not have the Law do instinctively the things of the Law, these, not having the Law, are a law to themselves, in that they show the work of the Law written in their hearts, their conscience bearing witness, and their thoughts alternately accusing or else defending them… (Rom 2:14-15)

I will leave it up to someone else to discover what Paul is talking about here.

However, anyone who would like to check on whether God's commandments are "written on our hearts" can do so next Sunday. Just ask anyone, including an elder, "please, what is the fourth and eighth commandment?" and "if someone steals something...is he required to make restitution by paying double or triple?" Also, "under what circumstance does restitution only require adding a fifth more?"

Please try this yourself. See if you can find anyone who will say: "Why, the fourth commandment requires we keep the Sabbath and the eighth tells us we should not steal." "And a thief who is caught is required to pay double...unless, of course, he returns what he took before it is found out, in which case he must only add a fifth more." Pastor, if you can find anyone, having God's Commandments written on his heart, who gives you this reply...I will treat you and your family to the best steakhouse in town!

I can assure you we are *desperately ignorant* when it comes to God's Commandments and what He requires when we do something wrong. We seriously need teaching here. We desperately need repentance here.

> My people are destroyed for lack of knowledge. Because you have rejected knowledge, I also will reject you from being My priest. Since you have forgotten the law of your God, I also will forget your children (Hosea 4:6).

Please, lead us Pastor. In my next letter, I will share some of the specific ideas I have come up with on how to do this. I am sure you have some ideas as well. I look forward to discussing this with you.

Yours in Christ,

LETTER 21

STEP ONE: Education
Part IV: How Do We Teach?

Dear Pastor,

Before we launch on this project we need to admit the difficulty we will face! During my short time in seminary, there was a great deal said about persecution and suffering for doing the Lord's work. In fact one of my Professors put a crazy question on an exam asking: "Was the church better off or worse off from Constantine declaring Rome a Christian nation in AD 313?" I put myself in the shoes of a Christian of the time and thought "Okay, do I want my freedom or would I prefer being fed to the lions?" Right?!!

Pastor, I think that even if this is done gingerly, it could come pretty close to being fed to the lions! The problem, however, is that we have the choice to either suffer some for doing the Lord's work or decide to openly disobey Him. I certainly wouldn't recommend the latter.

Besides being very careful and deliberate, we also need to sort out who is responsible for what. Now, I know that technically the "church" is simply all those individuals who are Christians and God's commission to "teach the nations to obey" applies to all of us. But, nowadays, the church is also specific institutions that have budgets, buildings, and pastors. I think the Bible is pretty clear as to who has the highest priority of responsibility in this area. As I concluded in letter 16:

7. God chooses and calls certain men (priests, apostles, prophets, rabbis, pastors, shepherds, etc.) and gives them

the responsibility to teach and call on men to follow His instructions.

Those who God has called to lead us clearly have the first line of responsibility. Paul tells in Romans:

> How then shall they call upon Him in whom they have not believed? And how shall they believe in Him whom they have not heard? And how shall they hear without a preacher? (Rom 10:14)

So, Pastor, we must all look to you and the "institutional" church to teach us what God has said about how we should live together and govern ourselves. Only you can call us to OBEY His commandments and teach us HOW that should be done.

However, I think we should also be clear that Biblically *educating, training, and disciplining children lies with the parents! But Pastor, it is up to you to call them to this responsibility.*

You probably have better ideas than I on the adults. Maybe a study of Deuteronomy with the deacons and elders or something like that might work. Perhaps some sermons would help to get it started. For sure you should show the DVD *Indoctrination* by Colin Gunn to the church leaders.

When it comes to educating children, we have some valuable history to turn to regarding what works and what does not. A few decades ago, there was a big push to start "Christian schools." The schools that resulted were basically Christian versions of public schools. They used the same model and simply tried to make them "Christian." Like public schools they were unbearably expensive and as a result the movement is now in decline.

Many parents, where Christian schools were not possible, turned to the "homeschooling" model. That has turned out to be amazingly successful! Just refer back to what I found two letters back where regardless of parent or student the achievement was, on average, over thirty percentile points higher than public schools and comparable with some of the best private schools. In fact they were far better than the Christian schools.

Not only that, but the cost per student for the homeschool model is a fraction of that of the public-school model. Most public-school-type institutions require from six to fifteen thousand dollars per student per year. The average cost per child for homeschooling is less than five hundred dollars per year!

Pastor, this is so amazing! Upon reflection, you can see this is just one more testimony to the efficacy of God's Word! After all, the Bible is very clear that the responsibility to discipline and train children is with parents. Why are we so surprised when we turn to that model that it works better than any other? Pastor, do you think we may be slow learners?

Now, how do we capitalize on that model and still fulfill our Lord's commission to "teach the nations to obey My commandments?" No matter how we set it up, we must make sure we stay true to the Biblical model that requires parents to be responsible.

One way to do that would be to put a homeschool co-op project under the control of a "board of directors" made up of parents. You would probably want to restrict board membership to parents who were members of the church and who had one or more children in the system.

Pastor, I would strongly encourage you to resist trying to set it up so that some elder or associate pastor is on the board. There are far better ways to protect the church from the project going awry. Further, when you try to wrest control in some way from the parents you will be diminishing the project and departing, I believe, from the Biblical model.

The other temptation that should be resisted is making the project in any way "exclusive." Pastor, the more children you can involve in such a project, the more souls that will find there way into the Kingdom! We only need to look at Reverend Kumar, mentioned in Letter 19, to see that nearly every child trained in God's Word from preschool up will come to faith in Christ. Let us pray that such a project would be overrun with children from outside the church! We should strongly encourage participating parents to invite their friends and neighbors to be part of the co-op.

Most of the time when you walk through the church during the week it's quieter than a mausoleum, and that is probably a waste of the Lord's resources. Why shouldn't we give the co-op first priority access to the facilities? Also, since it is at heart an evangelical outreach, we should probably allocate at least two or three hundred dollars a child to help with the costs. This would also provide more than adequate control. Should the project somehow begin to stray, the prospect of denied access and or withdrawal of funds would keep it on course.

Speaking of being on course, you would probably want to insist that Bible reading, prayer, and worship were part of each day. We should also probably require the parent-board to come up with some benchmarks such as reciting one of the shorter catechisms, giving an oral presentation on some Bible lesson or the like for each year. Training in apologetics and creation science should also be included.

Pastor, such a project would easily qualify as a tax-exempt, non-profit endeavor, making it much easier to fund. We should certainly keep a separate accounting for the project but then report it under the church's tax-exempt umbrella. This is the very thing I did when Chairman of Christian Life Ministries. We allowed a Christian concert ministry under our 501(c)3 umbrella by simply combining their accounting report with ours. It worked out very well.

We should also make sure that we encourage as many of the parent board members to go to state/regional homeschooling conferences as possible by paying their expenses. Interaction here will promote others to adopt this model as well as provide fresh new ideas on how to do things even better.

Pastor, I'm sure you are aware of it, but there are a TON of home-schooling resources now available. There are countless books, videos, online lectures, etc. I am also sure the co-op will have no problem finding volunteers to help.

This idea of a homeschool co-op, incidentally, is not mine. It is a new idea that is just now getting started. Here is a website that describes some of a co-op's characteristics. Some excellent resources are given in the links at the end of the article: http://www.maybewewouldbeamazed.com/coops.html.

I have had peripheral experience with voucher schools and charter schools and actually taught in a public high school. Pastor, I can assure you we *must avoid, under any circumstance, government liaisons, government money, government textbooks, or anything which government offers. All these things come with strings attached. It is the very entanglement and control that we are now trying to escape.*

Being fed to the lions aside, I don't think this will be an idea that is that hard to sell to the congregation. Pastor, a good way to get started is to show the DVD *IndoctriNation* first to the elders/deacons and then to the congregation. Then pose some questions much like this. Which would you prefer?

- Educating kids in a place where every day is begun with prayer and Bible reading, or a place where prayer and Bible reading are never allowed.

- A place where they discover they were created by a loving

God, or a place where the name of God is not allowed.

- A place where they learn the Ten Commandments, or a place where the Bible is considered mythology and they are taught that right and wrong are completely relative.

- A place where they are taught to be civil and respectful of one another, or a place where they are exposed to sexual innuendos and foul language and where it is fairly easy to obtain drugs.

- And also a place where they will typically achieve in the 80th to 90th percentile, as opposed to the government schools where typical achievement is at the 50th percentile.

Pastor, you can also point out to the congregation that it is something Jesus commissions us to do. And the only cost is providing space, now idle and unused, some inexpensive moral encouragement and at most a tiny fraction of the church budget for computers, monitors and the like, which will remain church property. You can also remind them that this is not another church program. It is an independent organization that the church must encourage and nurture but never control. Pastor, I can guarantee you that this project will become the greatest evangelical tool you can ever imagine! Do you suppose that is why our Lord Jesus commanded it in His "Great Commission" to us? Under any circumstances, you had better be prepared for some church growth beyond what you would ever expect.

You can also point out to the congregation the experience of Rev. Kumar of RIMI ministries in India which we discussed in Letter 19. I shall never forget his reply when asked how many of the orphans they take in make a commitment to faith in Christ…"why, almost everyone," he said! So, instead of sending Christian children to government schools in hopes of winning a few to the Lord why don't we invite those going to government schools to come to ours where almost "everyone" will come to Christ.

Pastor, *please lead us in repentance and change here.* We have been losing ground for nearly three generations. We have sent our nation's children to secularist schools only to see them emerge as pagans with poor character and no purpose in life. Lead us instead to provide the way for our nation's children to be "trained up in the way they should go." God commands it and our nation depends on it!

This is the first step in rescuing our nation and we can indeed rescue it—if only we will. *In fact, we will experience the greatest revival in our nation's history.* Pastor, you are the only one who can lead us to do this. Why would we not do this?

Yours in Christ,

P.S. The DVD *IndoctriNation* is available at indoctrinationmovie.com

LETTER

Strategy Part I
The Mission of the Church

Dear Pastor,

We have talked about this before but I think the most important thing, strategically, we must absolutely sort out: what are or are not the specific responsibilities of the church. In fact, I was discussing some of the things I have been writing with another local pastor. He said he was not convinced that all this should be the real "mission" of the church. He referred me to a book he had just read, DeYoung and Gilbert, *What is The Mission of the Church* (Crossway, Wheaton, IL, 2011). The book is a pretty good discussion of what might be called the "social gospel" versus the "salvation gospel." In the effort of the authors to somewhat narrow the mission of the church, on page 232, they ask "Is there a difference between a church and a bunch of Christians?" They suggest that "Perhaps we can talk about these two different entities as 'the church organic' and 'the church institutional.'"

As I thought about this it brought to mind my "Conclusion" number 7, in Letter 16 wherein I said "7. God chooses and calls certain men (priests, apostles, prophets, rabbis, pastors, shepherds, etc.) and gives them the responsibility to teach and call on men to follow His instructions. As part of our human nature God created in us a propensity to follow these leaders."

Pastor, I believe these whom God has "chosen" are identified in the New Testament as bishops or overseers and deacons (1 Timothy 3:2, 8), elders (1 Timothy 5:19), apostles, prophets, evangelists, pastors, and teachers (Ephesians 4:11). Don't you think that these are pretty much "the church institutional" to which the authors are referring?

These leaders God has called are distinguished from the followers of Christ in Ephesians where we are told: "And He (God called out and chose) gave some as apostles, and some as prophets, and some as evangelists, and some as pastors and teachers, for the equipping of the saints (the followers of Christ or what these authors call the "church organic") for the work of service..." (Ephesians 4:11-12).

Pastor, what this scripture seems to say is that the "church institutional" has been given the "mission" to equip the "church organic." In other words it seems to say that your job (as the "church") is to equip or teach us, the congregation, to do all the good works God commands.

Paul makes this distinction again when he encourages Timothy to: "Instruct them to do good, to be rich in good works, to be generous and ready to share, storing up for themselves the treasure of a good foundation for the future, so that they may take hold of that which is life indeed" (1 Timothy 6:18-19). Here again Timothy, the "institutional church," is to "instruct" those God has placed him over...the "church organic" to do the "good works."

The Lord Jesus said: "Let your light shine before men in such a way that they may see your good works, and glorify your Father who is in heaven" (Matthew 5:16). But don't you think He was primarily instructing the multitudes (the organic church) rather than His disciples (the institutional church)?

In fact, Pastor, think about what we call the "great commission" in Matthew 28. That was not given to "the multitudes." It was given to just the eleven disciples on a Galilean mountain. Pastor, don't you think this means that from a Biblical perspective, the institutional church has the very limited "mission" to evangelize the nations, to baptize them, and to teach the nations to obey God's commandments?

If this is true, then, all of these things like ministering to the poor and needy, healing the sick, making sure that justice is served, saving the planet, and all the other "good works" are not your mission as the church institutional. Pastor, I believe the mission of the church, when it comes to these good works, is to teach us how to Biblically go about doing them and what our Biblical responsibility is for each one. It seems to me that the mission of the church is to show us how to correctly do the good works and it is the mission of Christians to actually go and do the good works.

Wouldn't you agree?

Now, I know that these "missions" are not absolutely exclusive. By that I mean that Biblically, all followers of Christ are clearly encouraged to share their faith with those they encounter and all pastors are expected not to cross the street to avoid some elderly lady who has fallen and needs help getting up.

However, all this being said and even with this very narrow scope for the church's mission, I believe we *are failing* as the institutional church to fulfill that mission.

- The Bible tells us *how* to teach the nation's children but we're failing. The church has not taught us what the Bible says about this or called us into accountability.

- The Bible tells us HOW to minister to the poor but we're failing…The church has not told us how to Biblically go about this or called us into accountability.

- The Bible tells us HOW to do justice but we're failing to do that…The church has not told us what God's Word has to say here or called us into accountability.

- The Bible tells us HOW to choose righteous leaders but we're not doing that…The church has not told us how or called us into accountability.

In short, Pastor, I am convinced that until the church begins to teach us what God's Word has to say about how we should live together and govern ourselves and make us understand our responsibilities here, we are going to continue to make a hash of it. Children will continue to be lost to apostasy, the poor will continue to have their characters ruined and be mired in dependency, we will continue to burden ourselves with unjust laws and irresponsible spending, and will again and again elect those committed to secular humanism who will continue to lead us into ruin.

Don't we desperately need to repent and change our ways here?

Which brings us to the second most important thing we need to settle: Can it be done? Can we make the nation of America into disciples of Christ? Can we teach them to obey all God commanded? I must confess we do not seem to be winning the battle presently. Some pastors have even said something to the effect that: "We are just a minority now and those others out there are so big and strong…We just need to realize that like the children of Israel, we are on our way into exile!"

That has to be complete nonsense! The Lord has *commanded* us to "Go therefore and make disciples of all the nations...teaching them to observe all that I commanded you..." (Mat 28:19-20). He precedes this with the statement "All authority has been given to Me in heaven and on earth" (Mat 28:18). Pastor, He even says "...and upon this rock I will build My church; and the gates of Hades shall not overpower it" (Mat 16:18). This is pretty simple language and very resolute. These are not "suggestions" or "it would be nice if" or "possibly this or maybe that;" these are clear imperative statements and commands.

So, if the creator of the universe clearly tells me "Go do this, I have all the authority, and I will always be right there with you and further I promise that not even Satan himself will be able to stop you!" Pastor, we have only two choices...we either do not believe our Lord or we CAN do what He commands us.

There just might be a few that will try to excuse their inactivity by saying... "Well, even if all that is true, we still don't know for sure if it is the Lord's will." Pastor, the Lord has not only told us He has all authority and commanded us to go...He even tells us to pray "... Thy kingdom come, Thy will be done on *earth* as it is in heaven!" Incidentally, He is not talking about the "hereafter." This prayer is about forgiving the guy down the street and bread for tonight's dinner...it is clearly the "here and now." The Lord is telling us that we should even pray for this to happen.

Now, I know this is not a very nice way to say this but even Jesus, when the occasion warranted talked about "whitewashed graves." Pastor, we must face up to the fact that preaching to the choir every Sunday, having a week of "vacation Bible school" and sending turkeys to the innercity every Thanksgiving is *not going to get the job done! It is just not working.* Nowhere in God's Word, Pastor, does it say, "... here is what you should do...I know you can't do it, but I will give you credit for trying." God's Word does not tell us to do something God knows is impossible! If He says we can...then we can! He promises us: "I can do all things through Him who strengthens me" (Philippians 4:13).

Now, if it is His will and we *can* do what He commands and it is still *not* getting done, we have only one conclusion...We are either sitting on our behinds not doing enough or we are going about it the wrong way. Pastor, I think it is time we roll up our sleeves, go back to the instruction book and as the TV character, Larry the Cable Guy, says: *Get'r done!*

Actually, Pastor, I am not only convinced we can do this…I think it will probably be far easier than we think. It will probably take a lot longer than we hope but it most certainly can be done. We can rescue our nation.

Before we take the next step, though, I think we should also consider the ways and means we use to go about the task. I have had a number of thoughts about what God's Word has to say about this, but I will share it with you in my next letter.

Thanks for being patient with me.

Yours in Christ,

LETTER 23

Strategy Part II
Our "Ways and Means"

Dear Pastor,

Before we go any further here, we must never, never forget that no amount of laws, public policy, good politicians, good works, or anything else we may do will rescue our nation should we fail to observe "Step One," which we have already discussed. It is what the Lord Jesus has commanded us and it is what we did in this nation from its founding in the 1600s all the way up to my grandfather's time. If we do not once again bring up our nation's children in the way they should go everything else will be an exercise in futility. John Adams put it most eloquently in a speech to the military in 1798 when he gave this warning:

> We have no government armed with power capable of contending with human passions unbridled by morality and religion . . . Our Constitution was made only for a moral and religious people. It is wholly inadequate to the government of any other. (http://www.free2pray.info/5founderquotes.html)

With this ever in our mind, Pastor, here are some more thoughts I had on how we should proceed. We need to be settled in our minds on *why and how* we are going to take on this task. I'm sure you would agree that *the strategy we use must be as biblical as what we wish to accomplish*!

First we should be sure that all of what we do is in response to God's command that: "*...you shall love your neighbor as yourself; I am the lord*" (Leviticus 19:18). This command is amplified by the command:

"If you meet your enemy's ox or his donkey wandering away, you shall surely return it to him. If you see the donkey of one who hates you lying *helpless* under its load, you shall refrain from leaving it to him, you shall surely release *it* with him" (Exodus 23:4-5).

Pastor, don't you think we are here being given the responsibility to proactively do what we can to protect our neighbor's God-given rights, his freedoms, and his property. To turn our backs here would fly in the face of this commandment. *So first and foremost when we see our neighbor losing these rights, freedoms, or property...God clearly commands us to do all we can to help him*!

Jesus, himself confirmed this, quoting the commandment to the rich young ruler; "...You shall love your neighbor as yourself" (Matthew 19:19). He even went so far as to say that our identity is established in obeying this commandment; "By this all men will know that you are My disciples, if you have love for one another" (John 13:35).

Secondly, in thinking about HOW we go about this task, we should keep in mind that God's word tells us: "Do not be overcome by evil, but overcome evil with good" (Romans 12:21).

Pastor, what that means to me is that we must, strategically, resist ranting and raving about how bad this policy or that one is. We must refrain from pointing out how scurrilous this politician is or what a failure this or that institution may be.

While all that "evil" may be true, our best strategy will be to quietly overcome it by rolling up our sleeves and doing "good!" For instance, we must not criticize public schools but instead create educational institutions that do a far better job. If we create a way to educate children that is more economical, more effective, and produces smarter kids with better character and with a Biblical world view we will not need to "criticize;" we will only need to be sure we can keep up with the *demand*.

Thirdly, our public statements should always be couched on the effectiveness and workability of a proposal rather than whether it is, or is not, a "sin" or whether it is, or is not, Biblical. We can quietly be assured that any proposal that is Biblical...will always be the most effective and workable solution to any problem. That, of course, is because we as believers know that God created the entire universe and that the Bible is His personal instructions to us. Of course, after we win some proposal on its merits and it turns out to be the best way of doing whatever it is...We can, at that time, point out that it happens to be Biblical. (*Our real caution here, Pastor, is to make sure we truly understand his instructions on how to do what needs to be done! Historically, this is where Christians have made some serious mistakes!*)

Fourthly, we must be absolutely clear on this, the "Church" is *not* called to *govern society*! In fact I believe such a position is certainly not Biblical because only Christ has been given the authority to be both a *"priest and king"* (Hebrews 6:20 – 7:2). It has also been proven unworkable historically. One needs only to look at the results from medieval times through the fifteenth and sixteenth centuries when the church claimed authority to choose or dethrone kings and all manner of other "controls" over government. *Strategically, it is very important that we make it unmistakable, especially to our antagonists, that the church has no intention or desire to actually govern society*!

While this is true, Pastor, we must be equally quick to realize *the church, through God's Word, indeed, does have the answers on how to govern*! We have seen this documented in all of the previous letters and the truth of this may be seen historically.

Alexis De Tocqueville, after lamenting what a mess Europe was in the 1830s, contrasts that with his observation of America (A. Goldhammer, *Democracy in America*, Translated, 2004, Intro. pg. 14, Vol. 1, pg. 42):

> There is one country in the world (America) in which the great social revolution of which I speak seems almost to have attained its natural limits. It has been effected there with simplicity and ease. Or, to put it another way, one might say that this country has witnessed the effects of the democratic revolution that we are now undergoing (In France) without having had the revolution.

He goes on to explain, reflecting on America's legislative records:

> …they appoint magistrates, make peace and war, establish rules of order and adopt laws as if answerable to God alone. Nothing is more curious and at the same time more instructive than the legislation of this period. Here above all lies the key to the great social enigma with which the United States confronts the world today. As a characteristic example of that legislation, we may choose the code of laws adopted in 1650 by the small state of Connecticut. In drafting those laws, they hit on the strange idea of drawing on sacred texts:

(enacting) …provisions taken literally from Deuteronomy, Exodus, and Leviticus.

Pastor, we halve already set forth in Letter 9 as well as others how America, within the limits of human frailty, tried its best to set up our government as Biblical as possible. And for the first two hundred years, with few exceptions, we were the most free and thriving country on the planet. This history clearly proves that Biblical principles of government work best!

Pastor, a big "red herring" that our adversaries often try to use here is that most of our founding fathers in this nation were "Deists" and therefore America was never a "Christian" nation. In the first case, that is patently not true. The seminal work of Dr. Peter Lillback, *George Washington's Sacred Fire*, Reverend David Barton of WallBuilders.com, and others debunk this notion completely. In the second case, Pastor, it is not what they were…*It is what they did*! Please reread the quotation from De Tocqueville above: "…they establish rules of order and adopt laws as if answerable to God alone." Pastor, it is the culture, mores, and laws that establish whether a country is Biblical or is not Biblical.

A fifth thing that is very important: *We must stop looking at ourselves as some helpless religious minority in an alien environment! Pastor, first of all we are children of the Creator of the universe, and secondly, we are Americans! This is our country! Our forbearers founded this country and dedicated it to God! We had better realize that as a result, God gave us this nation and will hold us responsible if out of fear, disobedience, or stupidity we lose it.*

Abraham Lincoln was reputed to have said: "I do not need a majority to win the day…I only need a very dedicated minority!" Pastor, it is very clear, if we roll up our sleeves and go to work, we can undoubtedly rescue our country. And we must!

Along this line, we must also resist those naysayers who claim; "Our nation has gone too far, we are now beyond saving!" *Pastor, did our Lord ever say to someone: "Sorry, you are just too sinful…My grace is insufficient in your case?" No? Then let us suggest that those folks stop grumbling and instead help us rescue our nation*!

This brings me to another very strategic consideration. *Where we go from here is not a matter of who is right or who is wrong…It is a matter of whether we will obey God or refuse. Pastor, God has shown us in His Word how to set up a free and just society. If we obey, He will reward us with just that; if we refuse, we will lose our country and He will hold us accountable.*

Speaking of right and wrong, when we are contending with those who disagree we must never treat or talk of them as if they were Satan's children. We must realize that these folks sincerely believe that their ideas are the very best for our nation. I believe it is what the Bible means when it says we should "love our enemies." As believers, we are not to "destroy" those with whom we disagree; we are to treat them respectfully and patiently convince them, if possible, that there is a better way.

Finally, Pastor, as you may know believers came together about thirty years ago, quoted 2 Chronicles 7:14 to one another and began to "intercede" for America. We humbled ourselves, sought God's face and pleaded for mercy, only to see our country fall deeper and deeper into ungodliness. If we look very closely at that scripture… (if) "My people who are called by My name humble themselves and pray, and seek My face and *turn from their wicked ways*, then I will hear from heaven, will forgive their sin, and will heal their land." Pastor, I believe God is still waiting for us to "turn from our wicked ways!"

God is faithful and just. If, as has already been said, we roll up our sleeves and turn from our wicked ways there is no doubt; "*God will hear from heaven, forgive our sin and heal our land.*"

Pastor, "…He is our God, and we are the people of His pasture…" (Psalm 95:7). God has called you as our shepherd, therefore, only you can lead us to this task. Please lead us, Pastor, to be the rescuers of our nation; to be the "…repairer of the breach" (Isaiah 58:12).

Yours in Christ,

LETTER 24

STEP TWO: God's Word and Poverty
Part I

Dear Pastor,

Did you ever think about why there are so many people on welfare today? Why are there so many below the so-called "poverty line?"

In reading God's Word, I found this:

> However, there shall be *no poor among you*, since the LORD will surely bless you in the land which the LORD your God is giving you as an inheritance to possess, if only you listen obediently to the voice of the LORD your God, to observe carefully all this commandment which I am commanding you today (Deuteronomy 15:4-5).

A little bit further in Deuteronomy, I read this:

> "...And you shall again obey the LORD, and observe all His commandments which I command you today. Then the LORD your *God will prosper you abundantly* in all the work of your hand, in the offspring of your body and in the offspring of your cattle and in the produce of your ground, for the LORD will again rejoice over you for good, just as He rejoiced over your fathers; if you obey the LORD your God to keep His commandments and His statutes which are written in this book of the law, if you turn to the LORD your God with all your heart and soul. For this commandment which I command you today is not too difficult for you, nor is it out of reach" (Deuteronomy 30:8-11).

Even in the Book of Job I see:

> "And He opens their ear to instruction, and commands that
> they return from evil. If they hear and serve *Him*, They shall
> end their days in prosperity, and their years in pleasures" (Job
> 36:10-11).

Pastor, do you believe this? Do you believe that if we would "keep His
commandments and His statutes which are written in this book of the
law and repent from what we are now doing" that there would be "no
poor among us" and that God would "prosper us abundantly in all the
work of our hands" and we would end our "years in prosperity?"

*Pastor, I have some really good news! I believe this was not only
true for that time…I believe it is, in fact, true for all time! I believe it
was not only true for Israel… I believe it is true for any nation.*

Pastor, clearly, when I say it is true for any nation, I am not
talking about the ceremonial part of the law which was limited to the
nation of Israel. I am referring to the timeless instructions of, "(keep)
My charge, My commandments, My statutes and My laws" (Genesis
26:5) that God Himself charged Isaac to keep over a half century
before the nation of Israel ever was! These are the instructions, if
kept, which lead to "no poor among you."

Please have patience with me Pastor and I believe I can convince
you of this truth. Please also, just for the moment, put aside any
preconceived notions and hear me out before you make up your
mind.

First, let me say what I am *not* talking about here. I am not trying
to revive the so called "prosperity gospel." You know, where you give
to the church and get rich! You and I both know that prosperity is
only produced by preparation, hard work, opportunity, and a talent
of knowing what to do at the right time. And, of course it requires a
blessing from the Lord.

Pastor, I am also not talking about everyone always having
more money than they need. Or to put it another way, that there
would never be anyone short of funds or "down on their luck." That
is abundantly clear because in the Scripture quoted above only
one verse down says "If *there is a poor man with you*, one of your
brothers, in any of your towns in your land which the LORD your
God is giving you, you shall not harden your heart, nor close your
hand from your poor brother…" (Deuteronomy 15:7).

"The poor man with you," spoken of here is also the same as the
"…poor you have with you always" (Matthew 26:11) that Jesus is

talking about here in Matthew and the other Gospels. These two, the "no poor among you" and the "poor man with you" can both exist at the same time. There will always be the occasional widow or orphan, the handicapped or the injured with no family, etc. who are going to need a helping hand. These who will always be with us no matter what we do are the "poor man with you" spoken of by Jesus and here in Deuteronomy. Obviously, these will also be a small number unless there is some great natural disaster. Even then, the need should be temporary.

So what exactly is God's Word talking about when it says… "there shall be no poor among you?" We can get a better understanding of what "no poor among you" means by looking at the next verse down. Verse six, from the passage above says "For the LORD your God shall bless you as He has promised you, and you will *lend to many nations, but you will not borrow*; and you will rule over many nations, but they will not rule over you" (Deuteronomy 15:6) (emphasis added). Pastor, what God is promising in return for our obedience is a *robust economy with unlimited opportunity* and in that case "there will be no poor among you."

To shed a little more light on what it means to "have no poor among you" it might be helpful to take a look at the opposite extreme…to *have almost everyone among you poor*. That turns out to be Haiti. Haiti is the poorest country in the Western Hemisphere, with 80 percent living under the poverty line and 54 percent in abject poverty. About 40 percent of Haitians are small-scale subsistence farmers. According to the World Fact Book produced by US Government Publications, about half of the government's total expenditures come from foreign assistance.

Why is Haiti in this position? Haiti is plagued with a corrupt bureaucracy and a quagmire of regulations that completely stifle economic enterprise and opportunity. The International Finance Corporation of the World Bank surveyed 185 nations and rated them on how easy or hard it would be to start a small business in the country. Haiti ranked 184 out of 185! Pastor, the bureaucracy is so bad that in the 2010 earthquake, ships filled with emergency supplies could not get permission to dock and unload. As if this were not enough, half of the population is also illiterate (http://www. doingbusiness.org/data/exploretopics/starting-a-business).

Haiti is a perfect example of a country where nearly every command of God is unknown or in some way violated. They are not educating their children, those who are educated take no responsibility to love their neighbor as themselves, and the country is completely void of Biblical free enterprise. Most of the population claim to be Christian believers…but because they do not know God's commandments, nearly half of the population also practices Voodoo! From an economic perspective, the Biblical right to liberty and the pursuit of property are nowhere to be found in Haiti. Unless someone teaches them to know and observe God's instructions for how to live together and govern themselves they will continue in this abyss of poverty and hopelessness until the Lord returns.

So Pastor, considering what God's Word means when it says "there shall be no poor among you," this is a good example of the extreme opposite. Now I am sure you are probably asking, "Was there ever a country that even came close to having no poor among them?"

Pastor, over the first three hundred years of her existence, America came very, very close to that standard!

For the first three hundred years of this country's history I believe I can show you that… "there were no poor among us!" There were, of course, depressions, the Dust Bowl and drought, banks failing and individuals making catastrophic misjudgments over all those years and of course there were those trapped in "plantation slavery," but there were always freedom and opportunities for everyone else to "manage through" whatever came. Over those first three hundred years everyone who came to this country knew that if they worked hard and applied themselves, they could at least make a living for their families and, with a little good fortune, they might even get rich. Over that first three hundred years we enjoyed almost unlimited economic opportunity and freedom. Pastor, we defined this freedom as our "unalienable right to life, liberty, and the pursuit of property" given to us by our Creator. As a result there were "no poor among us," only those who due to misjudgment, tragedy, or whatever…"were temporarily a little short of cash." And, Pastor, these were always a small percentage and most were only in need until they could work through the difficulty they were experiencing.

Bear with me for just a little and let me explain what I mean. If you recall, the colonists came to America in the very early 1600s. They started out with crude tools, log cabins, and little or no help from the mother country.

By 1700 the Gross Domestic Product (GDP) was estimated, in 1990 dollars, to be $527 million! Pastor, by 1913 that number had grown to $517,383 million. We had increased our GDP by a thousand-fold to a half a trillion dollars! *A thousand-fold increase!* (These estimates are taken exclusively from the 2007 monograph *Contours of the World Economy, 1–2030 AD* by the British economist Angus Maddison.)

Dr. David Whitten, Auburn University, describes some of America's growth over this period in an article for EH.Net:

> The post-Civil War generation saw an enormous growth of manufacturing. Industrial output rose by some 296 percent, reaching in 1890 a value of almost $9.4 billion. In that year the nation's 350,000 industrial firms employed nearly 4,750,000 workers. Iron and steel paced the progress of manufacturing. Farm and forest continued to provide raw materials for such established enterprises as cotton textiles, food, and lumber production. Heralding the machine age, however, was the growing importance of extractives—raw materials for a lengthening list of consumer goods and for producing and fueling locomotives, railroad cars, industrial machinery and equipment, farm implements, and electrical equipment for commerce and industry. The swift expansion and diversification of manufacturing allowed a growing independence from European imports and was reflected in the prominence of new goods among US exports. *Already the value of American manufactures was more than half the value of European manufactures and twice that of Britain.* (emphasis added)
>
> (http://eh.net/encyclopedia/article/whitten.panic.1893)

Pastor...we did have some ups and downs but, trust me, we were the fastest-growing and most prosperous country on the planet! For all practical purposes... "there were no poor among us!"

I would like to share some more thoughts on how and why this occurred, some observations on what went wrong, and see if I can convince you about what we could do to rescue ourselves. This letter is too long, so I will do that in my next letter to you.

Yours in Christ,

LETTER

STEP TWO: God's Word and Poverty
Part II

Dear Pastor,

If you remember, in my last letter I showed historically the amazing economic success of America in her first three hundred years. Pastor, had that continued on through today, it would be easy to say something like… "Well, Americans are just an 'exceptional people;' we are just smarter or better or nobler or something such as that." That, of course, is why we were so successful. Now I think you would agree that on the face of it that has to be more pride than fact. That is especially obvious since today we are economically losing steam pretty quickly. Pastor, I believe it is because we are also drifting away at an ever-increasing rate from obedience of God's instructions to us.

Here is what I have come to see from God's Word about the requirements for economic success and a robust economy. It also coincides completely with what I have seen in my fifty years of being in small business. And, Pastor, it is exactly what America had for its first three hundred years. A thriving economy needs:

1. **A nation or community of moral people.** By that I mean they have been culturally disciplined to respect just authority and be civil to one another…a requirement of the Fifth Commandment… "Honor your father and mother." They must also be disciplined to respect the property of their fellow men…from the Eighth Commandment, You

shall not steal, and the Tenth Commandment, You shall not covet (swindle) that which is your neighbor's. In other words, when children are daily cultured and disciplined to "love their neighbor as themselves" the results will be a nation of moral people.

2. **A nation or community where legitimate commerce is unrestricted.** Nowhere in God's Word can you find any restrictions on commercial activity. In fact, in the parable of the landowner when a worker complained about his pay, Jesus, in Matthew 20:13-15, uses these words: "But he answered and said to one of them, 'Friend, I am doing you no wrong; did you not agree with me for a denarius? Take what is yours and go your way, but I wish to give to this last man the same as to you. Is it not lawful for me to do what I wish with what is my own? Or is your eye envious because I am generous?'"

God's Word does talk at considerable length about illegitimate commerce but it does not restrict legitimate commerce. God's Word, for instance, says: "You shall have just balances, just weights...I am the LORD your God..." (Leviticus 19:36). However, there are no provisions in the Bible for requiring a "license" for your measuring device, having it "certified" or for any government inspectors running around checking every measuring device for accuracy! In fact, there is no penalty authorized by God's Law should you be found with a faulty measuring device. You will look in vain trying to find such a penalty. (God's Law does, however, provide solutions. Should you be cheated by a faulty measure, you can bring charges, and a clearly specified restoration is prescribed. The person must repay you double the value of what was measured wrongly. It specifies: "For every breach of trust...the case of both parties shall come before the judges; he whom the judges condemn shall pay double to his neighbor" (Exodus 22:9). *God's Word has a great deal to say about how to provide restitution when some illegitimacy occurs in commerce but nothing about restricting commerce.*

3. **A nation or community where legitimate commerce is also unregulated.** Not only can you find no restrictions

on legitimate commercial activity, but God's Law also clearly states: *"You shall not add to the word which I am commanding you,* nor take away from it, that you may keep the commandments of the LORD your God which I command you" (Deuteronomy 4:2) (emphasis added). Thus, the Bible provides no regulatory laws and then the Bible precludes making additional laws so we must conclude that God's Word clearly tells us not to regulate here. This can be discussed at length later, but the two greatest problems with regulations are: first, a "regulation" in order to work presumes the person writing it knows what is going to go wrong and when it is going to happen. Otherwise, the regulation will not effectively prevent the wrong. But only God Himself can know when and how something is going to go wrong! Secondly, regulations are boundless. Because there is no limit on what can go wrong…there is no limit on what will be regulated. Finally, every "regulation," takes away a "freedom" and regulations will ever continue to increase until there are no freedoms left! For the first three hundred years in America, during which American manufacturing grew to half that of Europe and twice that of Britain… *there were, basically no regulations restricting commerce! Commercial enterprises were, for all practical purposes, completely free and unrestricted! As a result, pastor, "there were no poor among us."*

Now, how did that happen? I am convinced, Pastor, it was first due to the circumstance of how our country began. Secondly it was dependent on the cultural heritage enjoyed by those who first settled this country. And, thirdly, it was the result of a very vocal and involved pastoral community.

First, in considering how our country started out, we began with small settlements such as Jamestown and Plymouth. As more and more colonists came to America the number of these settlements or villages grew but they were all independent of one another. They, of course, traded with each other but it would never have occurred to them that one village could tell another what they could and could not do. They enjoyed a freedom not experienced anywhere else. In Volume One of his *Democracy in America*, Alexis de Tocqueville described it this way:

In America, on the other hand, it may be said that the township was organized before the county, the county before the State, the State before the Union. In New England townships were completely and definitively constituted as early as 1650. The independence of the township was the nucleus round which the local interests, passions, rights, and duties collected and clung. It gave scope to the activity of a real political life most thoroughly democratic and republican. The colonies still recognized the supremacy of the mother-country; monarchy was still the law of the State; but the republic was already established in every township.

So, for the first 150 years or so Americans enjoyed this free and unrestricted commerce. In the late 1700s Britain, in need of funds, decided to tax American commerce with the Stamp Act. It produced such an uprising that it was repealed in 1766. Any restrictions on commerce through taxes or otherwise was a scandal to Americans!

This attitude simply reflects a long cultural heritage of the colonists' understanding that they were a free people. Reverend Moses Mather (1719–1806), born in Lyme, Connecticut, into a famous New England family of ministers, describes this heritage in his sermon "America's Appeal to the Impartial World," Hartford, 1775:

> The English, animated with the spirit of freedom, to their immortal honor, anciently claimed these privileges, as their unalienable rights, and anxious to preserve and transmit them unimpaired to posterity; caused them to be reduced to writing, and in the most solemn manner to be recognized, ratified and confirmed, first by King John, then by his son Henry the IIId. in the 3d and 37th years of his reign, at Westminster-Hall, where Magna Charta was read in the presence of the nobility and bishops, with lighted candles in their hands; the king, all the while laying his hand on his breast, at last, solemnly swearing faithfully and inviolably to observe all things therein contained, as he was a man, a Christian, a soldier and a king; then the bishops extinguished the candles and threw them on the ground, and every one said, thus let him be extinguished and stink in hell, who violates this charter: Upon which there was universal festivity and joy, ringing of bells, &c. and again by Edward the 1st. in the 25th year of his reign, by the statute called Confirmatio Cartarum. Afterwards, by a multitude

of corroborating acts, reckoned in all, by Lord Cook, to be thirty-two, from Edw. 1st. to Hen. 4th. and since, in a great variety of instances, by the bills of right and acts of settlement; whereby Magna Charta, that great charter of liberties, hath been established as the standard of right throughout the realm, and all judgments contrary thereto declared void; it was ordered to be read twice a year in all the cathedral churches, and sentence of excommunication to be denounced against all, who by word or deed, acted contrary to, or infringed it. (Ellis Sandoz, *Political Sermons of the American Founding Era, Vol. 1 [1730-1788]*)

So, the colonists had literally hundreds of years of enculturation knowing they were "endowed by their Creator with the unalienable rights of life, liberty, and the pursuit of property!"

Finally, and maybe most importantly, these understandings were supported by an active and vocal American pulpit. From a section entitled: "Chronology 1774-1781" Sandoz points out:

"Ministers, in sermons and reprinted sermons, are in the vanguard to justify independence, defend liberty as a fundamental good, and encourage their congregations to sacrifice. *Over 80 percent of the politically relevant pamphlets published during the 1770s and 1780s are either reprinted sermons or essays written by ministers*" (emphasis added).

Colonial ministers preached spirited sermons on freedom and liberty, quoting many different scripture texts. Reverend Jonathan Mayhew's sermon titled "The Snare Broken" (Sandoz, No. 8) upon repeal of the Stamp Act in 1766 quotes "If therefore the Son shall make you free, you shall be free indeed" (John 8:36) and "Now the Lord is the Spirit; and where the Spirit of the Lord is there is liberty" (2 Corinthians 3:17). Reverend John Allen, in the pamphlet "An Oration upon the Beauties of Liberty," 1773, (Sandoz No. 10) quotes Galatians 5:1 "It was for freedom that Christ set us free; therefore keep standing firm and do not be subject again to a yoke of slavery."

Pastor, many of the Colonial-era ministers were quite well educated and appealed to social philosophers, both ancient and then current to bolster their positions. See, for instance, the sermon by Jonathan Mayhew set forth in Sandoz:

JONATHAN MAYHEW (1720–1766). One of the celebrated names associated with early American opposition to British tyranny, Mayhew graduated from Harvard College in 1744 and received an S.T.D. from the University of Aberdeen, Scotland, in 1749. He was pastor of Boston's West Church from 1747, a position he retained for the remainder of his short life. According to Frederick L. Weis, Mayhew was regarded by some as the best preacher in the New England of his day (The Colonial Clergy and the Colonial Churches of New England [1936]).

Having been initiated, in youth, in the doctrines of civil liberty, as they were taught by such men as Plato, Demosthenes, Cicero and other renowned persons among the ancients; and such as Sidney and Milton, Locke and Hoadley, among the moderns; I liked them; they seemed rational. Having, earlier still learnt from the holy scriptures, that wise, brave and virtuous men were always friends to liberty; that God gave the Israelites a king [or absolute monarch] in his anger, because they had not sense and virtue enough to like a free common-wealth, and to have himself for their king; that the Son of God came down from heaven, to make us "free indeed"; and that "where the Spirit of the Lord is, there is liberty"; this made me conclude, that freedom was a great blessing. (Ellis Sandoz, *Political Sermons of the American Founding Era, Vol. 1 [1730-1788], No. 8 "The Snare Broken," 1766*)

In the late 1800s through the early 1900s, however, things began to change in our country. As you know, I talked about this in my letters on "Education," wherein I pointed out how we abandoned the teaching of our Nation's children to the secular progressives. Pastor, that is the same time we also began to turn over our very governance to secular progressives.

Pastor, in my next letter, I would like to show you some of the amazing things I have discovered about that time period. I think you will be really surprised.

Yours in Christ,

LETTER

STEP TWO: God's Word and Poverty
Part III

Dear Pastor,

Before I show you what I have discovered about how our nation began to change in the late 1800s, here are some thoughts on why I think this occurred. Pastor, I think it is related to whether we look to God's Word as the basis of how we should live together and govern ourselves. Or, whether we look only to ourselves for how we should live together and govern ourselves. Here is why I think this. During that same time period in the mid to late 1800s, the so-called Enlightenment was filtering into American thought. I found this definition in Wikipedia to be helpful:

> The Age of Enlightenment (or simply the Enlightenment or Age of Reason) was a cultural movement of intellectuals in the 17th and 18th centuries, which began first in Europe and later in the American colonies. Its purpose was to reform society using reason, challenge ideas grounded in tradition and faith, and advance knowledge through the scientific method. It promoted scientific thought, skepticism and intellectual interchange and opposed superstition, intolerance and some abuses of power by the church and the state. The ideas of the Enlightenment have had a major impact on the culture, politics, and governments of the Western world. (Wikipedia, "The Age of Enlightenment," http://en.wikipedia.org/wiki/Age_of_Enlightenment)

This period began with intellectuals such as Baruch Spinoza (1632-1677), continuing with Voltaire (1694-1778) and Friedrich Nietzsche (1844-1900) who notoriously said: "God is dead. God remains dead. And we have killed him" (*The Gay Science*, Section 125). Charles Darwin (1809-1882) with his books *The Origin of Species* (1859) and *The Descent of Man* (1871) was probably one of the most influential of the later Enlightenment intellectuals. Karl Marx and Friedrich Engels with their collaboration, *Manifesto of the Communist Party* (1848) and Marx's *Das Capital*, published posthumously in the 1880s were also very influential.

In the worst cases these enlightened ideas led to the suffering produced by atheistic communism and the atrocities of Hitler's Third Rich attempting to "purify" the races. The intellectuals who propounded both of these ideologies, of course, could show how they used reason and logic to come to their conclusions. They only wanted the best for mankind.

Other intellectuals reasoned their way into more benign varieties of socialism, one of which is the "welfare state." Wikipedia defines this as:

> A welfare state is a "concept of government in which the state plays a key role in the protection and promotion of the economic and social well being of its citizens. It is based on the principles of equality of opportunity, equitable distribution of wealth, and public responsibility for those unable to avail themselves of the minimal provisions for a good life. The general term may cover a variety of forms of economic and social organization" (http://en.wikipedia.org/wiki/Welfare_state).

Pastor, the message of these intellectuals was: "The Bible is outdated superstition and so we must use reason to make our own way!" However, once you give up on the authority of God's Word, Pastor, you are left with no basis or benchmark to judge whether this person's "reason" is right or that person's "reason" is right.

Which brings to mind the wisdom of Sir William Blackstone, cited in Letter 8: "...If our reason were always, as in our first ancestor before his transgression, clear and perfect, unruffled by passions, unclouded by prejudice...we would need no other guide but this." "But every man now finds the contrary in his own experience: that his reason is corrupt, and his understanding full of ignorance and error." Blackstone then concludes "Upon these two foundations, the law of nature and the law of (Biblical) revelation depend all human laws; that is to say, no human laws should be suffered to contradict these."

Pastor, doesn't it remind you of Proverbs 16:25, "There is a way which seems right to a man, but its end is the way of death?" God's Word, Pastor, surely must be the sole anchor or benchmark to judge every idea of man.

America had been so cultured into the Biblical basis of governance, however, that initially, Enlightenment ideas were slow to be embraced. Thomas Payne promoted the Enlightenment philosophy but was considered very controversial. Thomas Jefferson accepted the Bible as a source of morality but he apparently rejected the supernatural, producing a New Testament sans the miracles. Interestingly, when he ran for president in 1800, there were so many sermons preached against him that he was unable to win a majority in the Electoral College. He finally won only by getting a majority vote in Congress!

Overall, Americans resisted these enlightenment ideas because of their strong cultural history and the vocal opposition of American pastors. During this time period of the late 1800s, however, Americans began to fall victim to the sweet temptations of the welfare state and American pastors began to fall silent in the public arena.

Pastor, by 1900 America had virtually lost the unchanging Biblical anchor that, for three hundred years, had secured limited government, demanded personal responsibility, and secured our rights of life, liberty and property. After 1900, every difficulty that arose called for a new government agency, a new government program or a new government regulation to fix the problem and prevent it from happening again. *The American welfare state was being born.*

We still had the Constitution intended to limit government influence but because that was a product of man's hand, it could, by man's hand, be changed. Intellectuals very soon began to claim that it was a "living document" that had to be constantly reinterpreted to fit changing times. As we have seen, this process can make the Constitution say about anything someone would like it to say. If you don't agree, it is simply your opinion against theirs. Although, as I pointed out in Letter 9, the Constitution was clearly a product of Biblical understanding; it is no substitute for the anchor of God's unchanging and timeless Word.

So, Pastor, it seems to me these are the two factors that allowed our nation to change. First there was the siren call of enlightenment ideas assuring man that his reasoning was superior to the outdated superstition of Biblical teaching. The second was the fact that at the very time they were most needed the American pastoral community retreated from the scene, and allowed these ideas to go unchallenged. As a result, in 1900 we began to drift...slowly at first, but with increasing speed...into a welfare state.

As I promised, I will write you again and describe what I found about this change.

Yours in Christ,

P.S. Pastor, just as an aside, in the definition of "Enlightenment" given above it says "challenge ideas grounded in tradition and faith, and advance knowledge through the scientific method. It promoted scientific thought, skepticism and intellectual interchange and opposed superstition." There is something here that needs to be cleared up.

God's Word, as we both know, does not involve superstition, and does not conflict with scientific thought and the scientific method. "Come now, and let us reason together," says the Lord in Isaiah 1:18. Thus, our Lord is a God of reason, not of superstition.

Also, most of the noted scientists of the Enlightenment era believed in God as Creator and Lord. Isaac Newton said in a letter: "Gravity explains the motions of the planets, but it cannot explain who set the planets in motion. God governs all things and knows all that is or can be done." In *Pensees*, the philosopher Blaise Pascal wrote: "There is a God shaped vacuum in the heart of every man which cannot be filled by any created thing, but only by God, the Creator, made known through Jesus." Johann Kepler, Robert Boyle, William Kirby, and James Clerk Maxwell were also devoted followers of God, just to name a few. Lord Kelvin, considered the most competent physicist of his time, was an ardent opponent of Charles Darwin!

Pastor, I can assure you that even today there are thousands of scientists, including myself, who reject evolution and embrace the idea of a creator god. To be "politically correct" and retain their grants of funding, publish their work, and retain their academic positions they cannot admit that publically. At any rate, it is worth noting that to be enlightened, reasonable, and a scientist does not preclude accepting God as Creator and Lord and believing His Word to be the standard for living together and governing ourselves.

LETTER

STEP TWO: God's Word and Poverty
Part IV

Dear Pastor,

In Letter 24, we talked about God's promise of incredible blessing if we would obey the instructions He gave Isaac in Genesis 26:5, to "(keep) My charge, My commandments, My statutes and My laws" (later recorded in Exodus, Leviticus, Numbers, and Deuteronomy). God promises that should we do this...live together and govern ourselves according to His Word..."there will be no poor among you!" In Letter 25, we briefly outlined what God's Word requires in this area and considered Haiti, which did not follow these commands, and America which did follow them for the first three hundred years. We laid out the amazing difference between the two. Then in Letter 26, we looked at why after the tremendous economic success of our beginning, we began to abandon God's teaching about governance and walked away. The church seemingly lost interest in how we should live together and govern ourselves, in spite of all that God's Word has to say about the subject. Pastor, we seemed to have lost sight of "Thou shalt love thy neighbor as thy self."

Enlightenment progressives were delighted to see all those "superstitious religious" people finally give up and go away! It took no time at all for these intellectuals to set about trying to change things. Of course, because of our strong cultural history, the American people were slow to change but the abrupt absence of pastoral influence left little to no opposition to the changes they wanted to try.

Incidentally, Pastor, I am not trying to sound conspiratorial here. In referring to "Enlightenment progressives," or "intellectual progressives" I know that encompasses a lot of different people with remarkable differences. I believe, however, what identifies them as a single group in this case is their rejection of "absolute and unchanging moral values" and/or their rejection of taking the Bible's plain instructions to be the ultimate and unchanging authority of how we should live together and govern ourselves.

One of the things they seem to have in common is a desire to create a powerful central government. They seemingly believe they need the control to make sure everything is fair and things are done the way they believe to be proper.

Pastor, I wanted to see what changes took place in America as these progressives began to take over our government. I was startled! Many of today's writers look at changes since the beginning of this administration, some even look at the change since the sixties. Pastor, I wanted to look at what happened when the pastors walked away in the late 1800s. I believe that is when the real change began to take place.

I first went to the government web site that lists all of the federal agencies and departments. I then researched each agency to find when it was created. I presumed the number of agencies would be an indicator of the size and scope of the Federal government. The graph below shows these results.

Growth of Federal Agencies

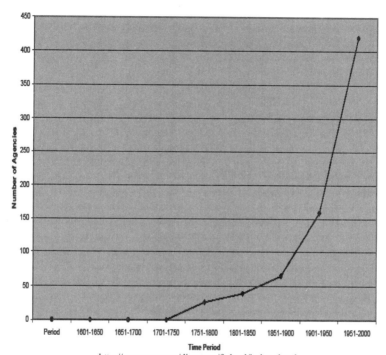

http://www.usa.gov/directory/federal/index.shtml

As you can see, there was no central government during the 1600s and early 1700s since every colony was answerable directly to the English Crown and that was thousands of miles of ocean away. After winning our independence the new federal government began creating the various positions and entities required by the new Constitution such as the House, Senate, Presidency, the Army, Navy, Core of Engineers, Post Office, etc.

In 1900, after nearly three hundred years as a nation, there were still only about 75 agencies that made up the entire federal government. Pastor, my daddy was born in 1901 and, historically, that is not very long ago! That is when these intellectuals really got started with their changes. Since then, as you can see, we have increased that number to over 500 federal agencies and departments!

Another indicator of the size of the central government can be found in the history of federal expenditures. I ran across the table of data on federal outlays posted on "WhiteHouse.Gov" referenced below. I simply graphed it out, extending it back to 1607 when the first colonists landed here. The White House web site projected the data out to 2017.

Pastor, can you believe this graph? The colonists came to the vast wilderness of this nation in 1607 with little more than hopes and dreams and by 1950 we were the richest, most powerful nation on the planet! There were truly "no poor among us;" we were lending money and help to other nations decimated by World War II, including Japan, Germany, Britain, and many others. And, as you can see from the graph of federal expenditures, the federal government was still practically limited to defending the shores and protecting life and property. Even the cost to fight World War II was just a blip on the graph relative to what was about to happen!

As we discussed in the Step One letters, by this time the secular humanists had built a firm grip on government schools and the federal court system. They were virtually uncontested as they secularized public schools, promoted evolution as science, and declared any other ideas religious superstition. Public prayer was eliminated in 1962 and public Bible-reading thrown out in 1963 again with little or no opposition from the pulpit.

A growing population of voters was being created that had no memory or knowledge of God's instructions for how we should live together and govern ourselves. Unfortunately and unlike our first three hundred years, the church took little to no interest in such things.

This was creating the perfect environment, however, for intellectual secularists to begin the creation of our "utopian welfare state." Frankly, Pastor, again unlike our beginning, the church has taken little to no interest in this either. At least up to now.

Intellectual liberals or progressives are not in complete agreement, of course, over just what the welfare state should encompass but they do agree that the more involved they and their cohorts are in deciding how we live our lives, the better off we will be.

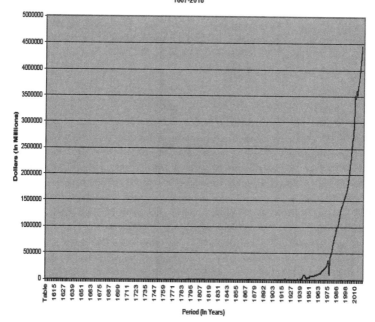

Creating dependence on the Federal government is a critical step in that process. They euphemistically call most of these programs "safety nets." While they had started promoting agricultural subsidies much earlier, the first big program was the Social Security Administration, created in 1935. It initially was a very modest program but, as all such programs do, it began to grow quickly. That was soon followed in 1964 when Lyndon Johnson initiated his "War on Poverty." That consisted of a plethora of programs but none were very well funded. Interestingly, it was not until Nixon, a Republican, took office in 1969, that substantial amounts of funds were allocated to these programs. Medicare, Medicaid, Prescription Part D, as well as Food Aid, Housing Subsidies, and many other programs too numerous to list have been added to these.

Pastor, at this point in time, I think we are close to half the population being dependent on one or more of these programs. No one can dispute we now have an ever growing number of poor among us! Of course, such dependence certainly solidifies the intellectuals' power base.

But Pastor, look at that graph. *Spending is out of control!* This spending is also unsustainable especially since a good part of the spending is borrowed money! Most importantly...*it is clearly not Biblical.* Pastor, we have stopped lending to other nations...now we are borrowing from other nations—*and at an ever-increasing pace!*

As you can see this is a train wreck about to happen. However, Pastor, I want to talk with you in my next letter about a way we have departed from Biblical teaching that is even more dangerous and debilitating. I think you will be able to see, we are in the process of regulating ourselves into Haitian-style poverty.

Yours in Christ,

LETTER

STEP TWO: God's Word and Poverty
Part V

Dear Pastor,

In Letter 25 I mentioned that one of the requirements for economic success and a robust economy is legitimate commerce being unregulated. I mentioned that the two greatest problems with regulations were these. Unless you believe a "regulator" is as omnipotent as the Lord Himself, he will be unable to know what will go wrong next and when it will happen. It is therefore futile to think you can prevent something from going wrong by writing some regulation against it. The second problem with regulations is that, by nature, they are boundless. If you sit down and make a list of everything that can go wrong, everywhere, and for all time...you will find you have a job that will last for several lifetimes! Pastor, I also pointed out that every "regulation" eliminates a "freedom" and because regulations are boundless..."freedoms" will soon all be eliminated.

The uselessness of regulations is best proven by an article entitled "Abolishing OSHA" published in 1995 by Indiana University professor of economics Thomas Kniesner and Bentley College associate professor of economics John Leeth. It appears in "Regulation," 1995, Number 4, pp. 46-56.

This article includes a graph published by the National Safety Council in 1994. The graph is titled: "Workplace Fatalities, 1928-1993." It shows the death rate per 100,000 workers in 1928 was near 15. For a number of reasons this rate declined at more or less a constant rate of one fatality less over each 5.6 year period. In 1994 it was down to 3.5 fatalities per 100,000 workers.

Our growing federal government, in 1970, created the Occupational Safety and Health Agency known as OSHA. One of its stated purposes was to eliminate workplace fatalities. Today they employ nearly 2,000 people and have a budget of at least hundreds of millions of dollars. They have written thousands of pages of regulations.

Pastor, go to: http://object.cato.org/sites/cato.org/files/serials/files/regulation/1995/10/v18n4-5.pdf and look at the graph. If you look at the point on the graph where OSHA was created in 1970 and try to find the effect of this agency, you will instead see *no perceptible change*! The creation of OSHA had absolutely no effect on job fatalities one way or another!

Not only are regulations unworkable, they are counter-productive. Niall Ferguson, MA, D.Phil., a noted professor of history at Harvard University, writing in the *Wall Street Journal,* June 18, 2013, had this to say:

> As the Competitive Enterprise Institute's Clyde Wayne Crews shows in his invaluable annual survey of the federal regulatory state, we have become the regulation nation almost imperceptibly. Excluding blank pages the 2012 Federal Register--the official directory of regulation—today runs to 78,961 pages. Back in 1986 it was 44,812 pages. In 1936 it was just 2,620.

Pastor, this does not include the Federal Tax Code. Ferguson further points this out:

> ...the Internal Revenue Service code (plus associated regulations) just keeps growing—it passed the nine-million-word mark back in 2005, according to the Tax Foundation, meaning nearly 19% more verbiage than 10 years before.

None of the above of course includes the some 21,000 pages of regulations that accompany the new healthcare law.

Pastor, they have been at this long enough and penned enough pages of regulations, that you would think we would be protected from any possible thing that could in any way go wrong. But, if you think about just the recent past...I believe the largest bankruptcy was Enron Corp., occurring in 2001, the largest environmental catastrophe was the BP gulf oil spill, occurring in 2010, the largest banking failures occurred in 2008, the so-called "banking bailout," and the largest scam was pulled off by Bernie Madoff in 2008. Pastor, I hope you can see that "regulations" simply cannot protect us from bad things happening, ever! They are absolutely useless!

Unfortunately, regulations do have consequences. What regulations can do, through eliminating freedoms, is destroy jobs and thus create poverty. Pastor, this has actually been scientifically investigated and quantified. In the Phoenix Center Policy Bulletin No. 28, Dr. Randolf Beard, had this to say in the article's abstract:

> On average, eliminating the job of a single regulator grows the American economy by $6.2 million and nearly 100 private sector jobs annually. Conversely, each million-dollar increase in the regulatory budget costs the economy 420 private sector jobs.

Pastor, this loss of jobs and opportunities would be enough to reject regulations out of hand, but there are also other more serious problems that regulating commerce can cause. Let me share with you my own personal experience.

In 2000, a business partner and I started a company to design and manufacture home standby electric generators. By God's grace and a lot of effort, we were able to develop an entirely new concept for this field, eventually producing a standby generator that not only had many new and desirable features but also had very, very low exhaust emissions. The five or six machines we made and sold through this development process were extremely well received by those who purchased them. In fact, we this year, 2014, filed a "provisional patent" on the new generator design. Just as we were completing the design, in 2008, the EPA issued a regulation on exhaust emissions for these devices.

Our machine produced far less emissions than the regulation specified. Even so, our little startup company was shut down by this regulation!

You see, Pastor, regulators must always be writing regulations to justify their existence, and big corporations are always on the lookout for ways to avoid competition. So with help from the big companies they wrote the regulation so that it required manufacturers to buy engines "certified" to meet the emission standard. They made sure this certification process would be very expensive. In our case, it was estimated that to have our design "certified" would require $80,000. And if we needed to make a small design change to improve the machine…it was another $80,000. In fact, every minor change required a new "certification" at another $80,000. If you are a large company that produces hundreds of machines per month this is not a big problem. If you are a small startup company with limited capital, as we were, it puts you out of business...even when your machine easily meets the standard!

As a result of this regulation, the large existing companies were thereby protected from new competition of small startup companies such as ours. Pastor, I think you can also see such regulation also greatly suppresses innovation and new ideas.

The really sad thing about this, however, was because there are so relatively few standby generators in the country...*this regulation will have absolutely no measurable affect on air quality!*

Biblically, Pastor, the worst thing about regulations is the immorality of them. They tend to "steal" opportunity from one's neighbor. As shown above, every one-million-dollar increase in regulatory budgets denies a job opportunity to 420 people in our country. And, of course, in our specific case they denied our ability to continue as a company. Pastor, this is about as far as you can get from the command to "love your neighbor as yourself."

The end of regulation, Pastor, is to smother out commerce and bring on corruption, poverty, and death. As we have shown in Haiti, the quagmire of regulation and corrupt bureaucrats has made the country the poorest in the Western hemisphere. One wherein starting a new business and creating jobs is virtually impossible. Pastor, in Haiti, regulations have become so oppressive there are finally no freedoms left!

For the first three hundred years of our nation's history we would have topped the list of how easy it was to engage in commerce. A person could come to America, buy a cow and sell milk to his neighbors; he could buy some scissors and a comb and make a living cutting hair; he could buy a car and give his neighbors a ride for hire...In fact he could set up a "lemonade stand" in the front yard and have his first lesson in commerce. Pastor, we have slipped down that list of countries to the point that all of the above are now regulated out of reach of most.

Over the last two or three generations we have been losing our "unalienable right to life, liberty, and the pursuit of happiness given to us by our Creator" at an ever-increasing pace. This is producing an ever-increasing growth of poverty and dependency.

Pastor, I will write again and we can discuss the solution that will reverse this whole problem and take us forward to a position where there will "be no poor among you."

Yours in Christ,

LETTER

STEP TWO: God's Word and Poverty
Part VI

Dear Pastor,

In the last five letters, I have pointed out how our nation enjoyed a thriving, robust, and prosperous economy for the first three hundred years, and then changed directions. Now, barely a hundred years later, we have a struggling economy, a smothering national debt and half our population on some kind of government handout.

Pastor, in the field of science and engineering, when something starts going badly, we simply revert to what was working and then try again. It works every time! We should undoubtedly do that here.

The change in direction mentioned above, about 1875-1900, occurred when the pastoral community gave up on the second part of the "Great Commission." Somehow those God had called out to be our spiritual leaders decided, at that time, they would try really hard to "make disciples of the nation" but give up completely on "teaching the nation to obey all God's commandments." At best, we might do a very little with church members, but we have completely and totally ignored everyone else. I think we covered that in the Step One Letters.

Because of this, we find ourselves with a present generation that is largely ignorant of what God's Word has to say about stealing, swindling, honoring parents, or in general "loving our neighbor." Pastor, virtually no one, including church members, have a clue as to what God's Word might say about how to make restitution when one of these wrongs does occur.

If we wish to revert to what was working, and "…having no poor among you," Step One is where we obviously must begin. Since we are now such a "multi-tasking" society, we clearly can also take Step Two at the same time.

So, to accomplish Step Two, first we simply must reestablish the three things laid out in Letter 25. Step One will begin to reestablish our nation as a *moral people*. Then, we must begin to reestablish *unrestricted commerce* and thirdly we must also begin to *deregulate commerce*.

Pastor, while this may sound like an economic problem, let me assure you this is a religious problem. It is a religious problem with economic consequences.

Pastor, it is this simple…God's Word tells us that if we obey His commandments we will have a robust economy. We proved that to be true in our first three hundred years as a nation. God's Word also says that if we disobey His commandments we will produce poverty and we have proved that to be true over the last one hundred years.

Pastor, a big part of lifting the smothering restrictions and regulations on our commerce, is going to require reducing the size of the incredibly large and invasive central government liberal progressives have created. In a large sense, we are reliving the plight of the Israelites when they asked for a "king" to "take care" of them! As you may recall, Reverend Jonathan Mayhew quoted earlier in Letter 25 had this to say about liberty and freedom.

> Having, earlier still learnt from the holy scriptures, that wise, brave and virtuous men were always friends to liberty; that *God gave the Israelites a king [or absolute monarch] in his anger, because they had not sense and virtue enough to like a free common-wealth, and to have himself for their king*; that the Son of God came down from heaven, to make us "free indeed"; and that "where the Spirit of the Lord is, there is liberty"; this made me conclude, that freedom was a great blessing. (emphasis added) (Ellis Sandoz, *Political Sermons of the American Founding Era, Vol. 1 (1730-1788), No. 8 "The Snare Broken," Johnathan Mayhew, 1766, pg. 1032.)*

We have, for all practical purposes, allowed these progressives to create a monarchical style government in this country. We may not have an actual king, but in practice, we have the equivalent. Pastor, we must return our federal government to the Constitutional limits that gave us this freedom and liberty.

We mentioned this once before, but to reassure ourselves this is possible, we should look again at 2 Chronicles 7:14…

"(If) My people who are called by My name humble themselves and pray, and seek My face and turn from their wicked ways, then I will hear from heaven, will forgive their sin, and will heal their land."

Pastor, I believe this is still true! We also have two other assets to draw from. The first is that we as a nation still have a certain "residual" morality in our culture. There remain a significant number of people who still have to some degree a Biblical view of what right is and what it is not. We yet retain a fleeting cultural instinct that we should obey the "Ten Commandments."

The second asset in this effort is a growing group of people who identify themselves as "Libertarians." The reason for this, interestingly, is because one of their objectives is to limit federal government to only that specified by the Constitution. And, coincidentally, as I pointed out in Letter 9, the Constitution is a document that in terms of governance could hardly be more Biblical. I am sure they would be in even more agreement if they knew that God's Word also severely limits tort claims. His law has no provision for "pain and suffering" damages and further specifies that if the claim is made falsely the claimant is liable for the costs…including the amount of damage falsely claimed!

Incidentally, Pastor, when it comes to economics and governance we should feel free to work with any and all allies such as these in areas where we agree. Years ago I had the privilege to work with Dr. E. V. Hill, pastor of Mt. Zion Missionary Baptist Church in Los Angeles. While he was speaking at a pastors' conference we were hosting, he had these very wise words of advice: "If I agree with someone 50 percent…I can work with him 50 percent, if I agree with him 90 percent, I can work with him on the 90 percent of those things where we agree." Pastor, we are not talking here about how or when we should baptize someone…We are talking about how *all of us* are going to live together and govern ourselves.

One other aside: These past five letters have referenced a lot of historians, a lot of economists, economic and historical data, and the like. The reason for this, Pastor, is that I think we have a responsibility to be educated enough to make the case for what we are advocating to those who do not accept God's Word as authoritative. Sort of like the admonition of "…always *being* ready to make a defense to everyone who asks you to give an account for the hope that is in you, yet with gentleness and reverence..." (1 Peter 3:15).

Pastor, I have always marveled at God's Word. When it comes to our salvation, His Word is so simple and plain that even a kid in grade school can understand the plan of salvation. He did not make us dependent on brilliant theologians or sage Bible commentators to figure it out. Anyone can read His Word and know for themselves what He requires of us. God is amazingly good and caring in this respect.

By the same token, we as believers do not need brilliant economists or sage politicians to know His rules for living together and governing ourselves. His Word is just as plain and simple here as it is in our instructions for salvation. Pastor, God assures us that these instructions (commandments) are "...not too difficult for you, nor is it out of reach" (Deuteronomy 30:11). God gives us no laws that restrict or regulate commercial or economic endeavors. He further commands that we NOT make such laws. God's Word does not promote communism, socialism, capitalism, or anything of the sort...His Word simply gives us complete individual freedom when it comes to legitimate commerce. Because of this the role of government is not to impose rules but to protect this individual freedom. God simply provides us the unalienable rights of life, liberty and the pursuit of happiness (property). However, as simple as God's Word is in this area, for we who believe Him, we should not go around quoting Scripture, etc. to unbelievers to make our points. As I pointed out in Letter 23 our strategy here is to objectively argue for the effectiveness and workability of these changes as I have laid them out in the last five Letters. After God's way does work, and it always will, we can point out that it happens to be Biblical.

Pastor, *I can guarantee you that to the extent we begin to teach the nation's children God's love and commandments, and begin to remove restrictions and deregulate commerce, we will have such a robust economy we will have no poor among us. On the other hand, if we continue what we are now doing, there will never ever be enough money in the entire world to eliminate the poor among us.*

Before we discuss the actual steps to bring this about we should talk about what to do with "the poor man with you" mentioned in Deuteronomy 15:7. Because we will never have a "utopia" on this earth..."the poor you will always have with you," as Jesus tells us in the Gospels. In my next letter, we can examine this.

Yours in Christ,

LETTER

STEP TWO: God's Word and Poverty
Part VII

Dear Pastor,

I mentioned in my last letter that if we continue to address the problem of poverty the way we do now, there is not sufficient money in the entire world to solve it. To the extent that we take the steps outlined of teaching our nation's children how to love their neighbor, take off restrictions, and deregulate commerce, we will in so doing create a robust and thriving economy and make it possible to solve the problem. In fact, with that kind of economy, the "poor that we will always have with us," will be a very small and easy-to-address problem. However, to solve it will require us to make sure we solve it the way God instructs us.

To do this, I found it helpful to do a "word search" on the words "poor," used 140 times, "hungry," used 46 times and "needy," used 52 times in the New American Standard Bible. The first thing I noticed is that God is really, really concerned about this. You find such Scriptures as "He who shuts his ear to the cry of the poor will also cry himself and not be answered" Proverbs 21:13, and

> ...They are fat, they are sleek, they also excel in deeds of wickedness; they do not plead the cause, the cause of the orphan, that they may prosper; and they do not defend the rights of the poor. Shall I not punish these people? Declares

the LORD, on a nation such as this shall I not avenge Myself?
(Jeremiah 5:28-29)

Pastor, I realize there have been a ton of books written on meeting the
needs of the poor. Probably one of the best is *Bringing in the Sheaves*,
by Dr. George Grant, and a classic in this genre is *Losing Ground*, by
Charles Murray. However, since we are making such a hash of meeting
the needs of the poor today we will just briefly here outline some of the
main Biblical principles that seem to be evident.

The first bastion against "need" has to be teaching children
from their youth up to be self-reliant. "...By the sweat of your
face you shall eat bread" (Gen 3:19), and "For even when we were
with you, we used to give you this order: if anyone will not work,
neither let him eat. For we hear that some among you are leading an
undisciplined life, doing no work at all, but acting like busybodies..."
(2 Thessolonians 3:10-11).

That some will lead an "undisciplined life;" incidentally,
precludes the government ever being able to provide for the needy.
Government is unable to make such value judgments. In fact, Pastor,
go through the Scriptures generated by the word search on poor,
hungry and needy...you will not find a single passage that assigns
responsibility in this area to the state. There are, of course, repeated
references warning the state to treat rich and poor alike. "You shall
do no injustice in judgment; you shall not be partial to the poor
nor defer to the great, but you are to judge your neighbor fairly"
(Leviticus 19:15). There are also dire warnings to those who would
use the state for their own advantage such as:

> Woe to those who enact evil statutes, And to those who
> constantly record unjust decisions, So as to deprive the needy
> of justice, And rob the poor of My people of their rights, In
> order that widows may be their spoil, And that they may
> plunder the orphans. Now what will you do in the day of
> punishment, And in the devastation which will come from
> afar? To whom will you flee for help? And where will you
> leave your wealth? (Isaiah 10:1-3)

As an aside, Pastor, lest we think we are not guilty here, almost everyone
in our congregation is, in one way or another, using the government
to take money from other people and appropriate it to themselves. Of
course, they would say "Social Security," and "Medicare" consists of
simply returning "my money" that I earned. I put that into the system

myself. Pastor, do the math. All the money they "put in" gets used up very quickly…in the first few years. After that it is all other people's money. Whether it is agricultural "price supports," business "credits" for this or that or "guaranteed industrial prices" for some product…all of it consists in taking other people's money and appropriating it to ourselves. That is clearly disobeying God's Commandments. It is stealing!

After the first bastion consisting of self-reliance, the second bastion against "need" is the family. "But if anyone does not provide for his own, and especially for those of his household, he has denied the faith, and is worse than an unbeliever" (1 Titus 5:8). Family members clearly have the first responsibility to provide for their own members.

The third remedy God prescribes for "the needy" is a combination of "creating opportunity" and or "lending to the needy." If there is a need that looks to be temporary and the person simply needs funds or the like to get him over a hurdle, God's Word clearly directs us to lend him what he needs: "…you shall not harden your heart, nor close your hand from your poor brother; but you shall freely open your hand to him, and shall generously lend him sufficient for his need in whatever he lacks" (Deuteronomy 15:7-8). Pastor, I think the Bible may be unique here, but we must also never be rewarded when lending to those in need. "Now in case a countryman of yours becomes poor and his means with regard to you falter, then you are to sustain him, like a stranger or a sojourner, that he may live with you. Do not take usurious interest from him, but revere your God, that your countryman may live with you. You shall not give him your silver at interest, nor your food for gain. I am the LORD your God…" (Leviticus 25:35-38).

In addition, we are commanded to intentionally create opportunities for those who are in need so they can independently sustain themselves. "When you reap the harvest of your land, moreover, you shall not reap to the very corners of your field, nor gather the gleaning of your harvest; you are to leave them for the needy and the alien. I am the LORD your God" (Leviticus 23:22). And again: "…Nor shall you glean your vineyard, nor shall you gather the fallen fruit of your vineyard; you shall leave them for the needy and for the stranger. I am the LORD your God" (Leviticus 19:10).

Pastor, this is an area where America excelled for our first three hundred years! On the simplest scale, a traveler with limited funds in this country could stop at almost any home or farm and receive food, shelter, and even clothes when needed in exchange for doing some task. It might be painting a shed, pulling weeds, or chopping wood...something that would make the traveler feel he had not just been given a "handout." A handout to someone who is able-bodied is demeaning no matter how you try to justify it.

On a larger scale, we met almost every need in this country through private associations. In chapter seven of his book, "Social Conditions of the Anglo-Americans," Alexis de Tocqueville, in the early 1800's had this observation:

> In no country in the world has the principle of association been more successfully used, or more unsparingly applied to a multitude of different objects, than in America. Besides the permanent associations that are established by law under the names of townships, cities, and counties, a vast number of others are formed and maintained by the agency of private individuals.

> The citizen of the United States is taught from his earliest infancy to rely upon his own exertions in order to resist the evils and the difficulties of life; he looks upon social authority with an eye of mistrust and anxiety, and he only claims its assistance when he is quite unable to shift without it..." "The same spirit pervades every act of social life. If a stoppage occurs in a thoroughfare, and the circulation of the public is hindered, the neighbors immediately constitute a deliberative body; and this extemporaneous assembly gives rise to an executive power which remedies the inconvenience before anybody has thought of recurring to an authority superior to that of the persons immediately concerned. If the public pleasures are concerned, an association is formed to provide for the splendor and the regularity of the entertainment. Societies are formed to resist enemies which are exclusively of a moral nature, and to diminish the vice of intemperance: in the United States associations are established to promote public order, commerce, industry, morality, and religion; for there is no end which the human will, seconded by the collective exertions of individuals, despairs of attaining.

Pastor, early America had "associations" that formed orphanages, helped immigrants assimilate into society, provided for widows of this group or another. On every occasion when a need was identified it almost immediately precipitated an association or organization to address the need at hand. Sometimes these were associated with churches but just as frequently were constituted simply of concerned citizens.

PASTOR, ON A NATIONAL SCALE, DON'T YOU THINK THIS IS WHAT GOD MEANS WHEN HE COMMANDS US TO "LOVE OUR NEIGHBOR AS OURSELF?" PASTOR, DID YOU KNOW THAT SUCH ORGANIZATIONS WERE OUTLAWED IN THE SOVIET UNION? DID YOU KNOW THAT THEY ARE PRACTICALLY UNKNOWN IN THE WELFARE STATES OF EUROPE? DO YOU KNOW WHY?

Alexis de Tocqueville made a very wise observation about despotic government. It is true whether you are considering a monarch, an oligarch, a politburo, or simply the strong centralized authority of a welfare state, which is itself as despotic as any of the above.

> Despotism, which is fearful by nature, looks upon the isolation of men as the surest guarantee of its own duration and ordinarily does all it can to ensure that isolation. No vice of the human heart suits it better than egoism: *a despot will be quick to forgive the people he governs for not loving him, provided they do not love one another.* (emphasis added)

Pastor, don't you think it is amazing that God knew when He commanded us to love our neighbor as ourself, it was the only way we could at the same time enjoy the unalienable rights he gave us of life, liberty, and the pursuit of property? Pastor, our freedom and liberty depend on our loving one another! Isn't that just amazing? Do you think that is why the intellectual left is presently so intent on dividing us into racial, economic, sexual, and whatever other kinds of categories to separate and divide us from one another?

This is another aside but the American welfare state, which has been in the making since pastors lost interest in these things, is utopian in nature. The intellectual left feels certain they can, using secular principles, make everything fair and right if given enough authority. Given the power of taxation, regulation, etc. they can take from the corporations and the wealthy and meet every need. They can make sure everyone has a good job, a fair wage, a good place to live, good medical care, and a proper retirement. In fact, they have even redefined these things as "human rights!"

They are certain that with sufficient control and authority they could meet all the needs of the poor, the hungry, and the needy. I believe, perhaps, that the unrealized and certainly unspoken fear is that we might once again come together and "love our neighbor as ourselves." in which case all these needs will be met by individuals and we find no need for government control or restrictions. We could then return to the freedom and liberty God intended us to have. Pastor, don't you see this as a Biblical issue?

Pastor, did you know there are still a number of the charitable associations De Tocqueville talks about still operating today. Probably the most well known is the Salvation Army founded in London in 1852. The founder's second son, Ballington Booth and his wife Maud came to America in 1887 to help establish that organization here. In 1896, the younger Booths founded their own organization called Volunteers of America ministering to those in need.

As part of my research for this letter, I had a tour of the Cleveland, Ohio branch of that organization. I also had a tour of Vocational Guidance Services, a regional organization in the Cleveland area founded over 120 years ago. They serve those who have "barriers" to vocational opportunities. Pastor, would you believe that about 65 people with serious mental or physical impairment are gainfully employed at their 55th Street location in the sewing shop. They produce 100 percent of all the U.S. Army and Navy women's dress slacks! They do it at competitive quality and price and make competitive wages as well. Between these two private organizations, over five thousand of those in need are provided opportunities for gainful employment to support themselves. It is what happens when we intentionally "not reap to the very corners of your field, nor gather the gleaning of your harvest."

Pastor, the most important difference here is the character-building that this kind of help provides. The expression on these people's faces told the story. They were clearly proud to be able to support themselves with legitimate work. It is the Biblical model of charity.

If you want to see the difference, take a tour of some of the neighborhoods in Chicago's South Side. That is what it looks like when government simply hands out benefits to mostly able bodied people. It is why God's Word never assigns responsibility to the state to help those in need. When government takes on this task, they more often simply destroy the character of those they try to help. Government is the problem here, not the answer.

Next letter, Pastor, we can discuss what specifically we can do to rescue ourselves from this dilemma.

Yours in Christ,

LETTER 31

STEP TWO: God's Word and Poverty
Part VIII

Dear Pastor,

In these past few letters we have been discussing the problem of poverty, how it was produced, and what the solution might be to end it. We found in God's Word that if we followed His instructions we would not have poverty. He, of course, warns us there would always be a few folks from time to time who would find themselves in need, but God's Word even gives us instructions here as well. We also saw that for the first three hundred years we enjoyed the amazing freedom and liberty, that God gave us in our unalienable rights of life, liberty, and the pursuit of happiness. As a result, we had a very limited federal government that took no interest in restricting or regulating commerce. That produced a very robust economy that propelled us into being the richest and most powerful nation on the planet.

Pastor, I believe we then followed in Israel's footsteps. Reverend Jonathan Mayhew, quoted in Letter 25, put it very succinctly:

> ...God gave the Israelites a king [or absolute monarch] in his anger, because they had not sense and virtue enough to like a free common-wealth, and to have himself for their king...

Reverend Mayhew, in his time, risked his life encouraging Americans to resist the imperial advances of Britain...our pastors in the late 1800's retreated into their church sanctuaries and turned over the responsibilities of education and governance to the secular humanists.

They were, of course, delighted and proceeded to secularize our schools and build for us a very "unbiblical" welfare state. To regain the freedom and liberty we once enjoyed and eliminate poverty…the welfare state must be dismantled.

Frankly, Pastor, it is so late in the process we don't just have a mouse to deal with…We have an elephant in the room! But, as the sage once said you can eat an elephant…You simply do it one bite at a time. We can dismantle the welfare state and return to our God-given freedoms if we just put our minds to it and do it one step at a time! Here are some specific steps that must be taken.

1. We first must convince our fellow citizens that such a welfare state not only denies our freedoms; it destroys our character and tempts us into dependency. It produces poverty. Freedom is a far better choice…it is what God offers us. Following His instructions ends poverty…and Pastor, following His instructions is not optional!

2. We can and must have all of the rules and regulations subject to a "sunset" regimen. Each one must be periodically reviewed to establish they are effective and needed otherwise they must be repealed.

3. We must amend every rule we can to exempt smaller enterprises. We must make sure we continuously define and redefine "smaller" to be as inclusive as possible.

4. Every program that can be, should be "privatized" and taken out of the hands of politicians.

5. Every program possible should be relegated to the individual states.

6. Every agency and department should be evaluated periodically to maintain its existence. If it fails this, it should be dismantled.

Pastor, these are some of the obvious "direct" steps to dismantle the elephant. "Indirectly," the size of the welfare state can be reduced by simply reducing the funds available to operate it. Congress clearly has the authority to reduce the budgets available to each particular agency or department and they should continuously be encouraged to do that.

Beyond that *every* citizen must be required to contribute to the cost of government. Our present "graduated" income tax that requires the wealthy to contribute over three fourths of the tax collected while nearly half of our citizens pay nothing at all is more akin to Robin Hood's law than Biblical justice. We just saw in God's Word "...you shall not be partial to the poor not defer to the great..." (Leviticus 19:15).

The other reason for this is just common sense. If someone is not required to pay for a good or service they are clearly not going to be concerned with either the cost or the size of the government that provides it.

Probably the best way to do this is to take the total funds currently raised by income tax and convert it into a "sales tax." To make sure the "poor" are not too burdened, you can easily exclude the tax from applying to *food* (whatever is eaten or drunk, excluding alcohol), *shelter* (houses, mortgages, rent, etc.) and *medicine* (drugs, doctors, hospitals, first aid, etc.). Pastor, I can assure you, when everyone is reminded how much tax they are paying every time they make a purchase...they will be very reluctant to ever raise them and will be equally motivated to reduce them.

Another way to limit the funds available to the state is for Congress to refuse to increase the "national debt ceiling." That would prevent Washington from borrowing more money. Those who wish to maintain the welfare state will scream that this will "shut down" the government. Of course, it does not...It simply limits the expenditures to the funds coming in. It is something we should be doing as a matter of course.

Limiting spending to income is what we require of state and municipal governments and it is something we most certainly should do for our national government. It can be done with a "Balanced Budget" amendment to the Constitution.

To be clear, these are *not* steps for the church to take. *The church, in its role of teaching and encouraging, must teach us that steps such as these are required to restore our nation to providing the freedoms and liberties God has given us.* The role of the church is to encourage young leaders to strive to carry out steps such as these at whatever level they find themselves. The role of the church is to show us how to elect these young leaders to office.

I became interested in this task in 1979 and worked very hard to elect President Ronald Reagan. He frequently and notoriously would say: "...Government is not the answer, government is the problem!" Pastor, he actually began to make some modest success at reducing the size of our federal government. He was able to do this through the efforts of a small flood of politicians from the local level all the way up to and including Congress that came into office at that same time.

And this happened because of a surge in public support generated by pastors! With the encouragement of pastors, at that time, many, many Christians became involved and took a real interest in governance. Jerry Falwell's Moral Majority, Pat Robertson's Christian Coalition, as well as the Southern Baptists, just to name a few, were very active and involved. And, it made a direction-changing difference!

Unfortunately, Pastor, this enthusiasm was based on cultural instincts and objections to abortion and other moral issues. It was not based on a clear Biblical understanding of God's instructions on how we should live together and govern ourselves. And…for this very reason, the religious fervor faded away quickly and church members again lost interest in governance.

Pastor, no change will occur until you instill within us a profound understanding that this is something God commands us to do! It is not just patriotism or civic duty…It is a command of God. It is one of the ways we "love our neighbor as ourselves." It is the way to end poverty!

If you will lead us to be as enthusiastic in this task as we are for church attendance, Sunday School and personal holiness, we will rescue our nation and, among many other blessings, find there will be no poor among us.

Yours in Christ,

LETTER 32

STEP THREE: God's Word and Family
Part I

Dear Pastor,

In the beginning, when God created us, He created the "family." God created Eve and brought her to Adam: "…And the man said, 'This is now bone of my bones, and flesh of my flesh; she shall be called woman, because she was taken out of man.' For this cause a man shall leave his father and his mother, and shall cleave to his wife; and they shall become one flesh" (Genesis 2:23-24). Thus, God made the father, wife, children model of the "family" the basic building block of society.

We again see this at Babel, when God created the separate nations each with its own language; the building blocks He used were the "families." "…From these the coastlands of the nations were separated into their lands, every one according to his language, according to their *families*, into their nations" (Genesis 10:5).

God takes great pains to record the family relationships and genealogies of those He chose to work through. There are ten genealogies in the book of Genesis stretching from Adam to the sons of Jacob. The entire book of Numbers is taken up with listing the genealogies of the twelve sons of Jacob over the four-hundred-year span down to the time of Moses.

The book of Judges lists the family relationships of those who led Israel from Joshua down to Samuel and King Saul. And the first book of Chronicles records the genealogies from Adam to the reign of King David. The second book of the Kings lists the family relationships all the way down to the exile, about 587 BC.

Finally the book of Matthew traces the genealogy of Jesus from Abraham and the book of Luke traces the genealogy of Jesus from Adam.

Pastor, you have said many times "the plain things are the main things and the main things are the plain things." One way to judge just how "main" the "family" is in God's Word is to see how many times it refers to the family. For example baptism is a pretty main thing and it is used (in all of its conjugations) in about 60-plus verses.

Here is what I did. I checked to see how many verses contained the various terms for the nuclear family such as the singular and plural of father, mother, son, daughter, etc. Wow! These terms appear in 6,155 verses! They are in almost as many verses as the word "Lord" at 6,599, and they are in almost twice as many verses as the word "God" at 3,815. The Bible has just over 31,000 verses so, on average, terms describing the family appear in nearly every fifth verse in God's Word. Wouldn't you say that God is pretty interested in the family…that the family is definitely one of the "main" things here?

Besides being the building blocks from which God created the nations, the main functions of the family are first and foremost, as we saw in Step One, to make sure our children know and obey God. As some theologian was reported to opine…we are always just one generation away from paganism.

> Now this is the commandment, the statutes and the judgments which the LORD your God has commanded me to teach you, that you might do them in the land where you are going over to possess it, so that you and your son and your grandson might fear the LORD your God, to keep all His statutes and His commandments, which I command you, all the days of your life, and that your days may be prolonged (Deuteronomy 6:1-2).

> And, fathers, do not provoke your children to anger; but bring them up in the discipline and instruction of the Lord (Ephesians 6:4).

The second important Biblical function of the family is to provide the first line of defense against poverty as we saw in Step Two.

> But if anyone does not provide for his own, and especially for those of his household, he has denied the faith, and is worse than an unbeliever (1 Titus 5:8).

> ...if any widow has children or grandchildren, let them first
> learn to practice piety in regard to their own family, and to
> make some return to their parents; for this is acceptable in the
> sight of God (1 Titus 5:4).

Thus, I think we can conclude that the family composed of man/woman/ children is not only a very important Biblical concept; it is the building block of society, and the very glue that God provides to hold society together.

What is so interesting to me about the institution of the family is that even though it is the very glue of society...it is amazingly fragile. This is clearly obvious because God so strongly protects the family by commandments. Almost everything that erodes or strikes at the institution of the family is a capital offense in God's Word. Striking father or mother, adultery, incest, sexual perversion including pedophilia, homosexuality, zoophilia, or bestiality and aborting one's children all carries the death penalty.

Before someone goes into a self-righteous holy huff saying how draconian to have all of these things punishable by death that it is unreasonable and could not possibly work...there are two things we should realize. First and foremost, this is God's Word and it is stated in clear and certain language! I think that dismissing God's Word puts one on pretty thin ice. If God, in His Word, considers this level of protection for the family necessary we probably should be very reluctant to dismiss it out of hand.

The second thing we should realize is that these penalties were in fact the actual law of the land in colonial America. De Tocqueville had this to say in the 1820s:

> As a characteristic example of that legislation, we may
> choose the code of laws adopted in 1650 by the small state of
> Connecticut.

> "Whosoever shall worship any deity other than the Lord
> God," they began "shall be put to death."

This was followed by ten or twelve similar provisions taken literally from Deuteronomy, Exodus, and Leviticus.

> "Blasphemy, witchcraft, adultery and rape were punishable by
> death. A son who failed to honor his father and mother was
> subject to the same penalty."
> (Alexis De Tocqueville, *Democracy in America*, Translator: A.
> Goldhammer, The Library of America 2004, pp. 42-43.)

De Tocqueville further pointed out that even though these death penalties were numerous, they were seldom carried out. The reason they were not, I think, is because they were simply the unquestioned socially accepted norms of the times. Colonial children also, as pointed out in Step One, were all taught to read from the *New England Primer*. That assured they knew and understood God's commandments as the standard of "right and wrong." As part of their education, they were literally brought "...up in the discipline and instruction of the Lord."

So, what do you think, Pastor? Is the institution of the "family" so bulletproof that it is no longer in need of these "draconian"-sounding civil statutes to protect it from deterioration? Can we confine ourselves to "winning the lost," and pay no attention as the laws protecting the family are modernized to include whatever relationships are presently accepted, or simply abandon these laws altogether?

Let's see, since 1900, as those laws have been modified, altered or abandoned altogether, the divorce rate is now approaching 50 percent...and that is among pastors. Out-of-wedlock births are between 30 and 70 percent depending on the group and a growing number of couples are simply deciding not to get married at all.

I believe if we simply continue what we are now doing the "Biblical family" will soon be a thing of the past. Do you think we could call what we are doing now true obedience to our Lord? Surely not!

Would "Step Three" then be to reinstate all of these laws? Well, not unless we are willing to execute half our population!

I hope you see that until we repent and decide to obey our Lord's commandment in Matthew 29:20, what I have called "Step One," we cannot reinstate all of these statutes as God commands us. However I hope you can also see if we do a good job with Step One for a couple of generations...these statutes will be enacted as a matter of course. As this happens we will also see the Biblical family restored.

Pastor, this is what God has called you to do. His sheep will not listen to the voice of any other...only you. If you call us into obedience, you can rescue our nation. If not, we will continue to be led into paganism and God's judgment. We are in your hands.

Yours in Him,

LETTER 33

STEP THREE: God's Word and Family
Part II

Dear Pastor,

As I mentioned in my last letter, most of the statutes God gives us in His Word to protect the family, are out of reach at this time. Because we have so miserably failed in Step One, these are simply too shocking to be acceptable. This will likely take a vigorous and successful effort of restoring Step One for at least two generations.

There are three Biblical precepts that could yet be pursued. Just these however, could well reverse the divorce rate and provide considerable stability to the "family."

The first is to start making efforts in each state to chip away and eventually reverse the "no-fault" divorce laws. This law was changed in the various states very, very recently. In fact, I spoke with the Ohio senator who chaired the committee that held hearings in the 1970s when it was being considered in Ohio. He told me he was expecting it to be controversial and was totally surprised when testimony was offered in committee by many who supported it but not one church, pastor, or religious organization offered testimony against the law. It passed easily! God forgive us! For all practical purposes, that doubled the divorce rate in Ohio.

This is an area where the attorneys in our church should be encouraged to start looking for solutions. Pastor, I think there was actually a second type of "marriage" made into law in Ohio called a "covenant" marriage. It had no support from the pastoral community and has probably fallen into the unknown and not used category. We certainly should look into that.

There is a second Biblical precept that could provide significant protection in keeping families intact. It is called the "virgin's dowry law."

Most Bible commentaries report the first time we encounter this in God's Word is in Genesis 29 when Jacob agrees to work for Laban seven years to marry Rachel. Then, after Laban switches his daughter Leah swindling Jacob, he works another seven years to marry Rachel herself.

However, if we back up to Genesis chapter 24, when Abraham sends his "senior" servant to Nahor to get a wife for Isaac it says: "And the servant brought out articles of silver and articles of gold, and garments, and gave them to Rebekah; he also gave precious things to her brother and to her mother" (Genesis 24:53). Considering they packed ten camels and trip supplies would surely have been packed on half or less…that would leave five camels packing about four or five hundred pounds each for gifts. That's over two thousand pounds of "gold, silver clothes and precious" things. Even though it was not named as a dowry…it is way over seven years of wages or what might be "saved" in that length of time by a laborer. Pastor, if that is not a dowry, it is close enough to be called a dowry.

While the "dowry" surely originates in God's Law as mentioned in Genesis 26:5, it was also a common practice of the time, even mentioned in the Code of Hammurabi:

> Even in the oldest available records, such as the Code of Hammurabi in ancient Babylon, the dowry is described as an already-existing custom. Daughters did not normally inherit anything from their father's estate. Instead with marriage, they got a dowry from her parents, which was intended to offer as much lifetime security to the bride as her family could afford. In Babylonia, both bride price and dowry were practiced. However, bride price almost always became part of the dowry. In case of divorce without reason, a man was required to give his wife the dowry she brought as well as the bride price the husband gave. The return of dowry could be disputed, if the divorce was for a reason allowed under Babylonian law. A wife's dowry was administered by her husband as part of the family assets. He had no say, however, in its ultimate disposal; and legally, the dowry had to be kept separate for it was expected to support the wife and her children. The wife was entitled to her dowry at her husband's death. If she died

childless, her dowry reverted to her family, that is her father if he was alive, otherwise her brothers. If she had sons, they would share it equally. Her dowry being inheritable only by her own children, not by her husband's children by other women.... (http://en.wikipedia.org/wiki/Dowry)

"Dowry" is only mentioned in the Bible four times, and then not with sufficient detail to leave it without questions. Most Orthodox Jewish scholars do not recognize it as Biblical Law.

All this being said, the practice strikes me as being worthy of consideration...especially today when the family is falling apart and in such desperate need of protection. Rushdoony points out:

In its Biblical form, the dowry had as its purpose an economic foundation for the new family. This aspect long lingered in America. "According to an old American custom, the father of the bride gave her a cow, which was intended to be the mother of a new herd to supply milk and meat for the new family." In cases of seduction and rape, the guilty party had to endower the girl with the dowry of a virgin. If marriage followed he lost permanently any right of divorce as well (Exodus 22:16-17; Deuteronomy 22:28, 29). If not, the girl in such a case went into her marriage to another man with a double dowry one of 50 shekels of silver from her seducer and another from her husband. Rushdoony, R.J. *The Institutes of Biblical Law*, The Craig Press, 1973, p. 177.

Pastor, if the "no-fault" divorce laws practically caused the divorce rate to double...I believe reinstating the Biblical dowry law would probably cut it in half! First, the dowry was a pot-load of money no matter how it was determined. It would be a very large deterrent against temptations of the husband to commit infidelity/adultery and risk losing it. Secondly, it could be reinstated contractually on a case-by-case basis and would not require passing of any new legislation. Don't you think this is something we should study, and then implement?

I'm sure the details could be worked out by the attorneys in our church...in fact it could even be funded through an insurance "instrument" for those grooms wanting to get married before actually putting a dowry together.

The third Biblical precept that we are violating is our belief that we should "lock up all those who break the law!" Or that we should "punish" law breakers with imprisonment. Nowhere in God's Word is imprisonment specified as proper restoration for a crime. In fact, God's Word does not even authorize us to "punish" someone... He reserves that to Himself. It almost always breaks up a family to imprison a father or mother. And it is clearly not Biblical!

One of my favorite Old Testament scholars is Rabbi Samuel R. Hirsh who published *The Pentateuch*, 1867-1878 (Translated 1967 by Isaac Levy). Volume II, Exodus, page 294. Hirsh has this to say about prisons:

> Punishments of imprisonment, with all the attendant despair and moral degeneration that dwell behind prison bars, with all the worry and distress that it entails for wife and child, are unknown in Torah jurisprudence (Biblical law). Where its power holds sway, prison for criminals does not exist.

An article from Wikipedia had this to say:

> Tough sentencing laws, record numbers of drug offenders and high crime rates have contributed to the United States having the largest prison population and the highest rate of incarceration in the world, according to criminal justice experts. The United States' prison population topped 2 million inmates for the first time in history on June 30, 2002. By this time, America's jails held 1 in every 142 U.S. residents. Since 1997, there has been a 5.4% increase in prison inmates and the numbers will continue to rise unless alternatives to incarceration are adopted.   (http://en.wikipedia.org/wiki/Alternatives_to_incarceration)

Pastor, our present attitudes about criminal justice and our present criminal justice system are Biblically scandalous. While the percentage of families being harmed by this may not be large, it is something we simply must go to God's Word, roll up our sleeves and take pains to change.

I must admit, I have no practical experience with the criminal justice system and as a result I'm in no position to offer advice. I can however say, with certainty from God's Word, if/when we return to "bringing up our nation's children in the way they should go," what I have called "Step One," most of our criminal justice problems will go away.

I can also say with considerable certainty that for those justice problems that remain, God's Word seems to divide them into "restorative" justice and "purging evil from the land" justice. For the first type, involving theft, swindling, torts, etc., God's Word gives us clear instructions how to make proper restitution. For the second type, involving murder, rape, child molestation, etc., God's Word mostly calls for capital punishment. Because we have done such a hash of teaching in this area, we probably will have to continue with imprisonment for the time being.

Pastor, we certainly should not neglect this area. There exists terrible injustice that God will undoubtedly hold us responsible for.

Yours in Him,

LETTER 34

STEP THREE: God's Word and the Family
Part III

(Because of my inexperience in jurisprudence, this letter was graciously provided by Pastor Mike Swiger, Exec. Director, True Freedom Ministries. See my introduction of Rev. Swiger in my "Acknowledgments")

Dear Pastor,

Another area where the church needs to lead the nation back to its Judeo-Christian heritage is in the area of Criminal Justice Reform. Did you know that right now America warehouses approximately two million citizens in prisons all across the country, at the cost of hundreds of billions of dollars annually? The American system of punishment and imprisonment is so far removed from the restorative justice model God codified on Mount Sinai, that I doubt Moses would recognize a single element of the system supposedly based upon the Ten Commandments. By the way, Pastor, did you know that our Founding Fathers considered the Bible as so fundamental to our legal system that they carved into the marble wall behind the United States Supreme Court the image of Moses receiving the law from the Hand of God?

As viewed in its entirety, the Biblical form of Justice can be divided into two major areas: Capital Punishment and Restorative Justice.

God dealt with those individuals who demonstrated themselves to be a threat to the peace and safety of society by permanently removing them through capital punishment. Because of the seriousness and irrevocable nature of this punishment, God required very high and exacting standards before the punishment could be applied (the uncontroverted testimony of two or more eye witnesses). This punishment was applied uniformly across all socio-economic classes, regardless of race or religious or gender or country origin (unlike the highly political and vengeful manner in which we apply it today). Furthermore, the punishment was applied immediately and publicly, therefore, ensuring the highest degree of deterrent to other would-be offenders.

So if a young man walks into a movie theater and guns down dozens of innocent citizens, the proper response should be to apply capital punishment immediately and publically. Instead, under our current system we are spending millions of tax payer dollars to house, analyze, defend, and eventually put on trial a man who is clearly guilty. We will put the victims' families through untold emotional pain and suffering throughout the trial, and when it is all said and done, we will spend tens of millions more to incarcerate him for the rest of his life. God's way is better.

For all of those crimes that do not rise to the level of capital punishment, God prescribed a system of restorative justice that emphasizes repairing the harm caused or revealed by the underlying criminal behavior. Restorative justice, while acknowledging the need for sanctions as a response to illegal and harmful behavior, requires and facilitates offenders to accept responsibility for the harm done, apologize for it, and make reparation to those harmed. God's justice is not primarily punitive but corrective.

In Biblical times, when someone was injured by neglect or indifference, restoration was required in order to return justice to the community. Once restoration was made the injured party was satisfied and the guilty party was exonerated. No prison time was involved. Restoration included money paid to return an injured person to health or for lost opportunity costs.

Exodus 21:35-36 provides a great illustration of the Biblical concept of restorative justice: *"When one man's ox butts another's, so that it dies, then they shall sell the live ox and share its price, and the dead beast also they shall share. Or if it is known that the ox has been accustomed to gore in the past, and its owner has not kept it in, he shall repay ox for ox, and the dead beast shall be his."*

Accidents happen. However, the aggrieved party must be made

whole. In this case cited above, one man's ox killed a neighbor's ox. The owner of the guilty ox had to sell his animal and share the proceeds with the owner of the dead ox. Further, both parties were to share the dead ox, whether the proceeds of its sale or its meat. The aggrieved party was made whole without the owner of the offending ox being subject to the criminal justice system, wasting incredible sums on hiring a defense lawyer, and being incarcerated at the public expense.

But what about when irresponsible behavior leads to criminal wrongdoing? According to the above passage, if the goring ox was known to be aggressive, and the owner did not take steps to protect the community, then a greater injustice would have been committed, requiring a greater act of restoration. In this case the owner of the goring ox comes away with only the dead ox, while the victim receives a new ox from the owner of the offending ox. Once again, the aggrieved party is made whole, and the community is spared the expense of incarceration.

The American system of incarceration as a form of punishment is completely foreign to the Bible. It does nothing to restore victims to their original condition, debilitates the offender, and breaks down the perpetrator's own family, all at the cost of untold billions to the tax payer. The only incarceration mentioned in the Bible is a "Debtors' Prison" where individuals who would not or could not repay their debts were sent to work off their obligations. Even here the amount of time was limited to seven years of labor, and the goal of the process was to restore the creditor to his original condition.

Pastor, I know many will say, "All this eye for an eye stuff is Old Testament theology, abrogated by the coming of Jesus Christ." This simply is not true. Jesus said in Matthew 5:17, "Do not think that I have come to abolish the Law or the Prophets; I have not come to abolish them but to fulfill them." This is just one example of the provisions of restorative justice is seen in the episode between Jesus and Zacchaeus in Luke 19:1-10.

Zacchaeus, confronted by the holiness of Jesus and convicted of his sin, determined to make things right with his neighbors. Instead of repaying the amount required by the Old Testament law—which equaled the amount defrauded plus a twenty percent penalty (Leviticus 6:5 and Numbers 5:7)—Zacchaeus offered far beyond what the law required. Jesus, upon hearing his confession and plan, commended his action and confirmed that he was, indeed, a child of Abraham. Justice, which Zacchaeus had violated, was about to be restored. Zacchaeus accepted responsibility for his actions, apologized, and then made restitution without incarceration at tax payer expense.

Pastor, many other passages and examples from Sacred Scripture could be used to illustrate the point that the American criminal justice system is broken and unbiblical. It is the responsibility of every Pastor to advocate for public policies which promote the practice of Biblical Justice: capital punishment for those who pose a danger to public safety and restorative justice according the Law of God.

Yours in Him,

LETTER 35

STEP FOUR: God's Word and Self-Governance
Part I

Dear Pastor,

Our Lord has given us many unalienable rights; among the most valuable is our freedom to choose those who will be given authority to govern us. He has also given us clear instructions in His Word on the character we should require of those who govern us.

> The God of Israel said…"He who rules over men righteously, who rules in the fear of God is as the light of the morning *when* the sun rises, a morning without clouds, *when* the tender grass *springs* out of the earth, through sunshine after rain." (2 Samuel 23:3-4)

Pastor, do you think choosing those who govern (politics) are any business of the church? Here is what Dr. Jonathan Mayhew had to say in 1750:

> It is hoped that but few will think the subject of it (civil magistracy) an improper one to be discoursed on in the pulpit under a notion that this is preaching politics instead of Christ. However, to remove all prejudices of this sort, I beg it may be remembered that "all Scripture is profitable for doctrine, for reproof, for correction, for instruction in righteousness." (2Timothy 3:16) Why, then, should not those parts of Scripture which relate to civil government be examined and explained from the desk (pulpit), as well as others? Obedience to the civil magistrate is a Christian duty; and if so, why should not the

nature, grounds, and extent of it be considered in a Christian assembly? Besides, if it be said that it is out of character for a Christian minister to meddle with such a subject, this censure will at last fall upon the Holy Apostles. They write upon it in their epistles to Christian churches; and surely it cannot be deemed either criminal or impertinent to attempt an explanation of their doctrine. (Sermon Preface: "A Discourse Concerning Unlimited Submission and Non-Resistance to the Higher Powers," Jonathan Mayhew, A.M., Pastor of the West Church, Boston, 1750. *The Pulpit of the American Revolution*, Thornton, John Wingate, Biblio Bazaar, pp. 47-8.)

These comments were taken from the Preface of his sermon. His text was Romans 13:1- 7. No sooner had Dr. Mayhew delivered the sermon than it was reprinted in a number of languages around the world and read throughout the colonies; acquiring the name "The Morning Gun of the (American) Revolution."

Let every person be in subjection to the governing authorities. For there is no authority except from God, and those which exist are established by God. Therefore he who resists authority has opposed the ordinance of God; and they who have opposed will receive condemnation upon themselves. For rulers are not a cause of fear for good behavior, but for evil. Do you want to have no fear of authority? Do what is good, and you will have praise from the same; for it is a minister of God to you for good. But if you do what is evil, be afraid; for it does not bear the sword for nothing; for it is a minister of God, an avenger who brings wrath upon the one who practices evil. Wherefore it is necessary to be in subjection, not only because of wrath, but also for conscience ' sake. For because of this you also pay taxes, for *rulers* are servants of God, devoting themselves to this very thing. Render to all what is due them: tax to whom tax *is due*; custom to whom custom; fear to whom fear; honor to whom honor (Romans 13:1-7).

This was the "proof text" British monarchs had used to elevate their authority over the church, what was then called the "Divine right of Kings."

The Bible commenter William Barclay had this to say:

At first reading this is an extremely surprising passage, for it seems to counsel absolute obedience on the part of the Christian to the civil power. But, in point of fact, this is a commandment which runs through the whole New Testament. In 1 Timothy 2:1-2 we read: "First of all, then, I urge that entreaties *and* prayers, petitions *and* thanksgivings, be made on behalf of all men, for kings and all who are in authority, in order that we may lead a tranquil and quiet life in all godliness and dignity." In Titus 3:1 the advice to the preacher is: "Remind them to be submissive to rulers and authorities to be obedient, to be ready for any honest work." In 1 Peter 2: 13-17 we read: Submit yourselves to every ordinance of man for the Lord's sake: whether it be to the king, as supreme; Or unto governors, as unto them that are sent by him for the punishment of evildoers, and for the praise of them that do well. For so is the will of God, that with well doing ye may put to silence the ignorance of foolish men: As free, and not using *your* liberty for a cloak of maliciousness, but as the servants of God. Honor all *men*. Love the brotherhood. Fear God. Honor the king. (Barclay, William, *The Letter to the Romans*, Rev. Ed. 1977, Westminster Press, p171.)

Romans 13:1-7 has been a difficult text for Bible-believing Christians for a very long time. The most difficult part is its universal/absolutism. It unequivocally states: The King is a minister of God, is established by God, and to disobey him is to disobey God. When we read Dr. Mayhew's explanation the difficulty is cleared away immediately. I believe the key is allowing Scripture to explain itself. Dr. Mayhew points out that this is certainly not the only Biblical command of God that is stated in universal/absolute terms. Ephesians 6:1 reads "Children, obey your parents in the Lord: for this is right," Ephesians 5:22 "Wives, submit yourselves unto your own husbands, as unto the Lord," and several others share this same characteristic. Here is what Dr. Mayhew had to say:

> If those who bear the title of civil rulers do not perform the duty of civil rulers, but act directly counter to the sole end and design of their office; if they injure and oppress their subjects instead of defending their rights and doing them good they have not the least pretence to be honored obeyed and rewarded according to the apostle's argument.

> Rulers have no authority from God to do mischief. They are not God's ordinance, or God's ministers, in any other sense than as it is by his permission and providence that they are exalted to bear rule...

It is blasphemy to call tyrants and oppressors God's ministers. They are more properly "the messengers of Satan to buffet us." No rulers are properly God's ministers but such as are "just, ruling in the fear of God." When once magistrates act contrary to their office, and the end of their institution,-- when they rob and ruin the public instead of being guardians of its peace and welfare,--they immediately cease to be the ordinance and ministers of God, and no more deserve that glorious character than common pirates and highwaymen. ("A Discourse Concerning Unlimited Submission and Non-Resistance to the Higher Powers," Jonathan Mayhew, A.M., Pastor of the West Church, Boston, 1750. *The Pulpit of the American Revolution*, Thornton, John Wingate, Biblio Bazaar, pp. 72 -4.)

This understanding brings us to another of God's commandments stated at the outset: the unalienable right to choose those who will be our leaders. "...select out of all the people able men who fear God, men of truth, those who hate dishonest gain; and you shall place these over them, as leaders..." (Exodus 18:21).

Pastor, we have made such a hash of this commandment that we now have mostly pirates and highwaymen as leaders in all of our political parties! We are "perishing for lack of knowledge," and the blame clearly lies with the church or more accurately...with our church pastors.

I do not know of a single church that has taught voting-age members how to get someone elected to office. A very small percentage made an effort to make sure members were registered to vote...An even smaller percentage told members how to determine the positions candidates had on important issues, and likely only a handful made efforts to make sure their members voted.

Please lead us to repent for turning our back on this commandment of our Lord. Show us how to get involved in bringing Biblical teaching back to this area. It can actually be fun and very rewarding. The following is how we obey our Lord's commandment to "choose those who rule over us" in 21st-Century America.

A good way to get started is to have a "Return to Good Citizenship Week." Some of the events could be as follows:

1. Get volunteers to pull a copy of the "party platforms" for each party from the internet. Read them aloud to the group and discuss each issue as to how Biblical it may or may not be.

2. Invite the County Party Chairmen from each county in your area to give a talk on party structure and processes; one County Chairman for each party on different times.

3. Ask the County Party Chairmen to bring a list of vacant Precinct Committeemen's Offices. These are the folks who represent their party in their neighborhood. Encourage members to run for these vacancies. It is a certain win and the candidate then becomes an official member in the parties' County Committee.

4. Invite your local Congressman to speak to the group. Offer a 10-minute time for a presentation and 15 minutes of Q&A.

5. Invite the State Senators and State Representatives to a similar meeting.

6. Call for volunteers and form committees to supervise a "Voter Registration Drive," a "Voter Education Drive" and a "Get Out the Vote Drive."

7. Pastor, please give us one or two sermons taken from Reverend Charles Chauncy, "Civil Magistrates Must Be Just, Ruling in the Fear of God" 1747, Ellis Sandoz, *Political Sermons of the American Founding Era.* Volume 1 (1730 – 1788) [1991].

Many believers think that winning politically is how we will rescue our nation. Pastor, I think you must surely see by now that as important as this is, it is a small part of what we must do. In fact, unless we do Step One, bringing our Nation's children up in the way they should go, we will soon have so few believers we could not win any elections no matter how hard we try.

I will give you my thoughts on choosing those who will rule us in the next few letters. Please let me know what you think.

Yours in Christ,

LETTER

STEP FOUR: God's Word and Governance
Part II: Appoint for Yourselves Judges and Officers

Dear Pastor,

How do you kill eleven million people? That is actually the title of a book just written by Andy Andrews. In it he points out that the reason Adolf Hitler rose to power in Germany was that ordinary God-fearing, church-going people were not engaged in the political process. Less than 40 percent of eligible voters participated in the election that brought Hitler to power! Andrews goes on to say:

> It is a fact that fewer than 10 percent of Germany's population of 79.7 million people actively worked or campaigned to bring about Hitler's change. Even at the height of its power in 1945, the Nazi political party boasted only 8.5 million members. So the remaining 90 percent of Germans—teachers and doctors and ministers and farmers—did...what? Stood by? Watched? Essentially, yes. Mothers and fathers held their voices, covered their eyes, and closed their ears. The vast majority of an educated population accepted their salaries and avoided the uncomfortable truth that lingered over them like a serpent waiting to strike. And when the Nazis came for their children, it was too late.

Mr. Andrews also points this out: "...did you know that during the past quarter century, no presidential election has been won by more than ten million ballots cast? Yet every federal election during the same time *period had at least one hundred million people of voting age who did not bother to vote!"*

Over the last 10 years, about 30 percent of eligible voters were not registered to vote and of those who were, nearly 35 percent did not bother to vote.

Pastor, those numbers are going to be about the same for our congregation.

This is bad news and it is good news. It is bad news because if we do nothing we are so unengaged that we are clearly about to lose our country. It is good news because so many citizens *are not* engaged in the political process. The reason this is good news is because, should we roll up our sleeves and go to work, even a half-hearted effort will bring about a *landslide* change in direction.

Pastor, God has commanded us to "choose" those who will rule over us: "You shall appoint for yourself judges and officers in all your towns which the LORD your God is giving you, according to your tribes, and they shall judge the people with righteous judgment" (Deuteronomy 16:18). Pastor, these judges or governing authorities are the very ones that Paul mentions in Romans: "Let every person be in subjection to the governing authorities. For there is no authority except from God, and those which exist are established by God" (Rom 13:1-5).

Pastor, if we get involved in the process and choose wisely these authorities will be "He who rules over men righteously, Who rules in the fear of God" (2 Samuel 23:3). If we shirk our duty here our rulers will be the kind that Reverend Mayhew describes, "(they will)… cease to be the ordinance and ministers of God, and no more deserve that glorious character than common pirates and highwaymen."

Pastor, will we choose those who will rule righteously and in the fear of god or will we do nothing?

Won't God hold us accountable for doing nothing?

With just a small effort, we could end the violence of abortion, the corruption, and the injustice that is enveloping our country. All we need to do is still perfectly legal.

There is no rule or law to prevent our church from doing all that is necessary. If every Bible-believing person did these three things, there would be a landslide change in our country!

1. Make sure every member is registered to vote.

2. Make sure every member is aware of what the candidates stand for or support.

3. Make sure every member votes.

Pastor, here is what the IRS has said…in their own words. It is a direct quote from Tax Guide for Churches and Religious Organizations (Publication #1828, Internal Revenue Service, page 7): http://www.irs.gov/pub/irs-pdf/p1828.pdf

Certain activities or expenditures *may not be prohibited,*

Depending on the facts and circumstances. For example, certain *voter education* activities (including the presentation of public forums and the publication of voter education guides) conducted in a nonpartisan manner do

Not constitute prohibited political campaign activity. In addition, other activities intended to encourage people to participate in the electoral process, such as *voter education* and *get-out-the-vote drives, would not constitute prohibited political campaign activity if conducted in a nonpartisan manner.* (emphasis added)

Pastor, please help us do this. *The first thing we need to do is get everyone registered to vote!* Here is how to do this safely.

- This Sunday, find out how much of a task we have by asking everyone who is 18 or older and not registered to stand. Because members live in different counties, you might want to do this by counties. This will also give us an idea of how many registration forms we will need.

- Appoint one volunteer for each county. They must live in the county for which they are volunteering.

- Have them go to the County Board of Elections, and ask these folks for help. They can provide all the registration forms and instructions you will need. In fact, if you ask, they may be able to "deputize" the person to directly register people himself. (A phone book, a Google search, or a 411 call will give you the location and phone number for the County Board of Elections.) The people at the Board of Elections are friendly, nonpartisan and very willing to help.

- While at the Board of Elections make sure the volunteer gets a good supply of the forms called "Request for Absentee

Ballot." Give one to every member that might have any trouble getting to the voting place.

- Set up a table for each county in the church foyer. Put a sign on each table indicating which county it is and that the registration is "nonpartisan." It will take at least three Sundays to get everyone. Make sure any who need them receives a Request for Absentee Ballot.

Pastor, I would be willing to help. God has commanded us to: "Choose wise and discerning and experienced men from your tribes, and I will appoint them as your heads" (Deuteronomy 1:13). Pastor, don't you think if we did our best to obey God here that He would really bless our efforts?

Yours in Christ,

P.S. The Nazis have nothing on us, Pastor; we have killed *four times* that many unborn babies since 1973! Silence in the face of evil is itself evil. God will not hold us *guiltless*. As Dietrich Bonhoeffer noted, "*Not* to speak *is* to speak. *Not* to act *is* to act."

LETTER 37

STEP FOUR: God's Word and Governance Part III: Choose "He Who Rules Over Men Righteously..." (2 Samuel 23:3)

Dear Pastor,

Now that we have everyone registered to vote, we must now choose who should be elected. We must be very certain, however, that we do not fall under the apostle Paul's condemnation of: "...do you appoint them as judges who are of no account in the church?" (1 Corinthians 6:4).

God's Word commands: "You shall appoint for yourself judges and officers...and they shall judge the people with righteous judgment" (Deuteronomy 16:18).

To do this obviously requires two things.

First, *we must be clear on what the Bible defines as "righteous" or "just."*

And second, *we must determine what those who wish to lead believe and stand for.* Does their idea of what's right or wrong agree with what God's Word says is right or wrong?

If we are clear on these two things, Pastor, there is simply no need to tell anyone to vote for candidate Jones or to not vote for candidate Smith. Knowing these two things are all we need.

But, Pastor, I believe you are the only one who can show us what the Bible has to say about what is right or wrong. Aren't you the only one who can show us what God has said is just or unjust?

Pastor, if God's Word declares that taking the life of an unborn child is unrighteous, you must show us that. If God's Word declares that marriage is only righteous when it is between a man and a woman, you must show us that. If allowing the government to create a situation in which more and more people are becoming dependent on the state is Biblically unjust, you must show us that.

More than anything else though, Pastor, you must tell us if we knowingly vote for candidates that have shown they will defend or promote issues that are Biblically unjust or unrighteous...will not God hold us accountable? Is that disobedience in God's eyes? Is there any penalty?

Knowing where the candidates stand and what they believe is the easiest thing to discover. You can do this through some volunteers. Pastor, I can help.

In fact, Pastor, since this is our first time doing this we might want to keep it simple by limiting ourselves to Presidential, U.S. Senate and U.S. House races. There are two ways we could do this. We could just copy the chart below onto the churches' web site so that when a member wants to check on a particular candidate, they can go to these websites, find the name and see the endorsements or ratings given. You must, however, post the *entire chart* on the web site for it to be considered "nonpartisan."

Organizations That Rate or Endorse Candidates

- ADA: http://www.adaction.org/media/votingrecords/2010. pdf Americans for Democratic Action Ratings. A good rating from this organization indicates that a candidate is normally in favor of a larger role for government in public affairs.

- NTU: http://www.ntu.org/on-capitol-hill/ntu-rates-congress/2011-ntu-rates-congress-1.pdf   National Taxpayer's Union Ratings. A good rating from this organization indicates that a candidate is normally in favor of less taxes and government involvement in public affairs.

- NARAL: http://www.prochoiceamerica.org/elections National Abortion Rights Action League PAC Endorsements of Candidates. An endorsement from this organization indicates that the candidate has made a commitment to support the right to an abortion or has voted for some legislation that would support that position.

- NRL: http://www.nrlpac.org National Right to Life PAC Endorsement of Candidates. An endorsement from this organization indicates that a candidate has pledged support of opposing abortion or has consistently voted against legislation that promotes abortion.

- NRA: http://www.nrapvf.org/grades-endorsements.aspx National Rifle Association PAC endorsements and ratings. An endorsement or favorable rating from this organization indicates the candidate is supportive of the use and ownership of firearms. These candidates are also often found to be supportive of less governmental regulation in general.

The second way to provide the information is to have some volunteers produce voter information sheets. For each race (presidential, congressional, etc.) list the people running for the office and adjacent to each name list the endorsements and ratings of all of the organizations above that are available. Once again, you must list the endorsements and ratings that are available from *all of the organizations* to be "nonpartisan." Be sure to include with the voter information, of course, the above chart of organizations as shown so it can be determined what each organization promotes or stands for.

These information packets may be distributed to our members on a Sunday morning or in whatever way we choose.

Pastor, *if we provide voter information in the way it is described above, I can guarantee that it will qualify as being <u>nonpartisan</u> as required by law.*

The reason for this is the tax-exempt organization I was chairman of produced voter information this way for twenty years. It was challenged on two occasions. Both times, when reviewed by the Internal Revenue Service, it was passed as completely nonpartisan!

Not always agreeing on what is right or wrong or making an occasional mistake on where some candidate stands will not keep us from restoring our nation. *The most dangerous thing that can occur that will guarantee our nation's decline is for us to go on doing nothing!*

Pastor, as head of our flock, if you help us here, we can save our nation. But, if you instead do nothing, I am quite sure we will lose it. It really is up to you.

Yours in Christ,

P.S. So you will not need to go back to my previous letter, here again is the statement published by the IRS regarding what churches are allowed to do. Tax Guide for Churches and Religious Organizations (Publication #1828, Internal Revenue Service, page 7): http://www. irs.gov/pub/irs-pdf/p1828.pdf

Certain activities or expenditures *may not be prohibited*, depending on the facts and circumstances. For example, certain *voter education* activities (including the presentation of public forums and the publication of voter education guides) conducted in a nonpartisan manner do not constitute prohibited political campaign activity. In addition, other activities intended to encourage people to participate in the electoral process, such as *voter registration* and *get-out-the-vote drives*, would not constitute prohibited political campaign activity—*if conducted in a nonpartisan manner.* (emphasis added)

LETTER

STEP FOUR: God's Word and Governance Part III: Choose "He Who Rules Over Men Righteously..." (2 Samuel 23:3)

Dear Pastor,

At this point, Pastor, I believe we have all the eligible voters registered. We have found where all the politicians stand on the issues, but there is one more thing—the most important—that we still must accomplish.

We must make sure that everyone votes!

To do this will take a little bit of effort, but it is not that difficult. One important thing we need to do is to make an insert for the bulletin on Sunday, November 4, before Election Day on November 6.

Besides reminding us to *vote*, we should include the phone numbers for the different county board of elections we looked up during the registration drive like this:

- If you live in Baker County, you may call (107) 345-6789 to find your polling place. (Here the number is for the County Board of Elections)

- If you live in Coleen County, you may call (107) 567-1234 to find your polling place. (Here the number is for the County Board of Elections)

We should also note: If you need a ride to the polling place, please call the church office. Obviously we will need some volunteers here.

Pastor, if we really want to do this right, we should also get some volunteers, divide up the Church Directory and call everyone listed on Tuesday (Election Day), reminding them to vote. We also should be prepared to offer rides for those who need transportation.

As you can see, with only a little effort and a few days of work (mostly done by volunteers) we can make a huge difference! Doing this will put us well on the way to restoring Judeo-Christian principles to our public policy. All of this is not only legal for a church but...it is surely our Biblical responsibility.

Pastor, while all this can be done with volunteers, if you don't insist it be done...it won't!

Yours in Christ,

LETTER 39

Conclusions
Rescuing Our Country

Dear Pastor,

You are our "Shepherd!" God has created us with an amazing propensity to recognize your voice and follow you to the exclusion of most others! We are looking to you for leadership and teaching on how to be responsible and worthy followers of our Lord.

The Lord our God and Creator is a loving and kind Savior that has given us, in His Word, His instructions for how to live together and govern ourselves. These instructions include, above all else, what it means to love Him and to love our neighbors as ourselves. These instructions provide the maximum of life, liberty, and the pursuit of property with a minimum of restrictions while still enjoying peace and prosperity in our nation.

The last words while still here on earth of Jesus our Lord were directed to you, His disciples and shepherds. He instructed you to "make disciples of our nation" and to "teach our nation to obey His commandments."

Pastor, if you will obey Him, God will restore America to the greatness she once enjoyed! And we will experience the greatest "awakening" ever!

If you choose to continue what you are now doing, our nation will continue its decline into secular humanism until we come under His judgment!

Please, Dear Pastor, only you can rescue America.

Yours in Christ,

APPENDIX 1

Neat Things about God's Law

I thought I would share some of the surprising things I have learned, over this time, about God's law. Or, to put it another way…about God's instructions for how we should live together and govern ourselves.

Pastor, the *first* thing that amazes me with God's law is how simple it is to understand. Love and obey Him and love our neighbor as ourselves. How much easier could it be? I touched on this in Letter Four, quoting Martin Luther when he said: "For of this we must be certain no simpler speech has been heard on earth than what God has spoken (in the Bible)." Even a child can understand that when he sneaks a $25 book out of the library God's law requires him to return it, apologize and make a $5 (a fifth of $25) donation to the library (Leviticus 5:16). He can also understand that should he hide it, intending to keep it and then gets caught, the penalty becomes double or $50 (Exodus 22:4). We surely don't need some high-powered lawyer to understand what God is saying.

Now, I am not saying we can dismiss all the lawyers. There are always going to be contracts to be written, disputes to settle between folks, criminals to prosecute, and criminals to defend. I will say however, to the degree we can implement God's law instead of man's, we will need a lot fewer of them!

One of the reasons God's law enjoys this simplicity has already been discussed in Letter 12. Its simplicity comes from being "case" law rather than "regulatory" law. At this point, we need only to thank

Him for making it so easy to understand.

The *second* thing I noticed is that in God's law we are called to *restore* right order rather than PUNISH the offender. You can see that by doing a word study on "punishment." Using a computer Bible, I looked up "punish," "punishable," "punished," etc. as well as the words "penalty," and "vengeance." In the 175 times these occur in the New American Standard translation, 171 times it is God doing the "punishing!" Only in the most serious crimes of murder, etc. are we called to "punish" the offender by taking his life. Even here the Bible does not so much refer to it as punishing the offender but rather as "purging the evil" out of the land. God's Word implies that taking the offender's life is an act of restoring the land by "purging" the land of murderers.

Pastor, we have so isolated ourselves from God's instructions and so polluted our minds with humanistic ideas now that we do not understand the difference between restitution and punishment. The clearest illustration of this difference between punishing someone for doing wrong or restoring right order came about when I had my first company.

The vice-president of production came into my office to inform me that a few days ago some equipment came up missing. He said that they had narrowed it down to just a few people and upon questioning one young man confessed that he was responsible. The VP said, "The steps we have taken are current industrial policy in matters such as these. He has signed a statement that will go into his personnel file, and he agreed to leave without further ado if we promise not to press charges against him with the local police." The equipment was worth a few hundred dollars.

I thought a moment, and said: "You know, I have been reading in the Old Testament that in this kind of theft, if the person responsible pays double for what he took we should reinstate him with no penalty or record."

The VP looked surprised and said: "You must be crazy, if we do that, we will be robbed blind from now on!" But I insisted and ask him to send the young man in.

When he came in, I asked him if everything had been explained to him and did he understand what was going to happen. He said: "Yes."

I then said, "Okay, but now I would like to give you another choice." I told him that the Bible says that in this situation, if he would pay the company double for what he had taken, then we would reinstate him, remove the record from his file and treat him as if he had done nothing wrong. I also explained that, so it would not be a hardship, we could dock his pay over the next year. A look of incredulity swept over his face and he literally jumped to his feet. He said: "Oh wow! If you would do that for me, I promise you, I will make the best employee you have ever had!"

You know what, Pastor, he did! Incidentally, neither were we robbed blind after the incident. Now that I have had these years to reflect, it astounds me what a difference there was between man's effort to "punish the young man's crime" and God's laws which "restored right order."

In the first case, the company would have lost both the equipment and a good employee. The young man would have lost both his job and his reputation. Everyone would *lose* and no one would *gain*! On the other hand, with God's laws, the company got both a new upgraded piece of equipment and a really, really loyal and dedicated employee (worth more than gold). The employee kept both his job and his good reputation, learning a Bible lesson in the process. *Everyone gained...and no one lost!* Isn't that an astounding difference? Makes me want to go re-read Psalm 119, recounting how wonderful are the precepts, principles, statutes, laws and commandments of our Lord.

The *third* thing I noticed was of all the instructions (laws) God gives us to live by, how few of them there are in which He expects us to act or judge. In fact, I suspect there is considerable confusion on this. In Matthew 7:1 we are told; "Do not judge lest you be judged." Only to read in Deuteronomy 16:18 where we are told, "You shall appoint for yourself judges...and they shall judge the people with righteous judgment." Also in 1 Corinthians 6:3: "Do you not know that we shall judge angels? How much more, matters of this life?"

Pastor, I believe there are three rules for determining, Biblically, if a case is to be judged by us or not. Please let me know what you think.

Rule one is that we are restricted from judging anything involving the heart or mind. Only God knows a person's thoughts and beliefs and therefore only He is in a position to make those judgments. (You are correct; *the Inquisitions were not even close to being Biblical.*)

Rule two is we must only mete out those penalties specified by God's Word. If we are given no penalty to apply to the law-breaker it is obviously a law that God has reserved to Himself for judgment. We see this with God's law to "lend to the poor" Deuteronomy 15:7-8. In all of the many times this law is stated in the Bible, there is never any penalty specified. One who refuses to lend to the poor will certainly be judged by God and receive just punishment. But we are barred from doing that which God has reserved for Himself.

Rule three is that, in Biblical law, only the injured party can bring a case for judgment against someone. I believe lawyers call it "standing." That is why the Lord told the woman taken in adultery... "Neither do I condemn (judge) you; go your way" (John 8:11). Only her husband had standing to accuse her. Legally, the Pharisees that brought her did not, nor did Jesus, as an Israeli citizen. (After Jesus died on the cross, rose, and became king and ruler of the world He, of course, gained "standing" to judge everyone in the world!)

This last rule brings to mind the *fourth* interesting thing about Biblical law. There is a very limited need for police! Contrary to our current understanding about law enforcement, Biblically, it is everyone's responsibility to "enforce" the law. "Squealers" are definitely Biblical (Exodus 23:6). That does not mean we can dispense with policemen. It simply means that their job, Biblically, is not to "enforce" the law but to provide all the assistance and facilities needed for "citizens" to enforce the law. We would, of course, want to provide ourselves with the very best criminal investigators, forensic labs, secure places to hold law breakers prior to trial, etc., etc.

Pastor, I'm going to guess what your next question will be "What about crime prevention?" "Without a lot of policemen, won't we be overrun with criminals?" My answer is... Yes, of course! In our present position, we need all the policemen we can afford. The reason, of course, is because we have failed so miserably to obey the Lord's commission to "teach the nations to obey all my commandments." If we fail to "bring up the children of our nation in the way they should go" we will not find enough policemen to prevent crime! I have said this before but, again, our nation did a pretty good job of this for the first two hundred and fifty years. In fact, growing up in Oklahoma, even in the 1940s, it was certainly not "Camelot" but it was a far cry from what we have today. In all of the small towns where I grew up... no one locked their doors! If they did, you only had to go to the dime store, buy a "skeleton key" and you could unlock every door in town. In the sixteen years of my youth, I do not recall a single murder, and if you asked someone what a "mugger" was, you would get a blank stare. We did not even have the word in our vocabulary. Pastor, as we return to being obedient to our Lord's commission, including bringing up the nation's children in the way they should go, we will not only need less policemen, but we will find relief from a lot of the other problems we now face. As I pointed out, we clearly need to quickly get on to doing "Step One" today!

The *fifth* thing about God's law that we really need to pay some attention to is the fact that His law does not involve prisons! It implies the need for jails or some other way to hold someone who is to be tried, but under any circumstances God's law precludes penitentiaries. The first penitentiary in the world was established in 1829 when some religious folks got the state of Pennsylvania to build one. We did quite well without them for the two hundred years before that! As I mentioned in an earlier letter, one of my favorite Old Testament scholars is Rabbi Samuel R. Hirsh who published *The Pentateuch*, 1867-1878 (Translated 1967 by Isaac Levy). Volume II, Exodus, page 294. Hirsh has this to say about prisons:

> Punishments of imprisonment, with all the attendant despair and moral degeneration that dwell behind prison bars, with all the worry and distress that it entails for wife and child, are unknown in Torah jurisprudence (Biblical law). Where its power holds sway, prison for criminals does not exist.

We desperately need to repent here...Biblically; prisons are a scourge on our society.

The sixth observation is that God's law was never intended to *only* be used as some kind of "divine ruler" to measure someone's *personal* state of holiness. Of course, when we understand God's law and all that it requires, we clearly are brought face to face with His perfection, our "fallen" nature, and how desperately we need the love, salvation and grace He offers us. However, I am convinced that another of the intentions of God's law is to instruct us in how we are to live together and govern ourselves! I believe, within the limits of human frailty, God fully *expects us to obey* His laws. Pastor, God, Himself, tells us: "*For this commandment which I command you today is not too difficult for you, nor is it out of reach*" (Deuteronomy 30:11) (emphasis added). Admittedly, we might have problems truly loving our mother-in-law and that snot that lives down the street, but surely, we can resist killing our neighbor and robbing the local bank!

Pastor, to say, "We simply can never obey God's Law" is to create the disastrous situation we now find ourselves in where we have completely turned our back on God's instructions regarding how we should live together and govern ourselves. Why on earth would God give us these instructions if He knew we could not obey them? That would not be possible for a loving God!

There is one *seventh* and final observation about God's Word and His Law. I believe there is a sizeable group of Christians that believe in God and Jesus but think His Word is mostly allegorical. This makes it almost impossible to take God's Word and use it as basis or rule of how we should live together and govern ourselves. Those of us who are simple believers would love to have that group join our ranks…It will make rescue of our nation so much easier.

Please rethink some of these observations and then reconsider where you stand. Historically, for example, were you aware that archeologists take Bible history as a basically accurate account of the events it describes?

Any scientist will agree with you that the most basic elements that make up our universe are time (seconds), space (cubic centimeters), and mass (grams). Seconds, centimeters, and grams are referred to as the "cgs" or metric system of units. Pastor, you have on your desk the only "holy" book on the entire planet that not only claims to be the inspired word of God but that starts the creation account in a scientifically correct way! Check out the first sentence in the book. "In the beginning (*Seconds* began to tick away) God created the heaven (Speaking into existence *cubic centimeters*) and the earth (Speaking into existence *grams* of particles)" (Genesis 1:1). The next sentence: "And the earth was formless ("tohu"…confusion, unreality) and void ("bohu"…emptiness), and darkness (lack of light or energy) was over the surface of the deep" (Genesis 1:2). Then "…the Spirit of God was moving over the surface" (He created all of the laws of nature…physics, chemistry, etc.). Then God said, "Let there be light" (Genesis 1:2-3). Having created space, mass and time and all the *laws of nature*, God then created energy and set the universe in motion!

Pastor, if I found a book that claimed to be from the Creator of the universe and in three verses and less than fifty words could describe in a scientifically correct manner the origin of everything, I would tend to believe what followed. Wouldn't you?

Let me know, Pastor, if you disagree with any of this, but I think our understanding of these basic characteristics of God's law will help us apply it in the steps we must take to rescue our nation from decline and judgment.

APPENDIX 2

Civil Magistrates Must Be Just, Ruling in the Fear of God
—Charles Chauncy
Boston, 1747

CHARLES CHAUNCY (1705–1787). The most influential clergyman in the Boston of his time and—apart from Jonathan Edwards the elder—in all New England, Chauncy was graduated from Harvard and served as pastor of the First Church in Boston for sixty years. A thoroughly prosaic character who opposed enthusism and the revivalism espoused by Whitefield and Edwards, he prayed he would never become an orator; those who knew him well concluded that this was one prayer that undoubtedly had been answered. He was nonetheless a vigorous controversialist and prolific pamphleteer, devoting the decade of 1762 to 1771 to combating the British threat to send an Anglican bishop to America. It was an issue that rallied Congregationalists across New England in the period leading up to the Revolution.

The election sermon reprinted here was preached to Governor William Shirley, the council, and the house of representatives of Massachusetts on May 27, 1747. The bracketed passages in the printed text of this sermon were omitted during the oral delivery.

The God of Israel said, the Rock of Israel spake to me; he that ruleth over Men must be just, ruling in the Fear of God.
II Sam. xxiii. 3.

If we may judge by the manner in which these words are introduced, there are none in all the bible, applicable to civil rulers, in their publick capacity, of more solemn importance.

The last words of good men are commonly tho't worthy of particular notice; especially, if they are great as well as good, of an elevated station as well as character in life. This is a consideration that adds weight to my text. For it is enrolled among the last words of one of the best and greatest men that ever lived. Such was David, "the man after God's own heart," who was raised up from low life to the regal dignity, and stiled, on that account, "the anointed of the God of Jacob."

And was my text nothing more than his own private sentiments, formed with due care, upon long observation and experience, it might well deserve the particular attention of all in civil power; especially, as he was a man of extraordinary knowledge, penetration and wisdom, as well as piety; and, at the same time, singularly qualified to make a judgment in an affair of this nature, as he was called into publick service from a youth, and had for many years reigned king in Israel.

But it is not only David that here speaks. The words are rather God's than his. For they are thus prefaced, *The God of Israel said, the rock of Israel spake to me.* "That God who had selected the Jews to be his people, and was their God so as he was not the God of other nations; the rock on whom their political state was built, and on whom it depended for support and protection": This God spake unto David, either by Samuel, or Nathan, or some other inspired prophet, or himself immediately from heaven, saying, as in the words I have read to you, *He that ruleth over men must be just, ruling in the fear of God.* It is certainly some momentous truth, highly worthy of the most serious consideration of civil rulers, that is here delivered, or it would not have been ushered in with so much solemnity.

Some read the words, (agreable eno' to the original, as criticks observe) *there shall be a ruler over men that shall be just, ruling in the fear of God*; and refer them to Christ, as agreeing with other prophecies, which describe him as a "king that shall reign in righteousness," and be of "quick understanding in the fear of the Lord": But if they be allowed to look forward to him that has since "come forth out of Zion," they were also designed for the instruction and benefit of Solomon, David's son and appointed successor to the throne of Israel. And by analogy they are applicable to civil rulers, in their various stations, in all ages of the world.

In this view I shall now consider them, under the two following heads obviously contained in them.

I. There is a certain order among mankind, according to which some are entrusted with power to rule over others.

II. Those who rule over others must be just, ruling in the fear of God. The whole will then be applied to the occasions of the day.

I. I am to say, in the first place, there is a certain order among men, according to which some are entrusted with power to rule over others. This is evidently supposed in the text; and 'tis supposed, not as a bare fact, but a fact that has taken place conformably to the will of God, and the reason of things.

This, to be sure, is the truth of the case, in it self considered. Order and rule in society, or, what means the same thing, civil government, is not a contrivance of arbitrary and tyrannical men, but a regular state of things, naturally resulting from the make of man, and his circumstances in the world. Had man abode in innocency, his nature as a sociable creature, and his condition as a dependent one, would probably have led to some sort of civil superiority: As, among the inhabitants of the upper world, there seems to be a difference of order, as well as species; which the scripture intimates, by speaking of them in the various stile of *thrones, dominions, principalities, powers, archangels and angels.* But however it would have been, had man continued in obedience to his maker, government is rendered a matter of necessity by the introduction of sin into the world. Was there no civil rule among men, but every one might do that which was right in his own eyes, without restraint from humane laws, there would not be safety any where on the earth. No man would be secure in the enjoyment, either of his liberty, or property, or life: But every man's hand would be against his fellow; and mankind must live in perpetual danger, from that oppression, rapine and violence, which would make this world rather a hell, than a fit place to dwell happily in.

The present circumstances of the human race are therefore such, by means of sin, that 'tis necessary they should, for their mutual defence and safety, combine together in distinct societies, lodging as much power in the hands of a few, as may be sufficient to restrain the irregularities of the rest, and keep them within the bounds of a just decorum. Such a superiority in some, and inferiority in others, is perfectly adjusted to the present state of mankind. Their circumstances require it. They could not live, either comfortably or safely without it.

And from hence, strictly and properly speaking, does that civil order there is among men take rise. Nor will it from hence follow, that government is a mere humane constitution. For as it originates in the reason of things, 'tis, at the same time, essentially founded on the will of God. For the voice of reason is the voice of God: And he as truly speaks to men by the reason of things, their mutual relations to and dependencies on each other, as if he uttered his voice from the excellent glory. And in this way, primarily, he declares his will respecting a civil subordination among men. The sutableness of order and superiority, both to the nature of man, and his circumstances in the world, together with its necessary connection, in the nature of things, with his safety and happiness, is such an indication of the divine pleasure, that there should be government, as cannot be gainsay'd nor resisted.

Only it must be remembered here, a distinction ought always to be made between government in its general notion, and particular form and manner of administration. As to the latter, it cannot be affirmed, that this or that particular form of government is made necessary by the will of God and reason of things. The mode of civil rule may in consistency with the public good, admit of variety: And it has, in fact, been various in different nations: Nor has it always continued the same, in the same nation. And one model of government may be best for this community, and another for that; nay, that model which may be best for the same community at one time, may not be so at another. So that it seems left to the wisdom of particular communities to determine what form of government shall take place among them; and, so long as the general ends of society are provided for and secured, the determination may be various, according to the various circumstances, policies, tempers and interests of different communities.

And the same may be said of the manner of vesting particular persons with civil power, whether supreme or subordinate. This is not so fix'd by the divine will, as that all nations are obliged to one and the same way of devolving the administration of rule. The supreme authority in Israel, 'tis true, from which, of course, all subordinate power in that state was derived, was settled by God himself on David, and entail'd on his family to descend in a lineal succession. But it does not appear, that this was ever intended to be a rule obligatory on all nations of the earth: Nor have they kept to it; but have varied in their manner of designing persons for, and introducing them into, the several places of civil trust. And this seems to be a matter alterable in its nature, and proper to be variously determined according to the different circumstances of particular nations.

But 'tis quite otherwise in respect of government itself, in its general notion. This is not a matter of meer humane prudence, but of moral necessity. It does not lie with men to determine at pleasure, whether it shall or shall not take place; but, considering their present weak, exposed and dependent condition, 'tis unalterably right and just there should be rule and superiority in some, and subjection and inferiority in others: And this therefore is invariably the will of God; his will manifested by the moral fitness and reason of things.

And the will of God, as discovered in the revelations of scripture, touching government among men, perfectly coincides with his will primarily made known, upon the same head, by the constitution of things: Or rather, 'tis more clearly and fully opened. For kings, and princes, and nobles, and *all the judges of the earth*, are here represented* as *reigning and ruling by God*: Yea, they are stiled, *the ministers of God†*; and *the powers that be* are declared to be *ordained of God‡*: And, upon this consideration, *subjection to them* is demanded, *for conscience sake** and *whosoever resisteth*, is looked upon as *resisting the ordinance of God.†* From all which it is apparent, there is no more room to dispute the divinity of civil rule upon the foot of revelation, than of reason.

And thus we have seen, not only that some among men have rule over others, but that it is reasonable in itself, and agreeable to the will of God, it should be so.

And 'tis easy to collect from the whole, the true design of that power some are entrusted with over others. It is not merely that they might be distinguished from, and set above vulgar people; much less that they might live in greater pomp, and be revered as gods on earth; much less still that they might be in circumstances to oppress their fellow-creatures, and trample them under their feet: But it is for the general good of mankind; to keep confusion and disorder out of the world; to guard men's lives; to secure their rights; to defend their properties and liberties; to make their way to justice easy, and yet effectual, for their protection when innocent, and their relief when injuriously treated; and, in a word, to maintain peace and good order, and, in general, to promote the public welfare, in all instances, so far as they are able. But this leads me to the next head of discourse, which is what I have principally in view; *viz.*

II. Those who rule over others must be *just, ruling in the fear of God.* Here I shall distinctly say,

i. They must be just. They ought to be so in their private capacity; maintaining a care to exhibit in their conduct towards all they are concerned with, a fair transcript of that fundamental law of the religion of Jesus, as well as eternal rule of natural justice, "all things whatsoever ye would that men should do to you, do ye even so to them." But private justice, tho' necessary in all, yet is not the virtue here especially intended. The injunction respects those who rule over men; and 'tis as magistrates, not private members of society, that they are required to be just.

And this duty includes in it more than a negation of unrighteousness. 'Tis not enough that rulers are not unjust; that they don't betray the trusts reposed in them; that they don't defraud the public; that they don't oppress the subject, whether in a barefac'd manner, or in a more covert way; by downright violence, or under the cloak of law: 'Tis not enough, I say, that rulers don't, in these and such like ways, pervert judgment and justice; but, besides all this, they must be positively righteous. Being possess'd of an inward, steady, uniform principle of justice, setting them, in a good measure, above the influence of private interest, or party views, they must do that which is equal and right, in their various stations, from the king in supreme, to the lowest in authority under him.

It would carry me too far beyond the hour assigned me, should I make a distribution of rulers into their several ranks, and mention the more special acts of justice respectively required of them. I shall therefore content my self with speaking of them chiefly in the collective sense; pointing out, under a few general heads, some of the more important articles wherein they should approve themselves just. And they are such as these.

1. They must be just in the *use of their power*; confining it within the limits prescribed in the constitution they are under. Whatever power any are vested with, 'tis delegated to them according to some civil constitution. And this, so long as it remains the constitution, they are bound in justice to conform themselves to: To be sure, they ought not to act in violation of any of its main and essential rights. Especially, is this an important point of justice, where the constitution is branched into several parts, and the power originally lodged in it, is divided, in certain measures, to each part, in order to preserve a ballance in the whole. Rulers, in this case, in either branch of the government, are bounded by the constitution, and obliged to keep within the proper limits assigned them; never clashing in

the exercise of their power, never encroaching upon the rights of each other, in any shape, or under any pretence whatever. They have severally and equally a right to that power which is granted to them in the constitution, and to wrest it out of each other's hands, or to obstruct one another in the regular legal exercise of it, is evidently unjust. As in the British constitution, which devolves the power of the state, in certain proportions, on *King, Lords* and *Commons,* they have neither of them a right to invade the province of the other, but are required, by the rule of righteousness, to keep severally within their own boundaries, acting in union among themselves, and consistency with the constitution. If the prerogatives of the King are sacred, so also are the rights of Lords and Commons: And if it would be unjust in Lords or Commons, to touch, in any instance, the prerogative of the crown; so would it be in the crown, to invade the rights, which are legally settled in Lords and Commons: In either of these cases, the law of righteousness is violated: Nor does the manner in which it is done make any essential difference; for, if one part of the government is really kept from exerting it self, according to the true meaning of the constitution, whether it be done openly, or by secret craft; by compulsion or corruption, the designed ballance is no longer preserved; and which way soever the scale turns, whether on the side of sovereignty, or popularity, 'tis forced down by a false weight, which, by degrees, will overturn the government, at least, according to this particular model.

And the case is just the same in all dependent governments, as in those whose power originates in themselves: Especially, where the derived constitution, like that of Great-Britain, is divided into several ruling parts, and distributes the granted powers and priviledges severally among these ruling parts, to each their limited portion. The constitution is here evidently the grand rule to all cloathed with power, or claiming priviledge, in either branch of the government. And 'tis indeed a fundamental point of justice, that they keep respectively within the bounds marked out to them in the constitution. Rulers in one branch of the state should not assume the power delegated to those in another: Nay, so far should they be from this, that they should not, in any degree, lessen their just weight in the government; much less may they contrive, by an undue application to their hopes or fears, or by working on their ambition, or covetousness, or any other corrupt principle; much less, I say, may they contrive to influence them to give up their power, or, what is as bad, to use it unfaithfully, beside the intention for which it was committed to them. These are certainly methods of injustice; and, if put in practice, will, by a natural causality, weaken, and, by degrees, destroy those checks which rulers are mutually designed to have one upon another; the effect whereof must be tyranny, or anarchy, either of which will be of fatal consequence.

2. Another general instance wherein rulers should be just, relates to the *laws by which they govern.* [They have an undoubted right to make and execute laws, for the publick good. This is essentially included in the very idea of government: Insomuch, that government, without a right to enact and enforce proper laws, is nothing more than an empty name.

And this right, in whomsoever it is vested, must be exercised under the direction of justice. For as there cannot be government without a right of legislation, so neither can there be this right but in conjunction with righteousness. 'Tis the just exercise of power that distinguishes right from might; authority that is to be revered and obeyed, from violence and tyranny, which are to be dreaded and deprecated.

Those therefore to whom it belongs to make, or execute the laws of a government ought, in these exercises of their power, to square their conduct by that strict justice, which will be to them a sure rule of right action.]

To be sure, if they would be just, they must make no laws but what bear this character. They should not, when upon the business of framing and passing acts, suffer themselves to be swayed by any wrong biass, either from self-will, or self-interest; the smiles or frowns of men greater than themselves; or the humour of the populace: But should bring the proposed laws to a fair and impartial examination, not only in their reference to the temper, genius and circumstances of the community, but to that justice also which is founded in the nature of things, and the will of the supreme legislator: And if they should appear to be inconsistent with this eternal rule of equity, they ought not to countenance them, but should do what they can to prevent their establishment. And the rather, because should they enact that into a statute, which is unrighteous; especially, if it be plainly and grosly so, they would be chargeable with "framing mischief by a law": The guilt whereof would be the more aggravated, as power, in this case, would be on the side of oppression; and, what is as bad, as unrighteousness, by this means, would take a dreadful spread thro' the community. For as the laws are the rule for the executive powers in the government, if these are unjust, all that is done consequent upon a regard to them, must be unjust too. That would be the state of things which Solomon describes, when he says, "I saw under the sun the place of judgment, that wickedness was there; and the place of righteousness, that iniquity was there:" Than which, there cannot be given a more terrible representation of the unhappy effect of a disregard to justice in the making of laws.

But rulers, in order to their answering the character of just, must not satisfy themselves with making none but righteous laws; but must provide also, so far as may be, a sufficiency of such to restrain the sons of wickedness, men of avaricious minds, and no consciences, from that rapine and violence, those frauds and oppressions, in their various kinds and degrees, which their lusts would prompt them to perpetrate, to the damage of society, and in violation of all that is right and just.

Besides which, they should be particular in their care to guard the important and extensive article of commerce; calculating laws so as that they may have a tendency to oblige every member of the community, to use the methods of fairness and honesty in their dealings with one another: In order whereto, one of the main things necessary is, to fix the precise weight and measure, according to which these and those commodities shall be bought and sold; hereby rendring the practice of honesty easy and familiar, while, at the same time, it is made a matter of difficulty, as well as hazard, for this member of the community to defraud that, by palming on him a less quantity than he bargain'd, for, and expected to receive.

[A noble example of this expedient to promote justice, the scripture presents us with, in the history it gives of the laws by which the Jews of old were governed. It was not thought sufficient to prohibit their "doing unrighteousness in mete-yard, or weight, or measure;" and to command their having "just ballances and just weights, a just ephah and a just hin:" But the standard was fixt by law, according to which all weights and measures must be regulated; and it was kept in the sanctuary of God. And so exact was the government in its care to prevent all fraud, that it allowed no "weights, ballances or measures to be made of any metal, as of iron, lead, tin, (which were obnoxious to rust, or might be bent or easily impaired) but of marble, stone or glass, which were less liable to be abused."* And officers also "were appointed in every city to go about into shops, and see that the ballances and measures were just, and determine the stated measure of them: And with whomsoever they found any weight or measure too light or short, or ballance that went awry, they were to be punished by the judges."* .

This pattern of justice has been copied after by all governments acquainted with it; and the more particular their laws have been for the regulation of weights and measures, the better calculated have they been to promote honesty in private dealing.]

And if justice in rulers should shew itself by reducing the things that are bought and sold to weight and measure, much more ought it to be seen in ascertaining the medium of trade, as nearly as may be, to some determinate value. For this, whether it be money, or something substituted to pass in lieu of it, is that for which all things are exchanged in commerce. And if this, which is of such universal use in the affair of traffick, be a thing variable and uncertain, of one value this week, and another the next, 'tis difficult to conceive, how justice should take place between man and man, in their dealings with one another. If the measure we call a foot might gradually, in the space of a few months or years, lengthen into a yard, or shorten into an inch; every one sees, it would, if used as a measure in trade, tend to spread unrighteousness in a community, rather than justice. So, if the weight we call a pound might gradually, in the like space, increase or diminish one half; 'tis past dispute, it would be an occasion of general iniquity, rather than a means to promote honesty. And the case is really the same (however insensible we may be of it) with respect to the passing medium in a government. If what we call a shilling, may, in a gradual way, in the course of a few months or years, rise in value so as to be equal to two or three, or sink in proportion; 'tis impossible, in the nature of things, but a wide door should be opened for oppression and injustice. An upright man, in this case, would find it extreamly difficult to do himself justice, or others he might be concerned with in business. And for those of dishonest minds, and no principles of honour or religion, if men of craft and foresight, they would have it very much in their power to enrich themselves by being unjust to their neighbour.

I am sensible, the case may be so circumstanced in a government, especially if it be a dependent one, as that it may be extreamly difficult, if not impossible, while they have no money, to keep that which passes, in the room of it, from varying in it's real worth. But it is not very difficult; to be sure, it is not impossible, to pitch upon some certain standard, to which the current medium may be so related, as that it's true value, at different times, may be nearly ascertained: And if this was established as the rule in all public payments, as well as private contracts and bargains, it would be no other than what is right. It would certainly tend, not only to do every one justice, but to put it very much out of the power of men of no probity "to go beyond and defraud their brother:" Whereas, while the medium is connected with no established certain standard, but continually varies in it's real worth, it must be, in the natural course of things, an occasion of great injustice. [Some, on the one hand, under the fair pretence of a reasonable care to secure themselves, will injure those who lie at their mercy, by extorting from them more that is meet. And others, on the other hand, will take the advantage, to pay a just debt with one half the true value it was originally contracted for: Nor will the practice of unrighteousness be confined to these and such like instances, but unavoidably mingle itself with men's transactions in the whole business of trade, so as to put them upon making a prey of one another; as is too much the case among ourselves at this day.]

There is yet another thing, belonging to this head, wherein rulers should approve themselves just; and that is, the *execution of the laws.* [The power of executing as well as making laws (as has been hinted) is inseparable from government. And the demands of justice are to be comply'd with, in the one as well as the other. If 'tis just that rulers should make righteous laws, 'tis equally so, when they are made, that they should take effectual care to enforce a proper regard to them. Of what service would laws be, though ever so wisely calculated to promote the public good, if offenders against them should be connived at, or suffered, by one means or another, to go unpunished? And what might reasonably be expected in consequence of such a breach of trust, but that the best laws, together with the authority that enacted them, should be held in contempt? There is no such thing as supporting the honour of government, or securing the good ends proposed by the laws it establishes, but by unsheathing the sword, in a faithful and impartial execution of justice.

But here, that we may speak clearly, it may be proper to distinguish between those rulers to whom it belongs to *appoint and authorise persons to execute the laws*, and those who are *vested with authority for this purpose*. For the duty which justice requires is different, according to the nature of that power, wherewith these different rulers are betrusted.

It is certainly a point of justice, in those whose business it is to *empower others to execute the laws*, to select out of the community such as are well qualified for so important a trust. Every man is not fit to have the sword of justice put into his hands. And the main thing to be lookt at, in the choice of persons for this service, is their suitableness to it. Meerly their being men of birth and fortune, is not a sufficient recommendation: Nor, if they are eagerly forward in seeking for a post of honour or profit, is it a certain indication, that they are fit to be put into it: Neither, if they should offer money to purchase it, ought they, on this account, to be preferred to men of greater merit: Much less ought it to be looked upon as a turning argument in their favour, that they are fit instruments to serve the secret designs of those in superior station. These are considerations beside the true merit of the case: And those only ought to bear sway, which enter into the real characters of men, determining their qualifications for the trust that is to be reposed in them.

The advice which Jethro gave Moses is here proper, "Thou shalt provide out of all the people able men, such as fear God, men of truth, hating covetousness."* These are the men, men of understanding, courage and resolution; men of integrity, fidelity and honesty; men of piety and substantial religion; men of a noble generosity, setting them above the temptations, which those of narrow minds and selfish views, are easily drawn away by and enticed: These, I say, are the proper men to fill the various posts in the state. And it would be injustice to the public, for the persons concerned in the disposal of them, to neglect these, and bestow them on those of a contrary character. Men of low natural capacities, and small acquired accomplishments, are unmeet to be exalted to places of important trust. And should this be done, it would be acting over the evil, which Solomon complained of in his day, *Folly is set in great dignity*. And those are as unfit to be constituted guardians of the laws, who are indolent, inactive and irresolute; much more, if, together herewith, they are known to be of a vicious turn of mind. It can't be supposed, men of this character should be faithful in the execution of justice; and to devolve this care on them, would be to wrong the community, and expose authority.

Not that those, with whom it lies to appoint officers, are always to blame, when unqualified persons are put into places of trust; for they are liable, after all prudent caution, to be mistaken in their own judgment, and to be imposed on by misinformation from others. But then, they should take due care, when such persons are found, upon trial, to be unequal to the trust committed to them, to remedy the inconvenience: Nor otherwise will they continue innocent, however faultless they might be at first. 'Tis evidently the demand of justice, that such unmeet persons should be displaced, and others better qualified put in their room.

And 'tis equally just, that those who are capable of behaving well, but behave ill in their respective stations, should be testified against. And should they be so unadvised, as grosly to abuse their power; applying it to the purposes of tyranny and oppression, rather than to serve the good ends of government, it ought to be taken out of their hands, that they might no longer be under advantages to injure their brethren of the same community.

These are the demands of justice from those, who are to *put others into the executive trust.*

And justice is likewise required of *this sort of rulers*, according to the respective trust that is committed to them.

If 'tis their business to sit in the place of judgment, they must judge uprightly in all cases, whether civil or criminal, and not under a wrong influence from favour to the rich, or pity to the poor, or fear of the great, or affection or disaffection to any man's person whatsoever; having that precept in the divine law ever in their eye, "Ye shall do no unrighteousness in judgment: Thou shalt not respect the person of the poor, nor honour the person of the mighty: But in righteousness shalt thou judge thy brother."* And that also, "Thou shalt not wrest judgment, thou shalt not respect persons, neither take a gift; for a gift doth blind the eyes of the wise, and pervert the words of the righteous."†

If 'tis their business to enquire who have been offenders against the laws, and to exhibit complaints against them as such; they must be couragious and impartial, complying with their duty equally in respect of all, be their character what it will.

If 'tis their business to act as executioners of justice, they must faithfully inflict the adjudged sentence: In doing of which, tho' there may be room for the exercise of compassion, especially in the case of some sort of debtors; yet the righteousness of the law may not be eluded by needless, much less fraudulent delays, to the injury of the creditor.

In fine, whatever their trust is, whether of less or greater importance, they must exercise it with care, fidelity, resolution, steadiness, diligence, and an entire freedom from a corrupt respect to men's persons, as those who are concerned for the honour of government, and that it's laws may take effect for the general good of the community.]

To go on,

3. Another instance wherein rulers should be just, respects the debts that may be due from the public. A government may be in debt, as well as private men. Their circumstances may be such, as to render it adviseable for them to borrow money, either of other governments, or within themselves: Or, they may have occasion to make purchases, or to enter into contracts, upon special emergencies, which may bring them in debt. In which cases, the rule of justice is the same to magistrates, as to men in a private life. They must pay that which they owe, according to the true meaning of their engagements, without fraud or delay.

[They may also be in debt for services done by labourers, in this and the other secular employment. And here the rule of justice is that, "withhold not good from them to whom it is due, when it is in the power of thine hand to do it. Say not unto thy neighbour, go, and come again, and to-morrow I will give, when thou hast it by thee."* Or if the labourers are such as have nothing beforehand, but their day-labour is what they depend on for the support of themselves and families, the rule is yet more particular, "Thou shalt not oppress an hired servant that is poor and needy; at his day thou shalt give him his hire, neither shall the sun go down upon it; for he is poor, and setteth his heart on it: Lest he cry against thee unto the Lord, and it be sin unto thee."* And again, "Thou shalt not defraud thy neighbour, nor rob him: The wages of him that is hired, shall not abide with thee all night until the morning."†]

In fine, they may be in debt to their own officers, whether in higher or lower station, the proper business of whose office calls off their attention from other affairs. And as their time, and care, and tho't, are employed in the service of the public, a public maintenance is their just due. "Who goeth a warfare any time at his own charge? Who planteth a vineyard, and eateth not of the fruit thereof? Or, who feedeth a flock, and eateth not of the milk of the flock? Say I these things as a man? Or saith not the law the same also?"‡ For it is written, "For this cause pay you tribute; for they are God's ministers, attending continually upon this very thing.§ Render unto Cæsar the things that are Cæsar's."¶

Nor is it sufficient that they be supported according to the condition of men in low life. This may be tho't enough, if not too much, by those who imagine, that the more strait-handed they are upon the head of allowances, the more serviceable they shall be to the public. But there is such a thing in the state, as a "withholding more than is meet." And it really tends to the damage of a government. Too scant an allowance may unhappily prove a temptation to officers, to be hard upon those dependent on them; and what they may injuriously squeeze out of them, by one artful contrivance or another, may turn out more to the hurt of the community, than if twice that sum had been paid out of the public treasury, and this evil, by means hereof, had been prevented. Besides, 'tis no ways fitting, that men cloathed with honour and power should be brought down to a level with vulgar people, in the support that is granted them. Their outward circumstances should be elevated in proportion to their civil character, that they may be better able to support the visible dignity of their station, and command that respect which is due to men of their figure. He that is *governour should eat the bread of a governour*; and subordinate officers should be maintained, according to the rank they bear in the state: Nor ought their honourable maintenance to be tho't a matter of *meer* bounty; 'tis rather a debt, which can't be withheld without injustice.

[To be sure, where their stipends have been established, or, at least, they have had reasonable encouragement to expect such a certain acknowledgment for their service, righteousness requires that it be paid them: Nor may it be tho't that the same nominal sum, falling vastly below the real worth of the debt, will be sufficient to discharge it. It certainly is not sufficient, in the eye of justice, either natural or revealed; which respects no man's person, but will do that which is right to the lowest, as well as to the highest officer in the state.

And the case, in point of equity, is really the same, where a government has come into no special agreement; but the ascertaining the quantum proper for the support of it's officers, is left to it's own wisdom and probity. For an allowance is due to them by the law of righteousness: And it ought to be granted, both in proper season, and full proportion, that there may be no reason for complaint, either of penurious or unjust dealing.

I may add here, the distribution of rewards, in case of extraordinary service done for a government, falls properly under this head of justice. For tho' there may be bounty in it, there is also a mixture of righteousness. But however this be, it has been the practice of all nations to shew singular marks of respect to those who have distinguished themselves by their eminent labours for the public. And it is to be hoped, this government will never be backward, according to their ability, suitably to reward those who have signalized themselves, in doing service for their king and country.]

4. Another general instance wherein rulers should be just, concerns the liberties and priviledges of the subject. In all governments there is a reserve of certain rights in favour of the people: In some, they are few in kind, and small in degree: In others, they are both great and numerous; rendring the people signally happy whose lot it is to be favoured with the undisturbed enjoyment of them. And it would be no wonder, if they should keep a jealous eye over them, and think no cost too much to be expended, for the defence and security of them: Especially, if they were the purchase of wise and pious ancestors, who submitted to difficulties, endured hardships, spent their estates, and ventured their lives, that they might transmit them as an inheritance to their posterity.

And shall such valuable, dear-bought rights be neglected, or invaded by the rulers of a people? 'Tis a principal part of that justice which is eternally expected of them, as they would not grosly pervert one of the main ends of their office, to preserve and perpetuate to every member of the community, so far as may be, the full enjoyment of their liberties and priviledges, whether of a civil or religious nature.

Here I may say distinctly,

As rulers would be just, they must take all proper care to preserve entire the civil rights of a people. And the ways in which they should express this care are such as these.

They should do it by appearing in defence of their liberties, if called in question, and making use of all wise and sutable methods to prevent the loss of them: Nor can they be too active, diligent or laborious in their endeavours upon this head: Provided always, the priviledges in danger are worth contending for, and such as the people have a just right and legal claim to. Otherwise, there may be hazard of losing real liberties, in the strife for those that are imaginary; or valuable ones, for such as are of trifling consideration.

They should also express this care, by seasonably and faithfully placing a proper guard against the designs of those, who would rule in a dispotic manner, to the subversion of the rights naturally or legally vested in the people. And here 'tis a great mistake to suppose, there can be danger only from those in the highest station. There may, 'tis true, be danger from this quarter: And it has sometimes proved so in fact: An unhappy instance whereof was seen in the arbitrary reign of King James the second, in person at home, and by his representative here; as a check to which, those entrusted with the guardianship of the nation's rights were spirited to take such measures, as issued in that revolution, and *establishment of the succession*, on which his present majesty's claim to the British throne is dependent. May the succession be continued in his royal house forever! And may the same spirit, which settled it there, prevail in the rulers of the English nation, so long as the sun and moon shall endure!

But, as I said, a people's liberties may be in danger from others, besides those in the highest rank of government. The men who strike in with the popular cry of liberty and priviledge, working themselves, by an artful application to the fears and jealousies of the people, into their good opinion of them as lovers of their country, if not the only stanch friends to it's interests, may, all the while, be only aiming at power to carry every thing according to their own sovereign pleasure: And they are, in this case, most dangerous enemies to the community; and may, by degrees, if not narrowly watched, arrive to such an height, as to be able to serve their own ends, by touching even the people in their most valuable rights. And these commonly are the men, thro' whose influence, either as primary managers, or tools to others, they suffer most in their real liberties.

In fine, they should express this care in a constant readiness to bear due testimony against even the smaller encroachments upon the liberty of the subject, whether by private men's invading one another's rights, or by the tyranny of inferiour officers, who may treat those under their power, as tho' they had no natural rights, not to say a just claim to the invaluable priviledges of*Englishmen*.

The ancient Romans have set an illustrious example in this kind. Such was the provision they made to secure the people's priviledges, that it was dangerous for any man, tho' in office, to act towards the meanest freeman of Rome in violation of the meanest of them. Hence the magistrates who ordered Paul and Silas to be *beaten uncondemned, feared when they heard they were Romans*. And Lysias, the chief captain, was filled with the like fear for commanding, that Paul should be examined with scourging; when he understood, that he was born a freeman of Rome. And it would have a good tendency to secure to the people the enjoyment of their liberties, if these smaller instances of illegal power were carefully and severely chastised.

But justice in rulers should be seen likewise in their care of the religious rights and liberties of a people. Not that they are to exert their authority in *settling articles of faith,* or *imposing modes of worship,* so as that all must frame their belief, and order their practice, according to their decisions, or lie exposed to penalties of one kind or another. This would be to put men under restraint, as to the exercise of their religious rights: Nor are penal laws at all adjusted in their nature, to enlighten men's minds, or convince their judgment. This can be done only by good reason: And this therefore is the only proper way of applying to reasonable creatures.

Justice in rulers should therefore put them upon leaving every member of the community, without respect of persons, freely to choose his own religion, and profess and practice it according to that external form, which he apprehends will be most acceptable to his maker: Provided, his religion is such as may consist with the public safety: Otherwise, it would be neither wisdom nor justice in the government to tolerate it.

Nor is this all; but they should guard every man from all insult and abuse on account of his religious sentiments, and from all molestation and disturbance, while he endeavours the propagation of them, so far as he keeps within the bounds of decency, and approves himself a peaceable member of society.

Besides which, it would be no more than reasonable, if, as christian magistrates, they distinguished those in their regards, who professed the religion of Jesus, and in that way, which, to them, was most agreable to scripture rule. They should be guardians to such christian societies, by defending their constitution; by countenancing their manner of worship; by maintaining the liberties granted to them in the gospel-charter, in all their regular exercises, whether in church assemblies for the performance of the services of piety, or the choice of officers, or the administration of discipline; or in councils, greater or less, for the help and preservation of each other: And, in fine, by owning those who minister to them in sacred things, and providing for their support, according to that rule in scripture, as well as common equity, "They that preach the gospel should live of the gospel": Or if they are generally and wrongfully kept out of a great part of that support, which has been engaged, and is justly due to them, by taking their case into consideration, and doing what may be effectual for their relief.

This last instance of the care of rulers, I the rather mention, because it falls in so exactly with the circumstances of the pastors of the churches in this province. There is not, I believe, an order of men, in the land, more universally, or to a greater degree, injured and oppressed in regard of their just dues. While others have it, in some measure, in their power to right themselves, by rising in their demands, in proportion to the sinking of the current medium, they are confined to a nominal quantum, which every day varies in its real worth, and has been gradually doing so, 'till it is come to that pass, that many of them don't receive more than one half, or two thirds of the original value they contracted for. And to this it is owing, that they are diverted from their studies, discouraged in their work, and too frequently treated with contempt. And what is an aggravation of their difficulty, their only desiring that justice may be done them, often makes an uneasiness among their people: And if they urge it; to be sure, if they demand it, 'tis great odds but there ensues thereupon contention and strife, and, at last, such a general alienation of affection, as puts an entire end to their usefulness.

Suffer me, my fathers in the government, as I have this opportunity of speaking in your presence, to beseech the exercise of your authority, on the behalf, (may I not say) of so valuable and useful a part of the community: And the rather, because some special provision for their relief seems to be a matter of justice, and not meer favour; as it is by means of the public bills, tho' contrary to the design of the government, that they are injured. And might not this be made, without any great expence either of time or pains, and so as to be effectual too, to put it out of the power of people to turn off their ministers with any thing short of the true value of what they agreed with them for, when they settled among them? This is all they desire: And as it is nothing more than common equity, would it not be hard, if they should be still left to groan under their oppressions, and to have no helper?

The great and general court, it must be acknowledged, more than twenty years since, "upon serious consideration of the great distresses, that many of the ministers within this province laboured under, with respect to their support, resolved, that it was the indispensible duty of the several towns and parishes, to make additions to the maintenance of their respective ministers; and therein to have regard to the *growing difference in the value of the bills of credit*, from what they had sometimes been." And thereupon "earnestly recommended the speedy and chearful practice of this duty to the several congregations within this province." And that the recommendation might be universally known and comply'd with, "Ordered, that their resolve should be publickly read on the next Lord's day after the receipt thereof, and at the anniversary meeting of the several towns in the month of March next" following.*

And it is with thankfulness that we take notice of this instance of the care of our civil fathers; tho' we are sorry, we must, at the same time, say, it was generally treated with neglect by our congregations, as being void of power.

It will not be pretended, but that the distresses of the ministers, and from the same cause too, the sinking of the medium, are vastly greater now, than they were twenty years ago: And if it was then reasonable, in the great and general court, to recommend it to the several congregations, throughout the province, as their indispensable duty, to make additions to the maintenance of their ministers, and therein to have regard to the lower value of the bills of credit, from what they formerly were; it is certainly now high time to oblige them to this: Especially, as the grievances of the ministers have often, since that day, upon these occasions, been opened to their civil fathers, whose interposition has been humbly and earnestly intreated. But I would not be too pressing: Neither have I said thus much on my own account, who am not, thro' the goodness of God, in suffering circumstances myself, but in very pity to many of my poor brethren who are; because there may be danger lest guilt should lie on the government, if they take no notice of the sighing of so considerable a body of men; and because, I verily believe, the offerings of the Lord are too often despised, by reason of that poverty those are unrighteously reduced to, by whom they are presented.

But to return,

5. Another instance of justice in rulers relates to the defence of the state, and it's preservation in peace and safety. [The happiness of a people lies very much in their living peaceably among themselves, and at quiet with their neighbours. For which reason, rulers are bound in justice to use all prudent endeavours, that they may "sit every man under his own vine, and under his fig-tree, and have none to make them afraid." In order whereunto,

They should take care to prevent intestine jarrs and commotions in the government, by giving no occasion for murmurings and complaints; or if any should unhappily arise, by speedily removing the causes of them: By testifying a just displeasure against the fomentors of animosities, fewds and factions: By watching the motions of uneasy, turbulent and mobbish spirits, and checking the first out-breakings of them; or if, thro' the lusts of men, insurrection or rebellion should happen, by seasonably putting a stop thereto, lest afterwards the whole force of the government should be scarce sufficient for this purpose.

It may be, the late unnatural rebellion, which began in Scotland, was too much despised at first. It would not otherwise, 'tis probable, have risen to such a formidable height: Tho' the alwise holy God, by permitting this, and then remarkably succeeding the king's arms, under the command of his royal highness the duke of Cumberland, to put an end to this traiterous attempt against the throne of Great-Britain, took occasion, not only to lay the nation and it's dependencies, under more sensible bonds to give glory to him, in language like that of the 18th Psalm, "Great deliverance hath he given to his king, and shewed mercy to his anointed: Therefore will we give thanks unto thee, O Lord, and sing praises to thy name": But to do that also, which was proper to engage their more fervent prayers of faith, that he would go on to *clothe the king's enemies with shame, and cause the crown to flourish on his head,* and the head of his posterity forever.

Rulers also should endeavour to keep the state from being embroiled in foreign war, by contriving, in all prudent ways, to engage and continue the friendship of neighbouring nations; by bearing with lesser injuries from them, and not hastily resenting greater ones, so far as may be consistent with the public safety; by sacredly adhering to the treaties and contracts, they may have entred into with them; by expressing a due caution not to invade their rights or properties, or in any instance whatever to give them just cause of provocation: Or if this shou'd at any time happen, by appearing ready to make them all reasonable satisfaction.

Or if, after all, war should arise, by means of the pride, or avarice, or self-will and tyranny of unreasonable men, their concern should now be to look to the preservation of the state at home, by providing a sufficiency of warlike stores, in their various kinds; by guarding the exposed frontiers and coasts; and, in a word, by putting and keeping things in such a posture of defence, that neither their people, nor their interests, may easily fall a prey in their enemy's hands.

Besides which, it would be both wisdom and justice to carry the war into their enemies territories; doing every thing in their power to humble their pride, curb their malice, and weaken their strength; especially, where there may be most danger of being annoyed by them.]

6thly, and finally, rulers should be just to promote the general welfare and prosperity of a people, by discouraging, on the one hand, idleness, prodigality, prophaneness, uncleanness, drunkenness, and the like immoralities, which tend, in the natural course of things, to their impoverishment and ruin: And by encouraging, on the other hand, industry, frugality, temperance, chastity, and the like moral virtues, the general practice whereof are naturally connected with the flourishing of a people in every thing that tends to make them great and happy. As also, by rendring the support of government as easy as is consistent with it's honour and safety; by calculating laws to set forward those manufactures which may be of public benefit; by freeing trade, as much as possible, from all unnecessary burdens; and, above all, by a wise and sutable provision for the instruction of children and youth: In order whereunto effectual care should be taken for the encouragement and support, not only of private schools, but of the public means of education. Colleges ought to be the special care of the government, as it is from hence, principally, that it has it's dependence for initiating the youth in those arts and sciences, which may furnish them, as they grow up in the world, to be blessings both in church and state. It would certainly be unrighteous, not to protect these societies in the full and quiet enjoyment of such rights as have been freely and generously granted to them: And if they should not have within themselves a sufficiency for the support of their officers, it would be a wrong to the community, not to do what was further wanting towards their comfortable and honourable support.

And having thus, in a general and imperfect manner, gone over the more important instances, wherein rulers should be just, it might now be proper to enlarge on the obligations they are under to be so: But the time will allow me only to suggest as follows.

[They are obliged to be thus just, from the fitness and reasonableness of the thing in itself considered. 'Tis a duty that naturally and necessarily results from the relation they stand in to society, and the power they are vested with, in all righteous ways, to promote it's welfare. And it would, in the nature of things, be incongruous and absurd for men so scituated and betrusted, and for such good ends, to injure those over whom they are exalted, by abusing their power to the purposes of tyranny and oppression. Such a conduct would evidently and grosly break in upon that propriety and fitness of action, which is immutably and eternally required, in such a constitution of things, as rulers and ruled, and the relative obligations respectively arising therefrom.

They are also obliged to be thus just, in virtue of the will of the supreme legislator, made known in the revelations of scripture; which enjoins such precepts as those, "Judges and officers shalt thou make thee;—and they shall judge the people with just judgment. Thou shalt not wrest judgment;—that which is altogether just shalt thou follow."* And again, "Thus saith the Lord, Execute ye judgment and righteousness, and deliver the spoiled out of the hand of the oppressor: And do no wrong, do no violence to the stranger, the fatherless, nor the widow":† : To which laws of the great king of the world they owe an indisputed obedience, as they are, in common with the rest of mankind, the subjects of his government: Nor can they be freed from the charge of reflecting contempt on the divine majesty, and that sovereign authority by which he governs his creatures, if, in their administrations, they should express a disregard to them.

They are likewise obliged to be just, out of regard to the community, to which they are related; whose welfare is so dependent hereon, that if they act, in their respective stations, not from a principle of justice, but under the influence of worldly views and selfish designs, it may reasonably be expected, that "judgment should be turned away backward, and justice stand afar off"; that "truth should fall in the street, and equity not be able to enter": The natural effect whereof must be the ruin of a people. Whereas, if they "put on righteousness, and it clothes them; and their judgment is as a robe and a diadem: If they deliver the poor that cry, and the fatherless, and him that hath none to help him; and break to pieces the wicked, and pluck the spoil of his teeth"; they will approve themselves those "righteous ones in authority, who cause the people to rejoice": And the righteousness wherewith they rule them will be their exaltation.

In fine, it should be a constraining argument with rulers to be just, that they are accountable to that JESUS, whom God hath ordained to be the judge of the world, for the use of that power he has put into their hands. And if, by their unjust behaviour in their places, they have not only injured the people, but unhappily led them, by their example, into practices that are fraudulent and dishonest; I say, if they have thus misused their power, sad will be their account another day; such as must expose them to the resentments of their judge, which they will not be able to escape. It will not be any security then, that they were once ranked among the great men of the earth. This may now be a protection to them, and it often indeed screens them from that human vengeance, which overtakes those of less influence, tho' guilty of less crimes: But the "kings of the earth, and the great men, and the chief captains, and the mighty men," will in the day of the appearing of the son of God, be upon a level with the meanest of mankind, and as ready, if conscious to themselves that they have been unjust in their stations, to "say to the mountains and rocks, fall on us, and hide us from the face of him that sitteth on the throne, and from the wrath of the lamb: For the great day of his wrath is come, and who shall be able to stand?" A most affecting consideration, and should powerfully excite those who rule over others, to a righteous exercise of their power; especially, as they will by this means, if in other respects also they have behaved well, obtain the approbation of their judge; who will, as they have been "faithful over a few things, make them ruler over many"; placing them at his own right hand, in his kingdom.

II. I now proceed to say, in the second place, Those who rule over men, must *rule in the fear of God*.

The fear of God, being not only in itself a considerable part of religion, but also a grace that has a special influence on all the other parts of it, is commonly, and not unfitly, used in scripture to signify the whole of it. This seems to be the meaning of the phrase here: And the thing intended is, not only that rulers should be endowed with an inward principle of religion, but that they should exercise their authority, in their whole administration, under the influence of so good and powerful a disposition.

He that ruleth over men, must rule in the fear of God. As if the royal prophet had said, "It is necessary, civil rulers should have upon their minds a becoming sense of God and religion: And it should govern their public conduct. Whatever they do, in their several stations, should be done under the guidance of an habitual awe of God, a serious regard to his governing will, and their accountableness to him. This is the principle that should have a predominating sway in all exertments of themselves in their public capacity." This I take to be the true sense of the words.

To be sure, 'tis the truth of the thing. Civil rulers ought to be possessed of a principle of religion, and to act under the direction of it in their respective stations. This is a matter of necessity. I don't mean that it is necessary in order to their having a right to rule over men. *Dominion is not founded in grace*: Nor is every pious good man fit to be entrusted with civil power. 'Tis easy to distinguish between government in it's abstracted notion, and the faithful advantageous administration of it. And religion in rulers is necessary to the latter, tho' not to the former.

Not but that they may be considerably useful in their places, if the religious fear of God does not reign in their hearts. From a natural benevolence of temper, accompanied with an active honest turn of mind, they may be instrumental in doing good service to the public: Nay, they may be prompted, even from a view to themselves, their own honour and interest, to behave well in the posts they sustain, at least, in many instances. But if destitute of religion, they are possessed of no principle that will stimulate a care in them to act up to their character steadily and universally, and so as fully to answer the ends of their institution.

'Tis a principle of religion, and this only, that can set them free from the unhappy influence of those passions and lusts, which they are subject to, in common with other men, and by means whereof they may be betrayed into that tyranny and oppression, that violence and injustice, which will destroy the peace and good order of society. These, 'tis true, may be under some tolerable check from other principles, at least, for a while, and in respect of those actings that are plainly enormous. But no restraints are like those, which the true fear of God lays upon men's lusts. This habitually prevailing in the hearts of rulers, will happily prevent the out-breaking of their pride, and envy, and avarice, and self-love, and other lusts, to the damage of society; and not only so, but it will weaken, and gradually destroy, the very inward propensities themselves to the various acts of vice. It naturally, and powerfully, tends to this: And this is the effect it will produce, in a less or greater degree, according to the strength of the religious principle, in those who are the subjects of it.

And a principle of religion also, and this only, will be effectual to excite rulers to a uniform, constant and universal regard to truth and justice, in their public conduct. Inferiour principles may influence them in particular cases, and at certain seasons: But the fear of God only will prompt them to every instance of right action, and at all times. This will possess them of such sentiments, give such a direction to their views, and fix such a happy biass on their minds, as that their chief concern and care will be, to behave in their offices so as to answer the good ends for which they were put into them. In one word, they will now be the subjects of that divine and universal principle of good conduct, which may, under God, be depended on, to carry them thro' the whole of their duty, upon all occasions, under all difficulties, and in opposition to all temptations, to the rendring the people, over whom they bear rule, as happy as 'tis in their power to make them.

To be sure, without a principle of religion, none of their services for the public will meet with the divine approbation. 'Tis therefore, in respect of themselves, a matter of absolute necessity that they be possess'd of the true fear of God. It won't suffice, should they behave well in their places, if they have no higher view herein than their own private interest; if they are influenced, not from a due regard to God, his honour and authority, but from love to themselves. This will spoil their best services, in point of the divine acceptance: Whereas, if they act from a principle of religion, what they do in a way of serving their generation will be kindly taken at the hands of a merciful God, and he will, thro' Jesus Christ, amply reward them for it, in the great day of retribution.]

Application

It now remains to apply what has been said to rulers and people.

And 'tis fit I should first turn the discourse into an address to your Excellency, as it has pleased God and the king to advance you to the first seat of government, among those who bear rule in this province.

The administration, sir, is devolved on you in the darkest day, it may be, New-England ever saw; when there was never more occasion for distinguishing talents in a governour, to direct the public counsels, and minister to the relief and comfort of a poor people, groaning under the calamities of war and debt, and, what is worse than both, an unhappy medium, that fills the land with oppression and distress. We would hope, it was because the Lord loved this people, that he has set you over us; and that he intends to honour you as the instrument in delivering us from the perplexing difficulties wherewith our affairs are embarrass'd.

We have had experience of your Excellency's superiour wisdom, knowledge, steadiness, resolution, and unwearied application in serving the province: And would herefrom encourage our selves to depend on you for every thing, that may reasonably be expected of a chief ruler, furnished with capacities fitted to promote the public happiness.

We rejoice to see so many posts in the government, at the disposal of your Excellency, either alone, or in conjunction with your council, filled with men of capacity, justice and religion: And as the public good is so much dependent on the nomination and appointment of well qualified persons to sustain the various offices in the province, we promise our selves your eye will be upon the faithful of the land, and that, while you contemn every vile person, you will honour them that fear the Lord. And should any attempt by indirect means to obtain places of trust which others better deserve, we assure ourselves your Excellency will resent such an affront, and testify a just displeasure against the persons who shall dare to offer it.

The opinion we have of your Excellency's integrity and justice, forbids the least suspicion of a design in you to invade the civil charter-rights of this people. And tho' you differ in your sentiments from us, as to the model of our church-state, and the external manner of our worship; yet we can securely rely on the generosity of your principles to protect us in the full enjoyment of those ecclesiastical rights we have been so long in possession of: And the rather, because your Excellency knows, that our progenitors enterprized the settlement of this country principally on a religious account; leaving their native land, and transporting themselves and their families, at a vast expence, and at the peril of their lives, into this distant, and then desolate wilderness, that they might themselves freely enjoy, and transmit to us their posterity, *that manner of worship and discipline*, which we look upon, as they did, most agreable to the purity of God's word.

Your Excellency knows too well the worth of learning, and the advantage of a liberal education, not to be strongly dispos'd to cherish the college, which has, from the days of our fathers, been so much the glory of New-England: And we doubt not, you will be always tender of its rights, and exert your self, as there may be occasion, for its defence and welfare.

And as your Excellency is our common father, we repair to you as the friend and patron of all that is dear and valuable to us; depending that you will employ your time, your thought, your authority, your influence and best endeavours, to ease our burdens, to lead us out of the labyrinths we have run into, and to make us a happy and prosperous people.

We can wish nothing better for your Excellency than the divine presence enabling you to act, in your whole administration, under the influence of a steady principle of justice, and an habitual awe and reverence of that God, for whom ultimately you derived your authority, and to whom you are accountable for the use of it. This will recommend you to the love, and entitle you to the praise of an obliged happy people; this will yield you undisturbed ease of mind under the cares and burdens of government; this will brighten to you the shades of death, embalm your memory after you are dead, and, what is infinitely more desireable, give you boldness when great and small shall stand before the Son of man, and procure for you that blessed euge, from the mouth of your divine Saviour and Master, "Well done, good and faithful servant: Enter thou into the joy of thy Lord."

Permit me, in the next place, with a becoming respect, to apply myself to the honourable his majesty's council, and the honourable house of representatives; whose desire has ordered me into this desk.

Through the goodness of God, we see the return of this anniversary for the exercise of one of those charter-rights, granted to our fathers, and continued to us, on the wise and faithful management whereof, the public happiness is very much dependent.

His majesty's council, this afternoon to be elected, is an happy medium between the king and the people, and wisely designed to preserve a due ballance between the prerogatives of the one, and the privileges of the other. And as they constitute one branch of the legislature, they have a share in framing and passing all acts and orders. To them it appertains to assist the chief ruler with their advice upon all emergent occasions, especially in the court's recess. And without their consent, none of the civil posts in the government can be filled; in consequence whereof, no judges can be appointed, no courts erected, no causes tried, no sentences executed, but by persons who have had their approbation: All which, by shewing the weight of this order of men in the state, bespeaks the importance of this day's business, and, at the same time, demands a proportionable care and faithfulness in the discharge of it.

It is not, gentlemen, a trifling concern you have before you; an affair wherein you may act with carelessness or inattention; with a party or partial spirit; out of affection to friends, or complaisance to superiors; much less upon the corrupt design of making instruments to be imployed and managed to serve your own private schemes. It is not for yourselves only that you are empowered and called to vote in the elections of this day, but for your God, your king and your country: And you will be unjust to them all, if you give your voice as moved by any considerations, but those which are taken from the real characters of men, qualifying them to sit at the council-board.

You all know, from the oracles of God, how men must be furnished, in order to their being fit to be chosen into places of such important trust; that they must be wise and understanding, and known to be so among their tribes; that they must be *able men, and men of truth, men that fear God, and hate covetousness.* And 'tis to be hoped, we have a sufficiency of such, in the land, to constitute his majesty's council. It would be lamentable indeed, if we had not. 'Tis your business, gentlemen, to seek them out. And with you will the fault principally lie, if we have not the best men in the country for councillors; men of capacity and knowledge, who are well acquainted with the nature of government in general, and the constitution, laws, priviledges and interests of this people in particular: Men of known piety towards God, and fidelity to their king and country: Men of a generous spirit, who are above acting under the influence of narrow and selfish principles: Men of unquestionable integrity, inflexible justice, and undaunted resolution, who will dare not to give their consent to unrighteous acts, or mistaken nominations; who will disdain, on the one hand, meanly to withdraw, when speaking their minds with freedom and openness may expose them to those who set them up, and may have it in their power to pull them down, or, on the other, to accommodate their conduct, in a servile manner, to their sentiments and designs; in fine, who will steadily act up to their character, support the honour of their station, and approve themselves invariably faithful in their endeavours to advance the public weal.

These are the men, 'tis in your power, my honourable fathers, to choose into the council; and these are the men for whom, in the name of God, and this whole people, I would earnestly beg every vote this day: And suffer me to say, these are the men you will all send in your votes for, if you are yourselves men of integrity and justice, and exercise your elective-power, not as having concerted the matter beforehand, in some party-juncto, but under the influence of a becoming awe of that omnipresent righteous God, whose eye will be upon you, to observe how you vote, and for whom you vote, and to whom you must finally render an account, before the general assembly of angels and men, for this day's transaction.

We bow our knees to the alwise sovereign Being, who presides over the affairs of the children of men, in humble and fervent supplications, that he would govern your views, direct your tho'ts, and lead you into a choice that he shall own and succeed, to promote the best interests of this people.

And when the elections of this day are over, and the several branches of the legislature shall proceed upon the affairs of the public, we promise ourselves you will act as those, who have upon their minds a just sense of the vast importance of the trust that is reposed in you.

To you is committed the defence of the province, the guardianship of it's liberties and priviledges, the protection of it's trade, and the care of it's most valuable interests: And never was there a time, wherein it's circumstances more urgently called upon you to exert yourselves, in seeking it's welfare.

Religion is not in such a flourishing state, at this day, but that it needs the countenance of your example, and the interposition of your authority, to keep it from insult and contempt. We thankfully acknowledge the pious care, the legislature has lately taken to restrain the horrid practice of cursing and swearing, which so generally prevailed, especially in this, and our other sea-port towns, to the dishonour of God, and our reproach as wearing the name of christians. And if laws still more severe are necessary, to guard the day and worship of God from prophanation, we can leave it with your wisdom to enact such, as may tend to serve so good a design. And tho' we would be far from desiring, that our rulers should espouse a party in religion; yet we cannot but hope, they will never do any thing to encourage those, who may have arrived at such an height in spiritual pride, as to say, in their practice, to their brethren as good as themselves, "stand by thy self, come not near me; for I am holier than thou": Concerning whom the blessed God declares, "These are a smoke in my nose, a fire that burneth all the day." And as for those, be their character, persuasion, or party, what it will, who, under the notion of appearing zealous for God, his truths or ways, shall insult their betters, vilify their neighbours, and spirit people to strife and faction, we earnestly wish the civil arm may be stretched forth to chastise them: And if they suffer, 'twill be for disturbing the peace of society; the evil whereof is rather aggravated than lessened, by pretences to advance the glory of God and the interest of religion.

We are thankful for the good and wholesome laws which have been made, from time to time, for the suppression of vice, in it's various kinds; and, in particular, for the restraint that has been laid upon those, who may be inclined to excessive drinking. Alas! that such multitudes, notwithstanding, are overtaken with this fault. Hard drinking is indeed become common all over the land. And 'tis astonishing to think what quantities of strong drink are consumed among us! Unless some, well capable of forming a judgment, are very much mistaken, more a great deal is needlessly and viciously consumed than would suffice to answer the whole charge, both of church and state. A reproach this, to any people! And if something further is not done by the government, to prevent the use that is made of strong drink, it will, in a little time, prove the destruction of the country, in the natural course of things; if God should not positively testify his displeasure against such horrid intemperance. It may deserve your consideration, my fathers, whether one occasion of this scandalous consumption of strong drink, has not been the needless multiplication of taverns, as well as more private licensed houses, that are too commonly used for tipling, and serve to little purpose, but to tempt people, in low life sinfully to waste their time, and spend their substance.

[It would also redound much to the advantage of the province, if our civil fathers could contrive, some way or other that might be effectual, to prevent people's laying out so much of the fruit of their labour, in that which is needless and extravagant. It will not be denied, by any capable of making observation, that the excesses, all ranks of persons have unhappily run into, need correction. 'Tis owing, in a great measure, to our pride, discovering it self in the extravagance of our garb, as well as manner of living, that we are brought low. And, if some restraint is not laid upon this vicious disposition, so generally prevalent in the land, we may complain of our difficulties, but 'tis not likely, without a miracle, they should be redressed.]

But there is nothing more needs your awaken'd attention, my honoured fathers in the government, than the unhappy state of this people by means of the current medium. Whatever wise and good ends might be proposed at first, and from time to time, in the *emission of bills of credit*, they have proved, in the event, a cruel engine of oppression. It may be, there was scarce ever a province under more melancholly circumstances, by reason of injustice, which is become almost unavoidable. Sad is the case of your men of nominal salaries: And much to be pitied also are those widows and orphans, who depend on the loan of their money for a subsistance: While yet, these last, of all persons in the community, should be most carefully guarded against every thing that looks like oppression. This sin, when widows and fatherless children are the persons wronged by it, is heinously aggravated in the sight of a righteous God; as may easily be collected from that emphatical prohibition, so often repeated in all parts of the bible, "Thou shalt not oppress the widow, nor the fatherless." But the oppression reigning in the land, is not confined to this order or that condition of persons, but touches all without exception. None escape its pernicious influence, neither high nor low, rich nor poor. Like an over-bearing flood, it makes its way thro' the province; and all are sufferers by it, in a less or greater degree, and feel and own themselves to be so.

And will you, our honoured rulers, by any positive acts, or faulty neglects, suffer your selves to be instrumental in the continuance of such a state of things? God forbid! We don't think you would designedly do any thing to countenance oppression, or neglect any thing that might have a tendency to remove it out of the land.

Neither can we think, that any former assemblies have knowingly acted, in the *emission of public bills*, upon dishonest principles: Tho' it may be feared, whether the righteous God, in holy displeasure at the sins both of rulers and people, may not have witheld counsel from our wise men, and scattered darkness in their paths: And if, in consequence hereof, there has been disunion in the sentiments of our civil fathers, concerning the public medium, and unsteadiness in their conduct, 'tis no matter of wonder: Nor, upon this supposition, is it hard to be accounted for, that injustice, by means of the paper currency, should have taken such a general and dreadful spread, thro' the land.

But, by what means soever we became involved in these perplexities, 'tis certainly high time to make a pause, and consider what may be done that will be effectual towards the recovering and maintaining justice and honesty, that we may be called the *city of righteousness, the faithful city*.

It would be culpable vanity in me, to attempt to prescribe to our honourable legislature; yet may I, without going beyond my line, after the example of the great apostle of the gentiles, reason with you of public righteousness, and its connection with a judgment to come.

You are, my fathers, accountable to that God whose throne is in the heavens, in common with other men. And his eyes behold your conduct in your public capacity, and he sees and observes it, not merely as a spectator, but an almighty righteous judge, one who enters all upon record in order to a reckoning another day. And a day is coming, it lingers not, when you shall all stand upon a level, with the meanest subjects, before the tremendous bar of the righteous judge of all the earth, and be called upon to render an account, not only of your private life, but of your whole management as entrusted with the concerns of this people.

Under the realising apprehension of this, suffer me, in the name of God, (tho' the most unworthy of his servants) to advise you to review the public conduct, respecting the passing bills, and to do whatever may lay in your power to prevent their being the occasion of that injustice, which, if continued much longer, will destroy the small remains of common honesty that are still left in the land, and make us an abhorrence to the people that delight in righteousness.

Let me beseech you, sirs, for the sake of this poor people, and for the sake of your own souls, when you shall stand before the dreadful bar of the eternal judgment, to lay aside all party designs and private considerations, and to deliberate upon this great affair, with a single view to the public good, and under the uniform influence of a steady principle of righteousness; for, as the wise man observes, "transgressors shall be taken in their own naughtiness," while "the righteousness of the upright shall deliver them, and their integrity shall guide them"; and again, "as for the upright, the Lord directeth their way."

If there needs any excuse for my wonted plainness of speech, I can only say; my conscience beareth me witness, that what I have said has proceeded, not from want of a decent respect for those who are my civil fathers, but from faithfulness to God, whose I am, and whom I desire to serve, as well as from an ardent love to my dear country, which I am grieved to behold in tears, by reason of "the oppressions that are done under the sun."

Custom might now demand an address to my fathers and brethren in the ministry; but as a sermon will be preached to the clergy to-morrow, by one who is every way my superior, and from whom I expect myself to receive instruction, I shall no otherwise apply to them than as they may be concerned in the exhortation to the people, which, agreably to the preceeding discourse, speaketh in the words of the inspired Solomon, "Fear God, and honour the king."

Be, first of all, concerned to become truly religious; men of piety towards God, faith in our Lord Jesus Christ, and the subjects of that regenerating change, which shall renew your whole inner man, and form you to a resemblance of the blessed Jesus, in the moral temper of his mind.

And let your religion now discover itself in all proper ways; particularly, in doing your duty to those, whom it hath pleased God to entrust with power to rule over you.

Be exhorted to "make supplications, prayers and intercessions, with giving of thanks, for the king in supreme, and for all in authority" under him, that by means of their wise, and gentle, and just administrations in government, we may "lead quiet and peaceable lives in all godliness and honesty."

And as subjection to civil rulers is so peremptorily demanded of you, by the laws of our holy religion, that you can't be good christians without it, let me caution you, on the one hand, not to "despise dominion," nor "speak evil of dignities": And, on the other, let me "put you in mind to be subject to principalities and powers, and to obey magistrates; submitting to every ordinance of man for the Lord's sake: Whether it be to the king, as supreme; or unto governours, as unto them that are sent by him, for the punishment of evil doers, and for the praise of them that do well: For so is the will of God."

And as rulers are the ministers of God, his authoris'd deputies, for the people's good, and continually, so far as they answer the ends of their institution, attend on this very thing: "For this cause pay you tribute also": And do it, not grudgingly, but with a chearful mind, in obedience to that glorious sovereign Being, who has said, "render unto Cæsar the things that are Cæsar's."

In fine, let me call upon you to "render unto all their dues." Abhor the little arts of fraud and deceit that are become so common, in this day of growing dishonesty. Make use of conscience in your dealings with your neighbour; and be fair and equitable, wherein you may have to do with him in a way of commerce. In conformity to the righteous God, love righteousness, and discover that you do so, by constantly living in the practice of it: Always bearing it in mind, that he, "whose eyes behold, and whose eyelids try the children of men," will hereafter descend from heaven, "to give to every man according as his work shall be." Behold! He cometh with clouds, and we shall, every one of us, see him. We are hastening to another world; and it will not be long, before we shall all be together again, in a much more numerous assembly, and upon a far greater occasion, even that of being tried for our future existence, at the dreadful tribunal of the impartial judge of the quick and dead. The good Lord so impress the thought upon the hearts of us all, whether rulers, or ministers, or people, as that it may have an abiding influence on us, engaging us to be faithful and just in our respective places: And now may we hope, of the mercy of God, thro' the merits of our saviour Jesus Christ, to be acquitted at the bar of judgment, pronounced blessed, and bid to inherit the kingdom prepared from the foundation of the world. Amen.

[*]Prov. 8. 15, 16.
[†]Rom. 13. 4.
[‡]Verse 1.
[*]Verse 5.
[†]Verse 2.
[*]Vid. Bp. Patrick on Levit. 19. 36.
[*]So speaks Maimonides, as quoted by Ainswerth on the above text.
[*]Exod. 18. 21.
[*]Levit. 19. 15.
[†]Deut. 19. 16.
[*]Prov. 3. 27, 28.
[*]Deut. 24. 14, 15.
[†]Lev. 17. 13.
[‡]1 Cor. 5. 7, 8.
[§]Rom. 13. 6.
[¶]Matth. 22. 21.
[*]The resolve refer'd to above, and in part quoted, it's tho't proper to insert at large; and is in these words.

At a great and general court or assembly for his majesty's province of the Massachusetts-Bay in New-England, begun and held at Boston, upon Wednesday May 26, 1725.

The following resolve pass'd both houses, and was consented to by his honour the lieutenant governour. Viz.

Upon serious consideration of the great distresses that many of the ministers of the gospel within this province labour under, with respect to their support or maintenance, their salaries being generally paid in the public bills of credit of this province, altho' many of the ministers contracted with their people in the time when silver money passed in payment; and the necessaries of life, such as cloathing, provisions, together with labour and other things, now demand so much more of the bills of credit than heretofore; Resolved, that it is the indispensable duty of the several towns precincts and parishes of this province, to make such additions to the salaries or maintenance of their respective ministers, as may honourably support and encourage them in their work; and therein to have regard as well to the time of the contract between the minister and people, and the specie therein mentioned, as to the great and growing difference in the value of the bills of credit, from what they have sometimes been. And this court do therefore most earnestly recommend the speedy and chearful practice of this duty, to the several congregations and religious assemblies within this province: And that this resolve be publickly read on the next Lord's day after the receipt hereof, in the afternoon before the congregation be dismiss'd; and at the anniversary meeting of the several towns or precincts in the province in the month of March next.

By order of the great and general court or assembly, Josiah Willard, Secr.

[*]Deut. 16. 18, 19, 20.
[†]Jer. 22. 3.

APPENDIX 3

Nineveh's Repentance and Deliverance

—Joseph Sewall
Boston, 1740

JOSEPH SEWALL (1688–1769). A Harvard graduate of 1707, Sewall spent a long and generally serene ministry at Old South Church in Boston, where he preached beyond his eightieth year. He was a strong Calvinist, yet he became a friend of George Whitefield, who preached in Sewall's pulpit during several visits to Boston. He was offered the presidency of Harvard in 1724, but he declined it after a peevish attack by Cotton Mather. He preached the artillery sermon in 1714 and the election sermon in 1724, and he was awarded a D.D. by the University of Glasgow in 1731. With his classmate Reverend Thomas Prince, he edited *The Compleat Body of Divinity* from collected papers of Samuel Willard (1726). His own papers were not collected, but *Sibley's Harvard Graduates* (vol. 5), lists twenty-nine writings by him.

Reprinted here is a fast-day sermon preached before the Massachusetts governor, the council, and the house of representatives on December 3, 1740. Always ready to look for underlying causes and strongly attached to his province, Sewall readily supported the patriot cause and permitted his meeting house to become a shrine of the American cause. In Charles Chauncy's words, Sewall "was a strenuous asserter of our civil and ecclesiastical charter-rights and priviledges. . . . He knew they were the purchase of our forefathers at the expence of much labor, blood, and treasire [*sic*]. He could not bear the thought of their being wrested out of our hands. He esteemed it our duty, in all wise, reasonable, and legal ways, to endeavour the preservation of them. . ." (Chauncy, *Discourse Occasioned by the Death of . . . Joseph Sewall* [Boston, 1769], p. 26).

> *And God saw their Works, that they turned from their evil Way, and God repented of the Evil that he had said that he would do unto them, and he did it not.*
> (Jonah III. 10)

In this book we have a very memorable and instructive history. The prophet Jonah, whose name the book bears, was call'd of GOD to go to Nineveh, the capital of the Assyrian monarchy, and cry against it: He criminally attempted to fly from the presence of the Lord, by going to Joppa, and from thence to Tarshish; but that GOD whom the winds and sea obey, raised such a storm as made the heathen mariners conclude there was something very extraordinary, and accordingly they propose to cast lots, that they might know for whose cause this evil was upon them. Jonah is taken, and cast into the sea; upon which it ceased from raging: And thus, by the wonderful Providence of GOD, he became a type of our Lord and Saviour Jesus Christ, who having appeased the wrath of GOD by his obedience unto death, lay buried in the earth three days, Matth. 12. 40. *For as Jonas was three Days and three Nights in the Whale's Belly: So shall the Son of Man be three Days and three Nights in the Heart of the Earth.* Jonah having cried to God, as *out of the Belly of Hell,* was delivered from his dreadful confinement. Chap. 2. v. 10. *The Lord spake unto the Fish, and it vomited Jonah upon the dry Land.* Thus the brute creation, even the mighty whales, obey the word of God's power, while men transgress his law. Jonah, being thus delivered from the depth of distress, obeys the second call of God to him, Ch. 3. v. 1. Happy is that rebuke, how sharp soever, which is sanctified to make us return to God and our duty. And here it is observ'd, in the third verse, that Nineveh was an exceeding great city, great to or of God,* "Things great and eminent have the name of God put upon them in scripture[,]" *of three days journey.* It is computed to have been sixty miles in compass, which may well be reckon'd three days journey for a footman, twenty miles a day, says Mr. Henry; or as the same author observeth, walking slowly and gravely, as Jonah must, when he went about preaching, it would take him up at least three days to go thro' all the principal streets and lanes of the city, to proclaim his message, that all might have notice of it." However, no greatness or wordly glory will be any security against GOD's destroying judgments, if such places go on obstinately in their sins. O let not London! let not Boston, presume to *deal unjustly in the Land of Uprightness,* lest the holy GOD say of them as of his ancient people, *You have I known of all the Families of the Earth: Therefore I will punish you for all your Iniquities,* Amos 3. 2. But to return, Jonah, in obedience to the divine command, cries against this great city, *Yet forty days, and Nineveh shall be overthrown,* v. 4. In the five following verses, we have the faith and repentance of the Ninevites described, which our Lord takes particular notice of, Matth. 12. 41. *The Men of Nineveh shall rise in Judgment with this Generation, and shall condemn it, because they repented at the preaching of Jonas, and behold, a greater than Jonas is here.* Let us then attend to these words *with reverence and godly fear, lest they also rise up in judgment against us in the terrible day of the Lord.* And here I would more particularly observe, 1. The People of Nineveh believed God, V. 5. Jonah, We May Suppose, Declared To Them The True And LivingGod, Who Made Heaven And Earth, And Publish'd His Message In His Name; And God Wrought Such A Faith In Them As Excited A Fear Of His Judgments, And Made Them Deeply Concern'd To Put Away Their Provoking Sins, That They Might Escape The Threatned Destruction. And This Impression Of Fear And Concern Was General; For We Find, 2dly, That They Proclaim'd A Fast, And Put On Sackcloth From The Greatest Of Them Even To The Least Of Them. Yea, There Was A Royal Proclamation For This By The Decree Of The King And His Nobles, V. 7. And This Great Monarch Humbled Himself Before The Most High, Who Cuts Off The Spirit Of Princes, And Is Terrible To The Kings Of The Earth. The King Of Nineveh Arose From His Throne, And Laid His Robe From Him, And Cover'd Him With Sackcloth, And Sat In Ashes, V. 6. Thus Did He Practically Confess, That He Had Behav'd Unworthy His Royal Dignity, And Deserv'd To Have It Taken From Him. And The Proclamation Requir'd The Strictest Abstinence, Let Neither Man Nor Beast Taste Any Thing. Not As If The Beasts Were Capable Of Moral Good Or Evil; But As These Had Been Abus'd By Them, They Would Have Their Moans And Cries Under The Want Of Food, Further To Excite Penitential Sorrow In Themselves. And All Are Commanded To Cry Mightily To God, V. 8. Yea, All Are Exhorted To Turn Every One From His Evil Way, And From The Violence That Is In Their Hands. The Ninevites Were Sensible, That To Outward Signs And Means Of Humiliation, They Must Add Repentance And Reformation. 3. We Have Their Encouragement To Attend This Duty, In A Time Of Impending Judgment, V. 9. Who Can Tell If God Will Turn And Repent. We May Suppose That Jonah Declar'd To Them The Grace And Mercy Of The God Of Israel, And Shew'd Them The Way Of Salvation Thro' The

Then Promised Messiah; That Tho' Their Bodies Should Be Destroy'd, Their Souls Might Be Sav'd In The Day Of The Lord. And They Might Well Infer Some Ground Of Hope As To Their Temporal Deliverance From This, That The Judgment Was Not Presently Executed; But The Space Of Forty Days Was Given Them For Repentance. However, As It Doth Not Appear They Had Any Particular Promise Respecting This Matter, So Their Faith And Hope Are Here Express'd As Attended With Doubt And Fear. Who Can Tell? A Like Expression We Have, Even Respecting God's Covenant People, Who Knows If He Will Return And Repent? Joel 2. 14. 4. We Have An Account Of Nineveh's Repentance, And God's Gracious Deliverance, V. 10.Godsaw Their Works, I.E. With Approbation And Gracious Acceptance. Their Works "Whereby They Testified The Sincerity Of Their Faith And Repentance."* Our Saviour Says, They Repented At The Preaching Of Jonas. Luke 11. 32. We May Conclude Therefore That His Preaching Was Accompanied With The Powerful Influences Of The Spirit Of God Convincing Them Of Their Many Hainous Transgressions, Awakening Them With Fears Of God's Judgments, And Prevailing Upon Them To Turn From Their Sins To The Lord. Had It Not Been For This Wonderful Work Of Grace Upon Them, They Had Been Like To The Sinners Of The Old World, Who Went On Securely, Tho' Noah Was A Preacher Of Righteousness To Them, 'Till The Flood Came, And Took Them All Away. Here Were Some, I Hope, And That Not A Few, Who Had Saving Repentance Given Them; And Others Were So Terrified And Awakened, That They Engaged At Least In An Outward And Publick Reformation. And May We Not Suppose That In This Wonderful Work, God Gave His Ancient People A Specimen And Earnest Of The Call Of The Gentiles? Now, Upon This Their Repentance It Is Said, God repented Of The Evil, And He Did It Not. Which Words Must Be Understood In Such A Sense As Is Consistent With The Divine Perfections. It Is Not Spoken Of God, As If He Could In A Proper Sense Be Griev'd For What He Had Done In Threatning The Ninevites; No, This Was Right, And He Had A Gracious Design In It: Nor, As If He Had Alter'd His Counsels Concerning Them. He Is Of One Mind, And Who Can Turn Him? Nor, As If He Acted Contrary To Truth And Faithfulness; No, The Threatning Was Conditional. And Accordingly When They Repented God Turned From His Fierce Anger, And Gave Them Deliverance; Which Is Agreable To That Rule Of His Government Which We Have Declar'd. Jer. 18. 7. 8. At What Instant I Shall Speak Concerning A Nation, And Concerning A Kingdom, To Pluck Up, And To Pull Down, And To Destroy It: If That

Nation Against Whom I Have Pronounced, Turn From Their Evil, I Will Repent Of The Evil That I Thought To Do Unto Them.

From the words thus explained to you, I would observe the following doctrines,

(1.) If we would seek the Lord in a right manner, we must believe him; the threatnings and promises of his word. (2.) It is the duty of a people to cry to GOD in prayer with fasting, when he threatens to bring destroying judgments upon them; and their rulers should be ready to lead in the right discharge of this duty. (3.) Our seeking to GOD by prayer with fasting must be attended with true repentance, and sincere endeavours after reformation. (4.) When a people do thus attend their duty, GOD will repent of the evil, and not bring destruction upon them.

I. *If we would seek the Lord in a right manner under his threatned judgments, we must believe him; the threatnings and promises of his word.*

The people of Nineveh believed GOD, and proclaimed a fast. We are not told what particular credentials Jonah produc'd to prove that he was a true prophet sent from GOD. His preaching might be more full and particular than is here recorded; and GOD set it home, so that they were made sensible they had to do with the true and faithful one, whose name is Jehovah; and accordingly they set themselves to entreat his favour with great seriousness. And thus we must believe, that the Lord is that powerful, holy, faithful, and merciful GOD, which he declareth himself to be in his word. We must realise it, that his word is sure and most worthy of credit, whether he threatens evil to the impenitent, or promiseth mercy to such as confess and forsake their sins; or we shall never be concerned to seek his face in a right manner. *Without faith it is impossible to please God,* in our approaches to him: For he that cometh to GOD, *must believe that he is, and that he is a Rewarder of them that diligently seek him.* Heb. 11. 6. Agreably, in a time of danger, that pious king Jehoshaphet, said to GOD's ancient people, *Hear me, O Judah, and ye the Inhabitants of Jerusalem, Believe in the Lord your God, so shall you be established; believe his prophets, so shall ye prosper.* 2 Chron. 20. 20. Certainly then, we who are born under the clear light of the gospel dispensation, must believe the Lord our GOD speaking to us in his word, if we would attend the duties of this day, so as to obtain mercy for ourselves, and this distressed people. We must believe that if we go on obstinately in our sins, and despite the warnings GOD has given us in his word and by his providences, we shall after our hardness and impenitent heart treasure up unto our selves wrath against the day of wrath; But if we forsake the way of sin, and return unto the Lord, he will have mercy and abundantly pardon. We must believe our Lord Jesus when he says to us, *Except ye repent, ye shall all likewise perish.* And we must also receive it as *a faithful saying, and worthy of all acceptation, that Christ Jesus came into the world to save sinners,* and will cast out none that come to him in the exercise of faith and repentance. O that there was such a faith in us! Then we should fly to GOD's name, as to our strong tower this day, and find him our defence and refuge in the day of trouble. *By Faith Noah being warnned of God of Things not seen as yet, moved with fear, prepared an Ark to the saving of his House; by the which he condemned the World, and became Heir of the Righteousness which is by Faith,* Heb. 11. 7.

II. *It is the duty of a people to cry to GOD in prayer with fasting, when he threatens to bring destroying judgments upon them; and their rulers should be ready to lead in the right discharge of this duty.*

Thus did the men of Nineveh, nor did their king refuse to humble himself and lie in the dust before that Almighty GOD, who threatned to destroy them. The order given was, "Let Man and Beast be covered with Sackcloth, and cry mightily to GOD." This then is a moral duty incumbent on all as GOD shall call. GOD's ancient people practised it. Thus when the children of Moab and Ammon came against Jehoshaphet to battel, he feared, *and set himself to seek the Lord, and proclaimed a Fast,* 2 Chron. 20. 1–3. And we have an account in scripture of more private fasting, Mark 2. 18, 20. Where we are informed that the disciples of John, and of the pharisees used to fast. And our Lord declares that after his departure, *His Disciples should also Fast.* And we have particular direction about religious fasting, 1. Cor. 7. 5. Here then, I would be a little more particular in describing the duty of fasting and prayer, in which we are this day engaged.

1. *In religious fasting we must chasten our bodies, by abstaining from meat and drink, and other pleasures which gratify the outward man.*

Thus must we acknowledge that we have abused GOD's good creatures, and are unworthy of the least drop and crumb even of the blessings of his common Providence. And in this way we ought to afflict and keep under our bodies, that our animal appetites may be bro't into subjection, and that our souls may be the more deeply humbled before GOD. Indeed the necessity of persons, respecting the weakness of some constitutions, is here to be regarded. However, when persons wantonly indulge their appetites, and find their own pleasures when GOD calls to weeping and mourning, is sinful and shameful. And GOD declares in his word, that this is a provoking evil, Isai. 22. 12–14. *In that Day did the Lord God of hosts call to weeping and to mourning, and to girding with sackcloth: And behold Joy and Gladness, slaying Oxen, and killing Sheep, eating Flesh, and drinking Wine; let us eat and drink, for to morrow we shall die. And it was revealed in mine Ears by the Lord of hosts, Surely this iniquity shall not be purged from you till ye die, saith the Lord God of hosts.* And surely the men of Nineveh will rise up in judgment against such, and condemn them; for we find they were very strict in attending these outward signs and means of humiliation. But then, it must be granted that this bodily abstinence will profit little, unless our hearts are broken for sin, and broken off from the pleasures of it.

2. In religious fasting we must *afflict our souls; have the heart inwardly pierced, and the spirits broken upon the account of our sins.*

That GOD who is a spirit, and forms the spirit of man within him, looks on the heart, and requireth us to worship him in spirit and truth. *The Sacrifices of God are a broken Spirit: a broken and contrite Heart, O God thou wilt not despise,* Psal. 51. 17. The call of GOD to his people on a day of solemn fasting, was that, *rent your heart,* Joel 2. 13. There must then be a deep and thorow conviction of sin, and contrition upon the account of it. We must look to Jesus whom our sins have pierced, and *mourn as one mourneth for his only Son, and be in bitterness, as one that is in bitterness for his First-born,* Zech. 12. 10. There must be hatred of sin, and indignation at it as the accursed thing which stirs up GOD's holy displeasure against us. There must be inward grief because GOD has been dishonour'd and his law broken by our sins: *That godly Sorrow which worketh Repentance,* 2 Cor. 7. 10. There must be holy fear of GOD's judgments. We must take shame and blame to our selves, and make that confession, Dan. 9. 8. *O Lord to us belongeth confusion of Face, to our Kings, to our Princes, and to our Fathers, because we have sinned against thee.* We must abhor our selves, lie down before GOD in deep abasement, and humble ourselves under his mighty hand: Thus must we go to GOD self-condemned, and willing to be reconcil'd to him upon his own terms; looking to Jesus as our advocate with the Father, and depending on him as the propitiation for our sins.

3. *We must cry mightily to GOD in prayer.* Earnest prayer, in this

and other places of scripture, is express'd by crying to the Lord, Psal. 130. 1. *Out of the depths have I cried unto thee O Lord.* Prayer is a great part of the duty of the day; and we must take care, that it be that *effectual fervent Prayer that availeth much,* Jam. 5. 16.[,] in-wrought prayer, that prayer which is wrought in the heart by the Holy Ghost. For this end, we must ask the spirit of grace and supplication to help our infirmities, and stir up the gift of GOD in us. Thus must we pour out our hearts before GOD, and say, in most humble importunity as Jacob, *I will not let thee go, except thou bless me.* For GOD said not to the seed of Jacob, seek ye me in vain, Isa. 45. 15. And therefore, if we approve our selves the genuine sons of that patriarch, we shall also have power with GOD, and prevail thro' the merits and intercession of our Lord Jesus Christ: we shall either obtain the blessing for GOD's people, as Elias did, tho' a man subject to like passions; or at least shall deliver our own souls. I might further set before you the prophet Daniel, who has given rulers a bright example of a publick spirit, greatly concern'd for the peace of Jerusalem. How earnest was he when he set his face to seek the Lord by prayer with fasting! Hear his repeated cries, Ch. 9. 19. *O Lord hear, O Lord forgive, O Lord, hearken and do, defer not, for thine own sake, O my God.* And when GOD call'd his people to sanctify a fast, the divine command is, Joel 2. 17. *Let the Priests, the Ministers of the Lord, weep between the Porch and the Altar, and let them say, Spare thy People, O Lord, and give not thy Heritage to Reproach; that the Heathen should rule over them: wherefore should they say among the People, Where is their God?* May Moses and Aaron, lift up their hands with their hearts to GOD in prayer this day, and receive the blessing from the Lord.

4. *We must turn, each one from his evil way.* Thus when the exhortation given was to cry mightily to GOD, it follows; Yea, let them turn every one from his evil way, and *from the Violence that is in their Hands.* And indeed, unless this be our care, our sins will cry louder than our prayers, and provoke GOD to cover himself as with a cloud, Isa. 59. 1, 2. *Behold, the Lord's Hand is not shortned that it cannot save: neither his ear heavy that he cannot hear. But your Iniquities have separated between you and your God, and your Sins have hid his Face from you, that he will not hear.* And when GOD had declared to his people that he rejected their assemblies and solemn meetings, he gives them that exhortation. *Wash ye, make ye clean, put away the evil of your Doings from before mine Eyes, cease to do*

evil, learn to do well, seek Judgment, relieve the Oppressed, judge the Fatherless, plead for the Widow, Isa. 1. 16, 17.

But this brings me to the 3d general head:

III. Our seeking to GOD by prayer with fasting, *must be attended with true repentance, and sincere endeavours after reformation.*

GOD saw their works, that they *turned from the evil way.* Here we may consider,

1. What is implied in this work of repentance and reformation.

2. Why we should thus engage in the work of repentance and reformation.

First, *What is implied in this work of repentance and reformation?*

A. 1. It implieth, *An holy and prevailing resolution to turn from those sins which we confess on the day of fasting.* When we appear before GOD to confess our sins and ask pardon for them; if we attend this duty in sincerity, we are convinc'd that it is an evil and bitter thing that we have forsaken GOD by transgressing his law; and we shall accordingly resolve to put away this accursed thing which separates between GOD and us, and engage to return to GOD and our duty. Thus did GOD's people on a solemn fast. *They entred into an oath to walk in God's law,* and solemnly promis'd, that they would reform the evils which had crept in among them; in taking strange wives, in profaning the Sabbath, in their cruel exacting upon their poor brethren, *&c.*Neh. 9. 38. 10. 29–31. And it is certainly seasonable and necessary for persons on such a day to resolve, relying on GOD for grace, to put away such and such sins as have more easily beset them, to take more care to keep themselves from their own iniquity, and to reform whatever hath been contrary to GOD's law.

Which leads me to say,

2. It intends, *That this resolution be put in practice in sincere endeavours to put away those sins and reform those evils, which have been confess'd and bewail'd before God.* This GOD requires of us. *Thus saith the Lord God, Repent and turn your selves from all your Idols, and turn away your Faces from all your Abominations,* Ezek. 14. 6. And after this manner did the children of Israel testify their repentance, when they cried to the Lord under the oppression of their enemies. *And they put away the strange gods from among them, and served the Lord and his soul was grieved for the misery of Israel.* Judg. 10. 16. Agreeably, when we have fasted and prayed, we must bring forth *fruits meet for repentance,* by engaging in a thorow reformation

of all sins of omission or commission. If we have omitted religious duties, secret or family prayer, self-examination, the ordinances of GOD's house; we must now conscienciously attend upon them. If we have neglected the duties of those relations which we sustain towards men, in publick or private life; we must now with care and diligence discharge them. If we have committed sins contrary to the laws of sobriety, righteousness and godliness; we must labour by the spirit to mortify them. In a word, we should cleanse our selves from all filthiness of the flesh and spirit, perfecting holiness in the fear of GOD. And in order to these things, we ought earnestly seek to GOD to put his laws into our minds, and write them in our hearts; for it is he alone that can work in us to will and to do, in beginning and carrying on this necessary work of reformation.

3. *That we return to God by Jesus Christ; to believe in, love and obey him.* The prophet Hosea complains, *They return, but not to the most High,* 7. 16. Whereas, when a reformation is sincere and general, we shall have a regard to the Lord our GOD in it, as to our chief good and highest end. We shall not be principally concern'd to serve a turn, and escape this or the other threatned judgment. As they, *When he slew them, then they sought him: and they returned and enquired early after God. And they remembred that God was their Rock, and the high God their Redeemer. Nevertheless, they did flatter him with their Mouth, and they lied unto him with their Tongues,* Psal. 7. 8. 34–36. But shall make it our great business to obtain peace with GOD thro' Jesus Christ the only Mediator, who has made peace thro' the blood of his cross. And then shall we endeavour to be stedfast in his covenant. The language of our hearts must be as Hos. 6. 1. *Come and let us return unto the Lord: for he hath torn, and he will heal us; he hath smitten, and he will bind us up.* 14. 3. *Asshur shall not save us, we will not ride upon Horses, neither will we say any more to the work of our hands, Ye are our gods: for in thee the Fatherless findeth mercy.* We must return to GOD as to our Lord and lawgiver, to obey and serve him; as to the object of our desire and choice, to take our full contentment in him: Thus it is said of GOD'S people *All Judah rejoiced at the Oath: for they had sworn with all their Heart, and sought him with their whole desire, and he was found of them,* 2 Chr. 15. 15. As to particular persons, it is necessary that they thus give up themselves to the Lord, and then keep the covenant of their GOD. And as to a people, considering them collectively, this must be their prevailing desire and practice: If they are generally

false & hypocritical, they will give GOD reason to complain of them, as of his ancient people, *O Ephraim, what shall I do unto thee: O Judah, what shall I do unto thee: for your goodness is as a morning cloud, and as the early dew it goeth away.* Hos. 6. 4.

Secondly, *Why should our days of fasting be thus attended with sincere endeavours after reformation?*

A. 1. *GOD demands this of us.* When that inquiry was made, Wherewith shall I come before the Lord, and bow my self before the high GOD? Shall I come before him with burnt-offerings? Will the Lord be pleased with thousands of rams or with ten thousands of rivers of oyl? The answer is, *He hath shewed thee, O Man, what is good, and what doth the Lord require of thee, but to do justly, and to love mercy, and to walk humbly with thy GOD?* Micah 6. 8. And therefore, when GOD'S people fasted in a formal customary manner, without engaging in the necessary work of reformation, GOD said to them, *Did ye at all Fast unto me, even to me?* And then it follows, *Execute true Judgment, and shew Mercy and Compassions every Man to his Brother. And oppress not the Widow, nor the Fatherless, the Stranger, nor the Poor, and let none of you imagine Evil against his Brother in your Heart,* Zech. 7. 8, 10.

2. *GOD makes precious promises to encourage and excite us to this duty.* Thus when GOD had exhorted his people to put away the evil of their doings; he adds for their encouragement, *Come now and let us reason together, saith the Lord; though your Sins be as Scarlet, they shall be white as Snow; though they be red like Crimson, they shall be as Wool. If ye be willing and obedient, ye shall eat the good of the Land.* And in the 55th Chapter we have that exhortation enforc'd with a promise of full and free pardon, v. 6, 7. *Seek ye the Lord, while he may be found, call ye upon him while he is near. Let the Wicked forsake his Way, and the unrighteous Man his Thoughts: and let him return unto the Lord, and he will have mercy upon him, and to our God, for he will abundantly pardon.* ver. 6, 7. Surely then, we must be basely ungrateful, if we are not drawn with these cords of a man, and bands of love. While we refuse to attend this great duty, we practically despise the riches of GOD'S goodness whereby he *leads sinners to repentance.* And this is another reason why we should engage in the work of repentance and reformation.

3. If we refuse to repent and reform, *we shall be condemned out of our own mouths, and fall under the threatned judgments of GOD.* One considerable part of the duty of a day of religious fasting is to make

an humble and penitent confession of our sins whereby we have
provoked a holy GOD to come out in judgment against us, and to
cry to him for grace that we may turn from them. Thus 'tis said
of GOD'S people on the day of solemn fasting recorded Neh. 9. *The
Seed of Israel stood and confessed their Sins, and the Iniquities of their
Fathers:* 2d v. But if there be no care to put away the sins which we
have confess'd, we shall give our Lord and judge reason to say to us as
to the wicked servant, *Out of thine own Mouth will I judge thee.* Now
this will be dreadful indeed, and must aggravate our condemnation, to
be thus self-condemned; and so to fall under the righteous judgment
of GOD. We have the proof of this written for our warning in the
doleful account which the Scripture gives of the sin and punishment
of GOD'S ancient convenant people. Tho' they had their days of
fasting, particularly on the seventh month, when the high priest was
to make an atonement for himself and the people, and enter into the
holy place within the vail, Lev. 16. Notwithstanding this, GOD said
to his people, If ye will not be reformed, but will walk contrary to
me, then will I also walk contrary to you, and will punish you seven
times for your sins. And GOD fulfilled his word. *They mocked the
Messengers of God, and despised his Words, and misused his Prophets,
until the Wrath of the Lord arose against his People, till there was no
Remedy,* 2 Chron. 36. 16. Jerusalem and the Temple were destroyed
by fire, and GOD'S people led into captivity to Babylon. And after
their merciful restoration, when they had filled up the measure of
their sins by disobeying and crucifying the Lord of Glory, and then
by rejecting the offers of the gospel made to them by his apostles; the
wrath of GOD came upon them to the uttermost by the Romans, and
they are made an execration and a curse unto this day.

IV. *When a people do thus turn from their evil way to the Lord, he
will repent of the evil, and not bring destruction upon them.* GOD saw
their works—and *God repented of the Evil that he had said he would
do unto them, and he did it not.* Judgment is GOD'S strange work; but
he delighteth in mercy. And when GOD threatens, it is with a reserve
of grace and favour to the penitent. *Remember therefore from whence
thou art fallen & repent, and do the first Works; or else I will come
unto thee quickly, and will remove thy Candlestick out of his Place,
except thou repent.* Rev. 2. 5. Thus GOD said to the prophet Jeremiah,

Take thee a Roll of a Book, and write therein all the Words
that I have spoken unto Thee against Israel, and against all
the Nations, from the Day I spake unto thee, from the Days of

Josiah, even unto this Day. It may be the House of Judah will hear all the evil which I purpose to do unto them; that they may return every Man from his evil Way, that I may forgive their Iniquity and their Sin, Jer. 36. 2, 3.

GOD knew perfectly well what they would do; but then he here lets his people know how ready he was to forgive the penitent and receive them into favour: It's true, such as repent may be afflicted in this life; but then it is with the tender compassion of a father, not with the deadly wound of an enemy. The first and purest times of Christianity were times of persecution; however, while the holy martyrs overcame by the blood of the Lamb, not loving their lives unto the death; the church was preserv'd, yea increased and multiplied. And as to a people, considering them collectively, I suppose no one instance can be produc'd in which GOD pour'd out his fury to destroy them, while a spirit of repentance and reformation prevail'd. And even in times of abounding iniquity, when the glory of GOD was departing from his people, and destroying judgments breaking in like a flood; GOD was pleased to make a remarkable distinction between the penitent, and such as were hardned in sin.

And the Lord said unto him, Go through the midst of the City, through the midst of Jerusalem, and set a Mark upon the Foreheads of the Men that sigh and that cry for all the Abominations that be done in the midst thereof. And to the others be said in mine hearing, Go ye after him through the City and smite: let not your Eye spare, neither have ye Pity, Ezek. 9. 4, 5.

But the time would fail me, should I attempt to speak particularly to this head; and I have in part prevented my self by what has been already said. I shall therefore only give a few hints further to confirm & illustrate the truth before us. The faithful and true GOD *declareth this in his word.*

When I say unto the Wicked, Thou shalt surely die: If he turn from his sin, and do that which is lawful and right; If the Wicked restore the Pledge, give again that he had robbed, walk in the Statutes of Life, without committing Iniquity; he shall surely live, he shall not die, Ezek. 33. 14, 15.

When Ephraim bemoan'd himself and repented, GOD manifested his fatherly compassions to him.

I have surely heard Ephraim bemoaning himself thus, Thou hast chastised me, and I was chastised, as a Bullock unaccustomed to the Yoke: Turn thou me, and I shall be turned; for thou art the Lord my God. Surely after that I was turned, I repented; and after that I was instructed, I smote upon my thigh: I was ashamed, yea, even confounded, because I did bear the reproach of my Youth. Is Ephraim my dear Son? Is he a pleasant Child? For since I spake against him, I do earnestly remember him still: Therefore my Bowels are troubled for him; I will surely have mercy upon him, saith the Lord. Jer. 31. 18–20.

Again, When a people do thus turn from their evil way to the Lord, *They are prepar'd to receive and improve GOD's merciful Deliverance after a suitable manner.* While a degenerate people are impenitent they will be ready to despise the riches of God's goodness and forbearance, and to wax wanton under sparing mercy. *Jeshurun waxed fat and kicked: thou art waxen fat, thou art grown thick, thou art covered with fatness; then he forsook God which made him, and lightly esteemed the Rock of his Salvation,* Deut. 32. 15. But when sin is embitter'd by the godly sorrow which worketh repentance we shall observe that caution after GOD has spoken peace, Psal. 84. 8. *Let them not turn again to Folly.* Such a people will be jealous over themselves and for the Lord of hosts, and be concern'd to improve all his gracious appearances for them to the honour of his great name. Accordingly, GOD says of his people, How shall I put thee among the children, and give thee a pleasant land? And then returns this answer, *Thou shalt call me, My Father, and shalt not turn away from me,* Jer. 3. 19. Again, this truth is evident *from the happy experience of the penitent.* We have a remarkable instance before us. Now, did GOD spare repenting Nineveh, and will he not spare his repenting covenant-people?

Yes surely,

If their uncircumcised Hearts be humbled, and they then accept of the punishment of their Iniquity: Then will I remember my Covenant with Jacob, and also my Covenant with Isaac, and also my Covenant with Abraham will I remember; and I will remember the Land.

And GOD was pleas'd to fulfill his promise to his people, 1 Sam. 7. and in other instances upon record in scripture. In a word, the Lord JESUS our great high priest, has offered a sacrifice of infinite value to make atonement for the congregation of his people, whether Jews or gentiles; and he lives in heaven to interceed for them: And therefore, when GOD's people look to him and mourn and turn to the Lord, he will turn from his fierce anger, and command salvation.

APPLICATION

USE 1. Learn that *true religion lays the surest foundation of a people's prosperity. Righteousness exalteth a Nation,* Prov. 14. 34. When we turn to GOD by Jesus Christ, and do works meet for repentance; we take the best way to obtain salvation from the help of his countenance, who is the Father of Lights, from whom cometh down every good & every perfect gift. It's sin that separateth between GOD and his people: When this accursed thing is therefore put away from among them, that GOD to whom belong the issues from death, will draw nigh to them with his saving health, and appear for their deliverance.

And *if GOD be for us, who can be against us? There is no Wisdom nor Understanding, nor Counsel against the Lord. The Horse is prepared against the Day of Battle: But Safety is of the Lord.* Prov 21. 30, 31. Certainly then, the one thing needful is to secure the presence and favour of GOD; and this we do when we return to him in hearty repentance, and then walk before him in new obedience. Blessed is that people whose GOD is the LORD: No weapon form'd against them shall prosper, and that good word shall be fulfilled unto them, *God is our Refuge and Strength, a very present Help in Trouble,* Psal. 46. 1. and v. 5. *God is in the midst of her, she shall not be moved. God shall help her, and that right early,* O that GOD would impress on our minds the firm belief of these things! O that he would affect our hearts suitably with them! That we might strive together in our prayers this day, crying to GOD with the prophet, *O Lord, revive thy Work in the midst of the Years, in the midst of the Years make known; in Wrath remember Mercy.* Hab. 3. 2.

USE 2. *Abounding iniquity will be the destruction of a people, except they repent.* If they persist and go on in the ways of sin, refusing to return to GOD, iniquity will be their ruin. *Sin is the Reproach of any People,* Prov. 14. 34. It hath both a natural and moral tendency to lay them low, and expose them to shame. Sin in the body politick, is like some foul and deadly disease in the natural body which turns the beauty of it into corruption, and weakens all it's powers. *Why should ye be stricken any more? ye will revolt more and more: the whole Head is sick, and the whole Heart is faint. From the Sole of the Foot, even unto the Crown of the Head, there is no Soundness in it; but Wounds and Bruises, and putrifying Sores: they have not been closed, neither bound up, neither molified with Ointment,* Isa. 1. 5, 6. And then, this deadly evil provokes the holy GOD to pour contempt upon a people, and lay their honour in the dust.

Thus GOD threatned his people, *Thou shalt become an Astonishment, a Proverb, and a By-word, among all Nations whither the Lord shall lead thee.* Deut. 28. 37. And in the 44th and 45th [verse:] *He shall lend to thee, and thou shalt not lend to him; he shall be the Head, and thou shalt be the Tail. Moreover all these Curses shall come upon thee, and overtake thee till thou be destroyed: Because thou hearknedst not unto the Voice of the Lord thy God, to keep his Commandments and his Statutes which he commanded thee.* And the threatning was fulfilled upon them. GOD said to his people, O Israel, Thou hast fallen by thine iniquity. And the weeping prophet laments their sins and ruin, *Jerusalem hath grievously sinned: all that honoured her, despise her, because they have seen her nakedness: yea, she sigheth, and turneth backward. Her filthiness is in her skirts, she remembreth not her last end, therefore she came down wonderfully: she had no Comforter.* Yea, after this remarkable deliverance granted to Nineveh, it's suppos'd about ninety years, when they returned to their former sins, the prophet Nahum foretells their ruin, Chap. 1.

USE 3. Let us then be sensible of the *destroying evil of sin,* and the *necessity of true repentance.*

GOD speaks to us this day as to his people of old, *Thine own wickedness shall correct thee, and thy Backslidings shall reprove thee: know therefore and see, that it is an evil thing and bitter that thou hast forsaken the Lord thy God, and that my fear is not in thee, saith the Lord God of hosts,* Jer. 2. 19. And as 44. 4. *O do not this abominable thing that I hate.* Most certainly they are guilty of great folly, who make a mock at sin. This is to cast fire-brands, arrows and death; and say, Am I not sport? The wise man observes, that *One Sinner destroyeth much Good,* Eccl. 9. 18. Thus *Achan took of the accursed Thing; and the Anger of the Lord was kindled against the Children of Israel,* Josh. 7. 1. Let us then fly from sin as the most pernicious evil, and see the necessity of our turning to the Lord by sincere repentance. O let that word of the Lord sink deep into our hearts this day! *Turn ye, turn ye, Why will ye die, O House of Israel?* Ezek. 33. 11.

Which leads me to the last use;

Let us all be exhorted *to turn, every one from his evil way; and to engage heartily in the necessary work of reformation.*

This, this is our great duty and interest this day, as we would hope to be made instruments in GOD's hand of saving our selves and this people. Let us then seriously consider that we have to do with that GOD who is able to save and to destroy. And settle that word in our hearts as a certain truth, *When he giveth Quietness, who then can make Trouble? and when he hideth his Face, who then can behold him? whether it be done against a Nation, or against a Man only.* Job 34. 29. And accordingly, let us turn from all sin to the Lord, and in this way hope and wait for his salvation. O let us take heed, lest there be in any of us *an evil Heart of Unbelief in departing from the living God.* To day, let us hear his voice, and not harden our hearts. May each one of us say with Job, *Now mine Eye seeth thee: Wherefore I abhor my self, and repent in Dust and Ashes.* And as it has pleased the Father to commit all judgment to the Son; let us look to him, and encourage our selves in him whom GOD hath exalted to be a *prince and a Saviour, to give repentance to Israel, and forgiveness of sins.* May our ascended JESUS, who has receiv'd of the Father the promise of the Holy Ghost, pour out this great blessing upon the whole land, and fulfill that word,

> Then will I sprinkle clean Water upon you, and ye shall be clean: from all your filthiness and from all your Idols will I cleanse you. A new Heart also will I give you, and a new Spirit will I put within you, and I will take away the stony Heart out of your Flesh, and I will give you an Heart of Flesh. And I will put my Spirit within you, and cause you to walk in my Statutes, and ye shall keep my Judgments, and do them. And ye shall dwell in the Land that I gave to your Fathers, and ye shall be my People, and I will be your God. Ezek. 35. 25–28.

Blessed be the Lord, his spirit has been, we hope, moving on the hearts of many to convince and awaken them. O let us not resist and quench the spirit! lest the threatning denounc'd against the sinners of the old world, should be fulfill'd on us, *My Spirit shall not always strive with Man, for that he also is Flesh.* Gen. 6. 3. Let us cherish his motions, and pray the more earnestly that he may be given in an extensive manner as a spirit of saving conversion and thorow reformation. And surely, If we duely consider the state of this sinful, distressed people, we shall be constrain'd to say with the prophet *It is Time to seek the Lord, till he come and rain Righteousness upon you.* Hos. 10. 12. And then with our fervent prayers, let us unite our best endeavours with regard to our selves, our families, and this people; that all iniquity may be put far from us, and that we may become zealous of good works. In this way we might hope GOD would say of us as of the remnant of Judah; *Then will I build you, and not pull you down, and I will plant you, and not pluck you up: for I repent me of the evil that I have done unto you.* Or as Isa. 65. 8. *Destroy it not, for a Blessing is in it.*

But the time requireth me to draw to a close. I would therefore proceed with due respect to make a particular application of what hath been said, unto our honoured rulers, who have call'd us to sanctify a fast with them; and have set apart this day to humble themselves under the sense of sin, and the tokens of the divine displeasure upon this province.

My fathers! Suffer the word of exhortation: Let GOD see your works; that you turn from every evil way; that GOD may also repent of the evil, and not bring it upon us. For how dreadful must it be if the example of the nobles and men of Nineveh should rise up in judgment against any of you: They repented at the preaching "of one Prophet sent to them by GOD, you have Moses and the Prophets"; Yea in these last days GOD has spoken to us by his Son that prince of the prophets, who is GOD manifest in the flesh. You have the sacred writings of the New-Testament, in which GOD reveals his wrath against all ungodliness and unrighteousness of men; and also his grace and mercy to the penitent by a redeemer. And as the judge of all the earth hath advanced you to rule over his people; so he declareth to you in his word, That *they who rule over Men must be just, ruling in the Fear of GOD;* and requireth you to lead in the work of reformation by your example, and by the right use of that power with which he hath betrusted you.

This people have observ'd many days of fasting and prayer, and yet there's sorrowful occasion to make that complaint; *For all this his Anger is not turned away, but his Hand is stretched out still.* You have also in this more private way sought the Lord some years past,* confessing your sins, and the sins of this people before him; notwithstanding which, the holy and faithful GODgoeth on walking contrary to us, and threatens to punish us seven times more for our sins. What means this heat of his anger? Why do we still complain, *Judgment is far from us, neither doth Justice overtake us: we wait for Light, but behold Obscurity; for Brightness, but we walk in Darkness. We grope for the Wall like the Blind, and we grope as if we had no Eyes.* Isa. 59. 9, 10. Alas! We must take up the lamentation which follows, v. 12–14.

Our Transgressions are multiplied before Thee, and our Sins testify against us: for our Transgressions are with us, and as for our Iniquities, we know them: In transgressing and lying against the Lord, and departing away from our God, speaking Oppression and Revolt, conceiving and uttering from the Heart, Words of Falsehood. And Judgment is turned away backward, and Justice standeth afar off: for Truth is fallen in the Street, and Equity cannot enter.

O it is time then, high time, heartily to engage in keeping the fast which GOD has chosen, and we have describ'd for our instruction and reproof, Isa. 58. 6, 8. *Is not this the Fast that I have chosen? to loose the Bands of Wickedness, to undo the heavy Burdens, and to let the Oppressed go free, and that ye break every Yoke? Is it not to deal thy Bread to the Hungry, and that thou bring the Poor that are cast out to thy House? when thou seest the Naked, that thou cover him, and that thou hide not thy self from thine own Flesh?*

Upon this GOD promiseth,

Then shall thy Light break forth as the Morning, and thine Health shall spring forth speedily: and thy Righteousness shall go before thee; the Glory of the Lord shall be thy Reward. Then shalt thou call, and the Lord shall answer; thou shalt cry, and he shall say, Here I am. 8, 9. v.

And 12 v[:] *They that shall be of thee, shall build the old waste Places: thou shalt raise up the Foundation of many Generations; and thou shalt be called, The Repairer of the Breach, the Restorer of Paths to dwell in.* Be intreated therefore to cry to GOD for grace that you may cleanse your hearts and hands from all sin, and so turn to the Lord; and then, let it be your constant care and diligent endeavour to do works meet for repentance. As GOD has exalted you above your brethren, let your light shine before them, that others seeing your good works may glorify your heavenly Father, and be excited to follow you. Let all that behold you, see your pious regards to GOD's worship and ordinances, his day and house. Do your utmost that the worship of GODmay be maintain'd in the power and purity of it, among this people. Let all due care be taken that men may fear this *glorious and fearful name*, the Lord our GOD, and not presume to take it in vain; for *because of swearing the land mourns*. Let the Lord's-day be strictly observ'd; for GOD hath set the Sabbath as a sign between him and his people, that he is the Lord who sanctifieth them. Let the most effectual means also be used that the great abuse of taverns may be reformed; that these be not converted into tipling and gaming houses for town- dwellers, to the dishonour of GOD and hurt of the common-wealth. Let the fountains of justice be kept open and pure, that judgment may run down as waters; and that such as thirst after righteousness may come freely, and be refreshed. And whereas the present difficulties which embarrass our affairs, do very much arise from the want of a suitable medium of trade, and different apprehensions in the legislature about supplying the treasury, whereby the publick debts are, in part at least, left unpaid, and the country naked and defenceless, in this day of calamity and war: I can't but humbly apprehend, that this awful frown of Providence calls aloud to you further to consider, whether there has not been great injustice and oppression with relation to the bills of publick credit which have pass'd among us, from their sinking and uncertain value; and to use your best endeavours that whatever bills shall pass for time to come in lieu of money, may be a just medium of exchange; for a *false Ballance is abomination to the Lord; but a just Weight is his Delight*, Prov. 11. 1. Whatever methods may be propos'd to extricate us out of our present distress, justice and equity must be laid in the foundation; or we may expect that the Lord who loves righteousness and hates wickedness, will confound our devices, and bring them to nought. But then, I presume not in the least measure to determine whether this or that way is right. May that GOD before whom all things are open and naked, direct Your Excellency and the whole court, into such paths of righteousness as shall lead to our deliverance and safety; that we may neither oppress one another, nor become a prey to an insulting enemy! May you be filled with the most tender and fatherly compassion for your people under the present distress and danger, and do all you can to relieve them! And if there should be a difference in your opinion about the way, may you be enabled to keep the unity of the spirit in the bond of peace, that the GOD of peace may be with you, who has promis'd to guide the meek in judgment!

But in vain is salvation hoped for from the hills, and from the multitude of mountains: Truly in the Lord our GOD is the salvation of Israel!

O GOD! We know not what to do; but our eyes are unto thee. We wait upon thee O Lord, who hidest thy self from the house of Israel; confessing that we thy servants, and thy people have sinn'd. Thy ways are equal, our ways have been very unequal. O Lord, righteousness belongeth unto thee, but unto us confusion of faces, as at this day, because we have sinned against thee. To the Lord our GOD also belongeth mercies and forgivenesses, tho' we have rebell'd against him. O Lord, hear, O Lord forgive, O Lord, hearken and do, defer not, for thine own sake, O GOD! for thy city, and thy people are called by thy name. Look to the face of thine Anointed, O merciful Father! Behold thy Son in our nature, who on earth offer'd a sacrifice of infinite merit to atone for the sins of thy people; and now appears in heaven, as a Lamb that had been slain, interceeding for us. We are unworthy; but the name in which we now ask thy divine help, is most worthy. O hear us, for thy Son's sake, and speak peace to thy people. Give ear, O Shepherd of Israel, thou that leadest Joseph like a flock, thou that dwellest between the cherubims, shine forth. Before Ephraim and Benjamin and Manasseh, stir up thy strength, and come and save us. Turn us again O GOD; and cause thy face to shine, and we shall be saved. O remember not against us former iniquities: let thy tender mercies speedily prevent us; for we are bro't very low. Help us, O GOD of our salvation, for the glory of thy name; and deliver us, and purge away our sins for thy name's sake: So we thy people and sheep of thy pasture, will give thee thanks for ever; we will shew forth thy praise to all generations.

And would you, our honoured rulers, to whom I again address my self, have the all-wise GOD present to shew you what his people ought to do in this very critical conjuncture, and to make you the joyful instruments of our deliverance; then abide withGOD by taking his word for your rule, by making his glory your highest end, and by seeking the public-weal in all things. Ask ofGOD a public spirit, and by all means labour to subdue a vicious self-love remembring the warning given us, 2 Tim. 3. 1, 2. *In the last Days perilous Times shall come. For Men shall be lovers of their own selves, covetous.* May you have the love of GOD and his people shed abroad in your hearts by his spirit; and be ready to sacrifice private views and personal interests to the publick good! Shake your hands from bribes of every kind, and when call'd to give your vote, consider seriously what is right in the sight of GOD, with whom is *no respect of persons, or taking of gifts*; and act accordingly. And if at any time you should be tempted to this great evil, as the best of men may; set that word of GOD in opposition to the temptation.

> He that walketh righteously, and speaketh uprightly, he that despiseth the Gain of Oppression, that shaketh his Hands from holding of Bribes, that stoppeth his Ears from hearing of Blood,

and shutteth his Eyes from seeing Evil: He shall dwell on high, his Place of Defence shall be the Munition of Rocks; Bread shall be given him, his Waters shall be sure. Isa. 33. 15, 16.

In this way you shall obtain the gracious presence of GOD with you. *The Lord is with you, while ye be with him,* 2 Chron. 15. 2. And if GOD be with you and for you, who can be against you? What can harm you? What can be too hard for you, if the Almighty is pleas'd to own you as his servants, and command deliverance for his people by you? Surely the mountains shall become a plain, crooked things straight, and the night shine as the day. Let me say to you therefore as 2 Chron. 15. 7. *Be ye strong, and let not your Hands be weak: for your Work shall be rewarded.* GOD will be your shield, and exceeding great reward. You shall see the good of GOD's chosen, rejoice with the gladness of his nation, and glory with his inheritance. And when the Son of Man shall come in his glory, and all the holy angels with him, then shall he say unto you, *Inasmuch as ye have done it unto these my Brethren, ye have done it unto me: Come ye Blessed of my Father, inherit the Kingdom.*

finis

[*] Urbs magna Dei. Calvin.
[*] Dutch annotations.
[*] Decemb. 10, 1736.

ACKNOWLEDGMENTS

I want to thank my wonderful wife, Anne, for putting up with me throughout the process of writing this book. Thanks also go to Dr. George Grant for his gracious help in sorting out how to get it published, referrals, and reviews, along with his kind comments. I wanted to comment more fully in letter 34 on the un-biblical nature of prisons and American criminal justice, but as I mentioned in Letter 33, I had absolutely no experience or accurate knowledge in this area. My dear friend Rev. Michael Swiger, True Freedom Ministries, offered to help by writing that letter for me, which he graciously did. Mike suffered imprisonment for nearly twenty years, came to faith in the Lord Jesus, and when freed some ten years ago, joined an Ohio prison ministry where he is now Executive Director. Mike speaks with great authority and I am very grateful for his help!

Thank you also goes to the many friends and loved ones who put up with my frequent debates and discussions over these letters as I was writing them. I can think of Dr. Ben Wherley and Mrs. Ellen Naylor, who provided written comments and other materials and Mrs. Jill Druhot for helping with researching the list of federal agencies. Thanks also, to my daughter-in-law, Amy Menefee, who put up with my endless discussions. And a special thank you to my publisher, David Dunham, and his wonderful team at Dunham Books, Joel Dunham and Crystal Flores.

I would also like to thank my Board, Edd Tate Parker, Ed Cup, and Robert Schmidt, for their encouragement and support, and supporters Ed Soeder, Bill Bares and Gary Winney. I am forever grateful to Mrs. Paula Parker and the countless friends who faithfully supported this work with their prayers.

Finally, my sincere and heartfelt gratitude goes to the Crossroads Foundation for underwriting the production of this book.

ABOUT THE AUTHOR

Jay Menefee grew up in rural Oklahoma, the only son of committed Christian parents, and committed his own life to Christ at the age of nine. He joined the U.S. Navy after high school and was honorably discharged as Petty Officer Third Class.

In 1957, Jay enrolled in Sam Houston State University in Huntsville, Texas, graduating with a Bachelor of Arts degree in physics and mathematics and a Texas secondary teaching certificate. After teaching high school for one year he was given a Teaching Fellowship at Sam Houston and graduated with a Master of Arts degree with a specialty in nuclear physics and mathematics. He also was given a life membership in Sigma Pi Sigma National Physics Honor Society.

In 1964 he was hired as Chief Physicist with the Harshaw Chemical Company in Cleveland, Ohio. Over the next five years Jay advanced to Manager of the Nuclear Products Group. While at Harshaw he took several courses towards his MBA degree at Kent State University but dropped out to start his own business in 1969.

Jay, along with three partners, started Bicron Corporation in Newbury, Ohio. He served as Chairman and CEO until he retired in 1987. Over those years, Jay also took several courses towards a Master of Divinity at Ashland Theological Seminary. He has been awarded five U.S. Patents, presented several technical papers, had them published in the Institute of Electrical and Electronic Engineering Journal, and he wrote Chapter One of a book entitled *Nuclear Medicine In-Vitro*.

Over the years, Jay has served as church trustee, chairman of the elder board, high school and adult Sunday school teacher, and mini-church group leader. In 1979, Jay felt a concern that the nation was drifting away from its founding principles. He started an organization called Ohio Roundtable in 1980, and served as Chairman of the Board for the next twenty years. The organization accomplished a number of objectives over those years, including leading a voter initiative to change the Ohio Constitution to limit the terms for state senators and state representatives. In 1981, Mr. Menefee was recruited to serve as the State Chairman for Citizens for America, a political organization founded by President Reagan.

Jay and his wife Anne celebrated their fifty-fifth wedding anniversary in 2014. They have two sons, a daughter-in-law, and two grandchildren.